W9-CMA-617

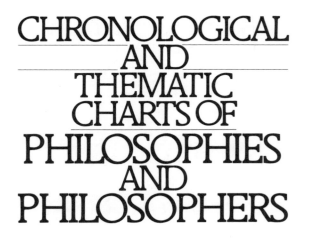

CHRONOLOGICAL AND THEMATIC CHARTS OF PHILOSOPHIES AND PHILOSOPHERS

CHRONOLOGICAL AND THEMATIC CHARTS OF PHILOSOPHIES AND PHILOSOPHERS

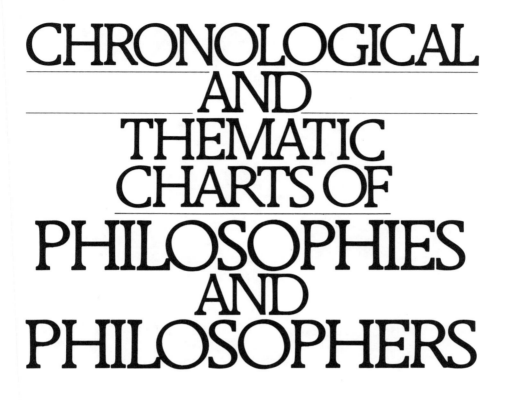

MILTON D. HUNNEX

ZondervanPublishingHouse

Grand Rapids, Michigan

A Division of HarperCollinsPublishers

CHRONOLOGICAL AND THEMATIC CHARTS OF PHILOSOPHIES AND PHILOSOPHERS
Copyright © 1961, 1971 by Chandler Publishing Company
Copyright © 1986 by Milton D. Hunnex

Requests for information should be addressed to:
Zondervan Publishing House
Academic and Professional Books
Grand Rapids, Michigan 49530

Library of Congress Cataloging in Publication Data

Hunnex, Milton D. (Milton De Verne)
  Chronological and thematic charts of philosophies and philosophers.

  Rev. ed. of: Philosophies and philosophers. [1971].
  Includes indexes.
  1. Philosophy—Introductions. 2. Philosophy—Outlines, syllabi, etc.
I. Hunnex, Milton D. (Milton De Verne). Philosophies and philosophers. II. Title.
BD21.H725 1986   102'.02   86-17308
ISBN 0-310-46281-9

Printed in the United States of America

99 00 01 /CH/ 19 18 17 16 15 14 13 12 11

CONTENTS

V.   PHILOSOPHERS   39

Summaries of Philosophers Whose Names Appear in Red on the Charts, Supplementing Information
Given Elsewhere in This Book

Alexander ▪ Aristotle ▪ St. Augustine ▪ Austin ▪ Ayer ▪ Bergson ▪ Berkeley ▪ Carnap ▪ Chrysippus ▪ Democritus ▪ Descartes ▪ Dewey ▪ Freud ▪ Hegel ▪ Heidegger ▪ Hobbes ▪ Hume ▪ Husserl ▪ James ▪ Kant ▪ Kierkegaard ▪ Köhler ▪ Leibniz ▪ Locke ▪ Marx ▪ Merleau-Ponty ▪ J. S. Mill ▪ G. E. Moore ▪ Nietzsche ▪ Peirce ▪ Perry ▪ Plato ▪ Plotinus ▪ Protagoras ▪ Russell ▪ Ryle ▪ Santayana ▪ Sartre ▪ Schlick ▪ Schopenhauer ▪ Socrates ▪ Spencer ▪ Spinoza ▪ St. Thomas Aquinas ▪ Tillich ▪ Vaihinger ▪ Whitehead ▪ Wisdom ▪ Wittgenstein

VI.   CHRONOLOGY WITH REFERENCES   49

A Chronological List of Important Philosophers, with Page and Chart References to Them in This Book

CHARTS

INDEX OF NAMES

INDEX OF TOPICS

{Part I}

This Book and Its Subject

ABOUT THE BOOK

This work is a *ready-reference* aid for the student who needs essential information in a hurry. It is neither an outline alone nor a condensed text but combines some of the functions of both. It stresses not only definitions and essential information but also *orientation* within a historical context.

This orientation is provided through the use of charts which take advantage of the fact that philosophical theories tend to recur in the history of thought and tend to cluster within the limitations of several possibilities of explanation. Through the use of charts, antecedent influences that lead to a particular philosophy may be suggested, as well as consequent influences and the relation to contemporary philosophy. Information accompanying the charts is also designed to aid orientation and understanding.

No attempt should be made to use this work as a substitute for study in texts and original sources. The student should not expect to master philosophy without recourse to the classic works in the field and certainly without the aid of one of many excellent introductory texts or readings and histories of philosophy.

Cross-referencing will be found throughout. The indexes and the Chronology with References locate most names and terms. Generally, terms and names need to be identified within a patricular *context*. They are usually grasped only in relation to other terms and names. Hence the student attempting to secure information regarding a particular philosophy or philosopher should seek it on the charts as well as in definitions or outlines.

The problems of philosophy are treated under three general headings. *Knowledge* (Part II), the *World* (Part III), and *Values* (Part IV). In addition, a special section outlines the theories of representative *Philosophers* (Part V). This section is limited to significant thinkers whose names *appear in red on the charts* and to their doctrines that are included within the scope of the study guide as a whole. Hence the number is limited and the philosophy outlined is restricted to those aspects that are relevant to the charts or problem at hand. For example, not all of the philosophy of Plato is outlined, but only those aspects related to the problems of knowledge, reality, and values—and these only in very sketchy form. The student should seek complete information elsewhere, particularly in translations of the works of Plato himself.

HOW TO USE THE BOOK

1. Consult the indexes or the chronology.
2. Thumb through the appropriate part related to your topic:

Philosophy, pp. 1–2.

Knowledge (epistemology, scientific method, truth, etc.), Part II.

Reality (physical reality, life, mind, metaphysics, etc.), Part III.

Values (axiology, ethics, aesthetics, education, and religion), Part IV.

Philosophers (men whose names appear in red on the charts: Alexander, Aristotle, St. Augustine, Austin, Ayer, Bergson, Berkeley, Carnap, Chrysippus, Democritus, Descartes, Dewey, Freud, Hegel, Heidegger, Hobbes, Hume, Husserl, James, Kant, Kierkegaard, Köhler, Leibniz, Locke, Marx, Merleau-Ponty, J. S. Mill, G. E. Moore, Nietzsche, Peirce, Perry, Plato, Plotinus, Protagoras, Russell, Ryle, Santayana, Sartre, Schlick, Schopenhauer, Socrates, Spencer, Spinoza, St. Thomas Aquinas, Tillich, Vaihinger, Whitehead, Wisdom, and Wittgenstein), Part V.

ABOUT PHILOSOPHY

The word *philosophy* is from the Greek *philein*, to love + *sophia*, wisdom.

Socrates committed himself to the belief that "the unexamined life is not worth living." For him—as for most of the Greek fathers of philosophy—the chief dignity of man was the exercise of reason in search for truth. For the Greeks, exercise of reason in the most general sense was philosophy. But man is also a creature of curiosity. "It is with wonder," Aristotle wrote, "that men begin to philosophize." Philosophy became the mother and sustainer of the sciences. Indeed, it became the most general of sciences, the science of sciences.

No discipline encompasses the core of liberal-arts education so fully as does philosophy. "To know the chief rival attitudes towards life," observed William James, "and to have heard some of the reasons they give for themselves ought to be considered an essential part of liberal education."

Philosophy attempts to examine life and the world as a

[1]

whole. Its method is *critical* and *constructive*. In its *critical function*, philosophy attempts to examine assumptions and ideas in the interest of clarification and understanding. This function embraces such problems as theory of knowledge and theory of value. It is essentially analytical. In its *constructive function*, philosophy attempts to take into account and organize *all* the facts in the interest of obtaining a view of the world as a whole. This effort is essentially *synoptic* and *speculative*. It involves such studies as *metaphysics* or theory of reality. Some philosophers believe that philosophy should confine itself to the *critical function*. Traditionally, however, philosophy has served to give expression to man's speculative interests—his efforts to understand himself in relation to the universe as a whole.

Philosophy is not a subject matter in the usual sense of being a special body of knowledge. Rather it is a discipline that appraises all kinds of knowledge claims either to clarify those claims, to criticize them, or to propose better ways of understanding them. While it is true that philosophy has become a highly specialized and technical discipline, it can still be said of it that it is "an unusually stubborn attempt to think clearly and consistently"—as William James once put it—whether one is analyzing what is being done in the use of moral language or proposing a theory concerning the nature of the good itself.

It will be helpful to note some distinctions between what scientists do and what philosophers do. Prior to the time of Galileo, when the modern scientific revolution got under way, there was little agreement as to what science was about. There was, e.g., no agreed-upon way of settling disputes about physical events or their causes. Science was called natural philosophy even up to Newton's day.

Today the various sciences have established rather definite ways of answering questions that used to be the subject of speculation. In general, questions for which there are in principle definite answers or agreed-upon ways of getting them are taken to be scientific questions. In contrast, other questions—such as, e.g., questions about the nature of reality, other minds, or what people ought to do—are questions that are left to philosophy. These are questions for which there are no generally agreed-upon answers or ways of getting them. They are open questions for which there may be no answers either because they are not properly questions at all, as skeptics might say, or they are questions whose answers must be "the gift of the gods" as Plato put it, or they are questions that involve other questions about language. In any event it is the philosopher who seeks out puzzling issues of this sort and who expects his answers to be disputed.

It would be silly, e.g., to wonder if the moon were made of green cheese or of some ethereal substance because we now know or can find out eventually what it is made of. But it wouldn't be silly to wonder what there is about green cheese or anything else that makes it a "physical" object or what it means to say that we "know" what it is. It *is* a matter of *wonder* that anything exists at all or that we can claim to *know* anything.

Philosophy today tends to be either *analytical* or *existential* (see Charts 23 and 24). English-speaking philosophers tend to favor the former approach. European philosophers tend to favor the latter approach. Important exceptions are the Marxists and the Neo-Thomists, as well as a number of recurrent traditional philosophical approaches.

The contemporary *analytical* philosopher is concerned primarily with clarifying all uses of reason and language, whether they constitute knowledge claims or value judgments. Ordinarily he doesn't advance claims concerning the nature of things that rival the claims of the scientist or anyone else, since he does not generally believe that he possesses special insight on these matters. He may attempt to promote a program for the use of an *ideal language* as do, e.g., philosophers like Russell and Carnap. This he would do in the interest of facilitating reasoning and communication. More likely he will accept the complexity of language and strive instead to effect some kind of "conceptual therapy" by exposing its misleading tendencies as do, e.g., philosophers like Austin and Ryle.

The contemporary *existential* philosopher, with whom we can include related kinds of philosophy like phenomenology, turns away from purely logical or linguistic analysis to the analysis of experience. His primary concern is directed to the components of the human situation. In this respect his interest is more nearly that of the traditional speculative philosopher, with the exception that he rejects the development of any philosophical system as such and he believes that traditional intellectualist approaches to philosophy are mistaken. He is likely to turn more to literary or theological expressions of his ideas, and his logic is likely to be dialectical rather than traditional or mathematical.

Those philosophers who are neither analytical nor existential will nonetheless attempt generally to effect some rapprochement with analytical or existential philosophy. In Europe, e.g., Marxism, existentialism, and phenomenology engage in considerable dialogue. Leading existentialists develop existential phenomenologies and embrace Marxism or react to it in varying degrees. In England there is no sidestepping the analysts by anyone, and in the United States there is perhaps the most vigorous dialogue between traditional philosophers of various kinds, on the one hand, and various forms of pragmatism, process philosophy, existentialism, and analytical philosophy, on the other hand, with analytical philosophy probably having the most followers.

This book does not discuss important developments since approximately 1970. For example, *creationism* as a theory of the nature and origin of physical and living reality is vigorously defended today. Also needing attention are the conflicting theories of the origin and nature of *human rights*, particularly as they relate to legal, moral, and philosophical questions. No attempt is made to include *Eastern philosophies*, philosophers, and religions, except where they directly influenced Western thought.

Finally, essentially pejorative terms, such as "secular humanism," are not specifically discussed. "Secular humanism" is used to refer to moral philosophies that renounce traditional and authoritarian views, especially those that invoke moral absolutes or the will of God. Its features can best be identified by referring to the various forms of *humanism, naturalism,* and *relativism,* as well as their corollaries—*existentialism, situationism,* and *subjectivism.*

{ Part II }

The Problem of Knowledge

RELEVANT QUESTIONS

What is mind? (concerning the faculty of knowing)
What is known? (concerning the object of knowing)
What is knowing? (concerning the nature of knowing)
What is true? (concerning the relation of knowing to reality)
What is valid? (concerning the method of correct reasoning)
What is scientific? (concerning the method of science)
Is genuine knowledge possible? (This question puts the challenge of *skepticism.*)
Is knowing innate or experienced or both? (On this question pivots the rivalry of *rationalism* and *empiricism.*)

THEORY OF KNOWLEDGE

The study of the theory of knowledge is called *epistemology* (Greek *epistēmē,* knowledge + *logos,* theory). The term was first used in 1854 by J. F. Ferrier, who distinguished the two main branches of philosophy as *ontology* (Greek *on,* being + *logos,* theory) and *epistemology.* Ontology is roughly synonymous with *metaphysics,* but the latter usually means both ontology as theory of being and epistemology as theory of knowledge.

Epistemology comprises the systematic study of the *nature, sources,* and *validity* of knowledge. It differs from *logic* and from *psychology.*

Logic is concerned with the specific and formal problem of correct reasoning, whereas *epistemology* deals with the nature of reasoning, with truth, and with the process of knowing themselves.

Psychology is concerned primarily with a *descriptive* study of behavior, phenomena, and the like, whereas *epistemology* deals with our claims to knowledge, with what we mean by "knowing."

For example: *Epistemology* asks, "Do we know an independent world or merely our experience?" The answers reveal two kinds of theories of knowledge, which may be grouped with regard to their degree of emphasis on the subjectivity or objectivity of knowledge (see Charts 1 and 2).

Subjectivistic theories of knowledge answer, "No, we do not know an independent world as the cause of our ideas. We cannot get beyond our experience or ideas, and we cannot speak of a knower experiencing them."

Objectivistic theories of knowledge answer, "Yes, we do know an independent world of material objects (some forms of *materialism* and *realism*) or of transcendent *ideas* (*Platonic idealism*)."

KINDS OF KNOWLEDGE

Russell makes the following distinction:

(1) Knowledge by *acquaintance* is the direct apprehension of

(a) sense data;
(b) objects of memory;
(c) internal states;
(d) ourselves.

(2) Knowledge by *description* is the mediated or thought-out knowledge of

(a) other selves;
(b) physical objects (as constructs and not sense data).

RATIONALISM VS. EMPIRICISM

Theories of knowledge divide naturally, theoretically, and historically into the two rival schools of *rationalism* and *empiricism.*

Rationalism believes that some ideas or concepts are independent of experience and that some truth is known by reason alone.

Empiricism believes that all ideas or concepts derive from experience and that truth must be established by reference to experience alone.

Neither rationalism nor empiricism disregards the primary tool of the other school entirely. The issue revolves on beliefs about (1) *necessary* knowledge and (2) *empirical* knowledge.

(1) *Necessary* or *a priori* knowledge is knowledge not given in nor dependent on experience, as, e.g., "Black cats are black," which is necessarily true by definition. This is an *analytic statement* (or, broadly speaking, a *tautology*). Its denial would be *self-contradictory.*

(2) *Empirical* or *a posteriori* knowledge is knowledge coming after or dependent on experience, as, e.g., "Desks are brown," which is a *synthetic statement.* Unlike the an-

alytic statement "Black cats are black," the synthetic statement "Desks are brown" is not necessarily true unless all desks are by definition brown, and to deny it would not be self-contradictory. We would probably refer the matter to experience.

Since knowledge depends primarily on synthetic statements—statements that may be true or may be false—their nature and status are crucial to theory of knowledge. The controversial issue is the possibility of *synthetic necessary knowledge*, i.e., the possibility of having genuine knowledge of the world without the need to rely on experience. Consider these statements:

(a) "The sum of the angles of a triangle is 180 degrees."
(b) "Parallel lines never meet."
(c) "A whole is the sum of all its parts."

Rationalism may believe these to be synthetic necessary statements, universally true, and genuine knowledge; i.e., they are not merely *empty* as the analytic or tautologous statements ("Black cats are black") and are not dependent on experience for their truth value.

Empiricism denies that these statements are synthetic *and* necessary. Strict empiricism asserts that all such statements only *appear* to be necessary or *a priori*. Actually they derive from experience.

Logical empiricism admits that these statements are necessary but only because they are not really synthetic statements but analytic statements, which are true by definition alone and do not give us genuine knowledge of the world.

Genuine Knowledge

Rationalism includes in genuine knowledge *synthetic necessary* statements (or, if this term is rejected, then those *analytic necessary* statements that "reveal reality" in terms of universally necessary truth; e.g., "An entity is what it is and not something else").

Empiricism limits genuine knowledge to *empirical* statements. Necessary statements are *empty* (i.e., they tell us nothing of the world).

Logical empiricism admits as genuine knowledge only *analytic necessary* ("Black cats are black") or *synthetic empirical* statements ("Desks are brown"). But the analytic necessary statements or laws of logic and mathematics derive from arbitrary rules of usage, definitions, and the like, and therefore reveal nothing about reality. (This is the *antimetaphysical* point of view.)

The Nature of Knowing

Knowing a statement (to be true) involves

(1) the fact that in some sense or by some criterion the statement is actually true;
(2) the *belief* that it is true; and
(3) evidence in support of it.

The Problem of Evidence

If evidence is *complete*, knowing is *certain*.
If evidence is *partial*, knowing is only *probable*.
Rationalism admits *synthetic necessary* evidence.
Empiricism admits *only synthetic empirical* evidence.

The Problem of Certainty

Can empirical knowledge be certain?

What evidence and how much evidence are required for any degree of certainty?

Fallibilism is the doctrine that no empirical judgment can be certain, i.e., that all empirical judgments are *fallible* or *probable*.

Antifallibilism is the doctrine that some empirical judgments are *certain* with adequate *confirmation*, e.g., the number of people in a room.

Theories of the *a Priori*, or the Nonempirical Element of Knowledge

Though primarily the tool of *rationalism*, the *a priori* is also present in empirical theories of knowledge. Three theories are

(1) *Theory of the intrinsic a priori*, wherein certain principles or ideas are believed to be *self-evident*, i.e., to be known *intuitively* because of their distinctness and clarity. An example would be the "I am conscious, therefore I exist" (the *Cogito ergo sum*) of Descartes (see Descartes, Part V).

(2) *Presuppositional theory of the a priori*, wherein the *a priori* is understood as the necessary condition of the possibility of intelligible experience or knowing. For instance, Kant presupposed *a priori* the subjective forms (*Anschauungen*) of sensibility: *space* and *time* (see Kant, Part V).

(3) *Analytical theory of the a priori*, wherein the *a priori* constitutes rules or postulates arbitrarily posited or agreed upon in advance as the basis for reasoning, i.e., what we propose to mean by certain words (see logical empiricism on this page).

Logic and the Laws of Thought

Fundamental to *necessary* knowledge are the three *laws of thought* enumerated by Aristotle. They are presupposed whenever anyone thinks about anything whatever:

(1) *Law of identity.* Any entity whatsoever is what it is and is not something else. As applied to propositions: If a proposition is true, it is true; if *p*, then *p* (e.g., "A rose is a rose").

(2) *Law of noncontradiction.* No entity whatever can be both what it is and not what it is with the *same* specification. As applied to propositions: It cannot be true both that a proposition is true and also that it is false; not both *p* and not-*p* (e.g., "A rose cannot be not a rose").

(3) *Law of excluded middle.* Any entity whatever is either *A* (some particular kind of thing) or it is not. Everything is either *A* or not-*A*, either *p* or not-*p* (e.g., "A thing is either a rose or it is not a rose").

These laws of thought are three of many laws of logic or reasoning. They cannot be proved or disproved. In order to demonstrate them, they must be assumed. To deny them is self-contradictory. They are presupposed in all rational—that is, consistent—thought and discourse.

Do the laws of thought apply to *all* of reality? Are they the basic rules of reality, or of thought only?

Rationalism holds that the laws of thought apply to everything whatever because they are the most *general truths* of reality. They apply not only to what we think and say but also to what we think and talk *about*.

Empiricism holds that the laws of thought are useful *verbal conventions* applying only to the *way* we think or talk, not necessarily to what we think and talk *about* or even necessarily to how we *must* think or talk (cf. skepticism, p. 9).

EPISTEMOLOGICAL ISSUES
Scientific Laws, Hypotheses, and Theories

Scientific laws may be defined as *descriptive generalizations* having *predictive value*, as, e.g., Newton's law of gravitation: Every particle in the universe attracts every other particle with a force directly proportional to the product of the two masses and inversely as the square of the distance between them.

Unlike theories, laws are *discovered* rather than *devised*. Their truth is highly probable; i.e., the mathematical likelihood of events occurring according to them is very high.

According to some philosophers, as, e.g., Hempel and other *logical positivists*, scientific laws are *universal hypotheses* which are "capable of being confirmed or disconfirmed by suitable empirical findings" (see pp. 6, 7, 14).

Hypotheses are particular explanatory statements, like "George took arsenic," which together with laws or theories, i.e., *general* statements, like "Arsenic is poisonous," explain certain claims or occurrences—in this case "George died."

Theories are general explanatory statements involving specifically *nonobservable* entities as, e.g., in the atomic theory, "There are protons and electrons."

Reasoning with theories is illustrated as follows:

All things are made of atomic particles. (atomic theory)
Hence a drop of coloring in a glass of water colors all of the water. (a fact explained by the theory)

Theories may be proposals to picture things a certain way, i.e., "useful fictions" or "explanatory *models*," as in *pragmatism* or *instrumentalism*, or general statements about what "really exists," as in *realism*.

Hypotheses and theories are (1) *provisional* yet *probable* because grounded in facts; and (2) *predictive* because capable of accounting for the facts.

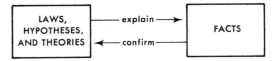

In establishing a particular hypothesis or general theory, *induction* leads to the generalization that is the theory proposed or suggests the hypothesis that is proposed. *Deduction*, on the other hand, determines whether the generalization or theory implies the facts serving as evidence. Confirming the facts makes the hypothesis or the theory probable.

Causality

Aristotle enumerated four causes (see Aristotle, Part V). Of these, mechanistic explanations admit only *efficient* cause, i.e., the actual force effecting change, and confine them to phenomena *preceding* effects. Purpose or goal, e.g., what one has in mind when doing something, is not admitted by the mechanist as a cause.

The causal principle has at least three general interpretations:

(1) *Empirical* (or *a posteriori*) interpretation. Cause is viewed as a generalization from the facts and dependent on the facts. Cause is the observed *constant conjunction* (Hume) of certain events; whenever *a*, then *b*.

(2) *Rational* (or *a priori*) interpretation. Cause is viewed as a *necessary connection* (Spinoza) between two events, wherein an appropriate effect *must* follow the cause according to the *principle of sufficient reason* (Leibniz). We know *a priori* that causality is a necessary principle of reality, that there can be no uncaused events (determinism), or that causality is a necessary principle of knowledge (Kant).

(3) *Pragmatic* interpretation. Cause is viewed as a useful or *guiding principle* of scientific explanation, although much of science may not need it. One version is the "recipe" theory, wherein cause is likened to a recipe for producing or preventing something. We produce *B* by producing *A* and speak of *A* as causing *B*; e.g., we cause iron to glow by heating it and therefore speak of the heating of the iron as the cause of its glow. Another version pictures the causal principle as a *proposal* to uncover uniformities in the world, i.e., a *procedural rule* which is neither true nor false because it is not *about* anything but is a *fruitful way* of looking at or dealing with anything.

Some considerations of causality are that

(1) Causality is *not* the same as *logical necessity*, as, e.g., in "Black cats are black."

(2) Causality in science is *not prescriptive*, as, e.g., in "The law commands obedience."

(3) Causality as a necessary *condition* (if effect, then cause) does not mean *necessary connection*. Necessary condition means that in the absence of a particular condition, a particular effect never occurs, as, e.g., "In the absence of oxygen, we never have fire."

(4) Causality as a *sufficient condition* (if cause, then effect) also does not mean *necessary connection*. Sufficient condition means that a particular condition is always followed by a certain effect, as, e.g., "If rain is falling, the ground is wet." Cause as *necessary* or *sufficient condition* is empiricist theory (J. S. Mill). Cause as *necessary connection* is traditional rationalist theory (Spinoza).

(5) Cause is usually taken to mean the whole set of conditions sufficient for the occurrence of the event. If the cause is *singular*, these *sufficient* conditions are also *necessary* conditions. If the cause is *plural*, these sufficient conditions are *not* all necessary conditions.

Scientific Explanation

"Why?" is an ambiguous question. It may be a request for either a *reason* or an *explanation*.

Reasons are given for holding *beliefs*, as, e.g., giving reasons for believing that the world is round.

Explanations are given for what *occurs* or is already the case, as, e.g., explaining why earthquakes occur or carbon monoxide is poisonous. These are *scientific* explanations, although "explain" can be used in other ways, as, e.g., to refer to making an idea clear.

One may have reasons for believing certain things, and these *reasons* may also be *explanations* for believing them, as, e.g., when one wants to believe what is true. On the other hand, one may give reasons why, e.g., he believes that God exists or that a certain kind of act is wrong. One may *justify* his beliefs. This is a *logical matter;* whereas the *explanation* of his beliefs about God or morality, i.e., the *psychological* question, is something else. He may, e.g., have had certain experiences or needs that *caused* the belief. These would *explain* the belief. Explanations have to do with causes.

Scientific explanations are scientific laws, hypotheses, or theories (see above). The laws, hypotheses, or theories *are* the explanation. An event is explained when it is "brought under" a law, hypothesis, or theory.

The *covering law model* of scientific explanation is as follows (Hempel):

All copper conducts electricity. (explanation)
This substance is copper.
This substance conducts electricity. (thing to be explained)

The statement about what is explained is deduced from the *explanation*, i.e., all the premises together, of which at least one is a *generalization*—a scientific law, hypothesis, or theory. If part of the explanation is only probably true, the explanation is probable. The generalization need not be empirical. It may be logical, as, e.g., "One person can't be at two places at the same time." In this case the explanation is *logical* rather than *empirical* or *scientific*.

A *scientific* explanation must have *predictive value;* i.e., it must be able to explain events other than the one it is invoked to explain and therefore be able to predict the occurrence of these events.

The Nature of Linguistic Meaning

Linguistic meaning is the meaning of words, phrases, or sentences. There are many other uses of "mean" such as, e.g.:

(1) That is no *mean* accomplishment. (insignificant)
(2) He was so *mean* to me. (cruel)
(3) I *mean* to help him if I can. (intend)
(4) The passage of this bill will *mean* the end of. . . . (result in)
(5) Once again life has *meaning* for me. (significance)
(6) What is the *meaning* of this? (explanation)
(7) He just lost his job; that *means* he will have to. . . . (implies)

(Alston, *Philosophy of Language*, p. 10)

Theories of *linguistic meaning* are:

(1) *Referential* theory, which holds that

(a) language is used to talk about things;
(b) the meaning of an expression is that to which it refers or the relation between the expression and its referent;
(c) reference is by *naming* (words stand *for* something) or *describing* (see Russell's theory of descriptions, p. 13).

(Russell, J. S. Mill, Frege, Church, C. I. Lewis, Carnap, and the early Wittgenstein in the *Tractatus*) (See Chart 23.)

(2) *Ideational* theory, which holds that

(a) words or expressions have meaning as they are used to refer to the *idea* that gives rise to them or to which they themselves give rise, e.g., as psychological effects in hearers.

(Locke, Stevenson, Grice, Leonard)

(3) *Behavioral* (or stimulus-response) theory, which holds that

(a) words or expressions have meaning as they are used to refer to the *situation* (stimulus) in which they are uttered and the responses which they elicit;
(b) meaning is a function of stimulus and response (Bloomfield);
(c) meaning is a function of behavioral disposition (Morris);
(d) meaning is a function of the conditions under which it is uttered (Quine);
(e) three factors are involved (Ogden and Richards): the *symbol* (i.e., words or expression), the *thought* (or interpretation), and the *referent* (or that referred to). (We get from words to things indirectly, by way of thought.)

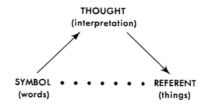

(Ogden, Richards, Bloomfield, Morris, Fries, Quine, Skinner)

(4) *Use* theory, which holds that

(a) meaning is a *function of use* (Wittgenstein of the *Investigations*);
(b) words or expressions have meaning as they are *used*, e.g., to perform *any speech act* (Austin) and not only to refer to something, i.e., to name or describe;
(c) *speech acts* (Austin) consist of

　　1. uttering sentences (*locutionary* acts);
　　2. what is done by the speaker in uttering the sentence (*illocutionary* acts as, e.g., announce); and
　　3. the effect on the hearer (*perlocutionary* acts as, e.g., encourage).

(d) Two sentences have the same meaning if they are used to *do* the same thing, i.e., if they have the same *illocutionary act potential*.
(e) To know what a sentence means is to know how to *use* it correctly.
(f) Meaning is not what sentences *have* but what persons do with them.

(Wittgenstein of the *Investigations*, Austin, Ryle, Alston, Warnock)

Meaning can be distinguished as *cognitive* or *noncognitive* (emotive) (see pp. 13, 14, 23, 27, 33, 34).

(1) *Cognitive* meaning is *empirically verifiable* or *confirmable*, has *truth value* (i.e., is true or false), and is genuinely *informative*.

(2) *Noncognitive* (emotive) meaning is expressive of the feeling or emotion of the speaker, as in, e.g., a *value judgment* (see pp. 23, 27, 28, 33, 34).

The Verifiability Theory of Meaning

According to this theory, meaning and truth are determined by *verifiability* or *confirmability*.

(1) The verifiability theory of meaning asserts that

there is *cognitive* (informative) *meaning* or *cognitive truth* only as verification or falsification is *actually* possible or, as in *operationalism*, when all necessary steps for demonstrating meaning or truth can be specified (see p. 14). Verifiability is the possibility of verification or falsification. Only verifiable or falsifiable statements are capable of truth or falsity since, properly speaking, only they are statements.

(2) The verifiability criterion of meaningfulness may be modified as the *confirmability* criterion of meaningfulness. Confirmability requires that an assertion be capable of being verified or falsified, i.e, verifiable or falsifiable in principle, by the specification of empirical evidence that would count for or against its truth or falsity.

With respect to the question of the verifiability theory of meaning, the opposition *rationalism* vs. *empiricism* becomes *metaphysicians* vs. *verificationists* (antimetaphysicians), i.e., those who hold knowledge to be in principle both verifiable and nonverifiable (rationalists) and those who hold that it *must* be verifiable (empiricists).

(1) *Rationalists* hold that the verifiability criterion is not itself verifiable and hence by its own definition not *meaningful* and not *true*. It is a theory of meaning and not the actual nature of meaningfulness. Statements are meaningful if *intelligible* (Mascall).

(2) *Empiricists* hold that it is a procedural rule justified by its *utility* and not by its *truth value* as such (Ayer, Hempel, Feigl, Carnap, *et al.*).

(3) The *use* of theory of meaning, however, holds that verifiability (or falsifiability) is not the exclusive criterion of meaningfulness. Use determines criteria or rules of meaningfulness. So far as the verifiability criterion applies, "A sentence has meaning only if it can be *used* to make an assertion, and it can be *used* to make an assertion only if it is possible to specify some way of verifying or falsifying the assertion" (Alston).

Verifiability is not the only way of making sense. The verifiability theory of meaning is a proposal to confine "meaningful" to the cognitive uses of language.

Truth
The Nature of Truth

(1) Truth may be *descriptive*, applying to *statements, propositions,* or *beliefs* that are (a) necessarily, i.e., analytically, true, as, e.g., "If *p* implies *q* and *p* is the case, then *q* is the case," *or* (b) contingently, i.e., empirically, true, as, e.g., "The earth is round." "Truth" functions as an adjective, e.g., *true beliefs.*

(2) Truth may be *instrumental*, applying to beliefs that guide thought or actions successfully, as, e.g., acting on the belief that fire burns helps one to avoid getting burned. "Truth" functions as an adverb, e.g., *one believes truly.*

(3) Truth may be *substantive* or *ontological*, referring to the real, as, e.g., "God is Truth." "Truth" functions as a noun.

(4) Truth may be *existential*, referring to one's way of life or ultimate commitment. One *lives* rather than *knows* the truth. "Truth" functions as a verb.

The Criteria of Truth

(1) *Correspondence* theory. That idea or proposition is

true which accurately and adequately resembles or represents the reality it is supposed to describe; e.g., "It is raining now" is true if as a matter of fact rain is now falling. This theory is usually that of *epistemological realism*, as, e.g., in Aristotle, Locke, and Russell. An objection is that it may be impossible to establish correspondence: "How can I know that my idea corresponds to its object even if in fact it does?" Ideas are radically different from objects. Austin modifies the theory to hold that the correspondence is in the nature of an appropriate *correlation* rather than congruity or resemblance. "The truth of a statement [is] a matter . . . of the words used being the ones *conventionally appointed* for situations of the type to which that referred to belongs" (Austin).

(2) *Coherence* theory. That idea or proposition is true which "fits in" or is consistent with or is necessitated by the totality of truth of which it is a part. This theory is usually, although not necessarily, held by *idealists,* as, e.g., Hegel, Bradley, and Blanshard. It is also held by nonidealists, like Carnap and Neurath. An objection is that this theory assumes a metaphysical unity which may not exist. Also, as Russell points out, *coherence* may be a *test* or even *necessary condition* of truth but it is not what is *meant* by truth.

(3) *Pragmatic* theory. That idea or proposition is true which *works* or *satisfies* or is capable of doing so (see pragmatic theories of knowledge, p. 11). More specifically:

(a) James gives a *personal* interpretation: "We cannot reject any hypothesis if consequences useful to life flow from it . . . If the hypothesis God works [for the individual] . . . it is true." Initially James defined truth as *that which works.* Later he defined it as

1. that which has "cash value," i.e., is *verifiable in principle;*
2. that which has *coherence,* i.e., fits present or anticipated facts; and
3. that which *favors higher values,* i.e., encourages progress.

(b) Peirce and Dewey give a *social* interpretation in terms of *predictive* power. Truth must be *socially* as well as *experimentally verifiable*—not just privately useful. Truth is public, not private. "The opinion which is fated to be ultimately agreed to by all who investigate is what we mean by truth" (Peirce).

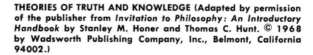

THEORIES OF TRUTH AND KNOWLEDGE (Adapted by permission of the publisher from *Invitation to Philosophy: An Introductory Handbook* by Stanley M. Honer and Thomas C. Hunt. © 1968 by Wadsworth Publishing Company, Inc., Belmont, California 94002.)

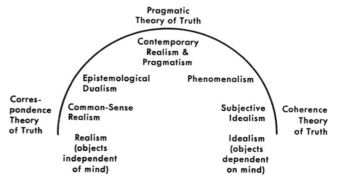

Truth is a "thing done" (*pragma*tism), a function of practical value, *made to happen,* i.e., brought about rather than discovered to be the case, as in correspondence theory (see p. 7). An objection is that something other than what is made to happen or could be made to happen, or works or could be made to work, is what is meant by truth and that, in any event, truth should refer to what *is now* or *was* the case, as well as to what *will be* or *could be* the case.

Method

The method of knowledge known as *scientific method* has a long history, reaching back to the *analytical method* of Aristotle (see Aristotle, Part V).

Aristotle developed the methods of

(1) *induction*—reasoning from the particular to the general; e.g., simple enumeration: $Fact_1$ + $Fact_2$ + $Fact_3$ . . . →Generalization.

(2) *deduction*—reasoning from the general to the particular; e.g., If all cases of *p* imply *q*, then this case of *p* implies *q*.

(3) *observation*—the use of empirical evidence; and

(4) *classification*—the use of definition.

Pythagoras developed the method of *mathematical enumeration.*

Democritus contributed the concept of *mechanism.*

In the early modern period:

(1) Galileo (1564–1642) revived the *mechanism* of Democritus.

(2) Copernicus (1473–1543) and Descartes (1596–1650) revived the *mathematical method* of Pythagoras.

(3) Aristotle's *inductive* and *deductive* methods were reformulated, substituting the *mechanism* of Democritus for Aristotle's *teleology* (see theories of reality of Democritus and Aristotle, Part V).

(4) Galileo approached contemporary *scientific method* by combining the *experimental empiricism* of Francis Bacon (1561–1626) with the *rationalism* of Descartes. (This synthesis resulted in a *material* and *mathematical* theory of reality. Descartes had neglected the *experimental* and *empirical;* Bacon, the *mathematical.* Together their deductive and inductive approaches approximated the scientific method. See Descartes, Part V.)

(5) Bacon initiated the tradition of *British empiricism* by reformulating Aristotle's inductive method as the scientific method which "derives *axioms* from the *senses* and *particulars,* rising . . . [to] the most general axioms" (Bacon). Induction becomes the remedy for the *idols of the mind* which "so beset men's minds that truth can hardly find entrance" (Bacon). These idols are

(a) the idols of the *tribe*—human and racial limitations;

(b) the idols of the *cave*—personal limitations;

(c) the idols of the *theater*—tendency to take sides; and

(d) the idols of the *marketplace*—difficulties of language and communication.

Though Bacon's method was subsequently modified, the emphasis on induction in the scientific method remained. John Stuart Mill's inductive methods for the determination of *empirical knowledge* derive from Bacon's method and are classic. They are

(1) the method of agreement;

(2) the method of difference;

(3) the joint method of agreement and difference;

(4) the method of concomitant variations; and

(5) the method of residues.

(See Mill's *System of Logic,* bk. III, ch. VIII, or any general introductory text or dictionary of philosophy.)

The scientific method became a series of steps varied according to the particular discipline or problem at hand. John Dewey (in *How We Think*) described it as *reflective thinking* and enumerated five steps in *problem solving* as the *pattern of inquiry* or scientific method:

(1) *awareness* of the problem—the indeterminate situation;

(2) *clarification* of the indeterminate situation as a problematic one by definition, observation, and the classification of facts;

(3) *formulation* of a possible solution—hypothesis (see p. 5);

(4) *deduction* of verifiable or testable consequences; and

(5) *verification* and reformulation as necessary leading to acceptance or rejection of the hypothesis and/or solution of the problem. (See any basic introductory text.)

The Problem of Induction

Whenever we say "All *A*'s are *B*'s," we are saying not only that all *A's have been B's in the past* but also that all future *A*'s will be *B*'s. Thus we give evidence from the past as reasons for making claims about the future. But will the future resemble the past? How can we know this? This is the *problem of induction.*

Inductive reasoning presupposes the *principle of uniformity,* i.e., the belief that scientific laws (like the universal law of gravitation) will hold in the future as they have in the past. But the principle of uniformity cannot itself be demonstrated without assuming that it is itself true.

To show that any future event will be like a past event, we have to assume uniformity, i.e., that it will be like a past event, as, e.g., *A* causing *B*. Induction cannot be demonstrated; i.e., we cannot *know* that the future will resemble the past, according to Hume, Russell, and skepticism generally.

Opposing views, as, e.g., Will, Strawson, and others, argue that skepticism disqualifies evidence by allowing nothing to count for induction, i.e., by *dis*qualifying evidence as soon as it applies to the case at hand. When future futures become present and past futures, they are disqualified as evidence for reasoning about other future futures.

The use of the principles of *uniformity* and *induction* is justified *pragmatically,* as was, e.g., the use of logic (see p. 4). Without these principles, knowledge would be impossible. With them, knowledge is or may be possible.

The Knowledge Situation

The *knowledge situation* concerns the question of the relation of the *knower* (self), *sense data* (experience), and *things known* (world). Theories of knowledge may be clearly delineated with regard to the manner in which the knowledge situation is described. Theories of knowledge may be identified as skepticism, subjectivism, objectivism,

THE KNOWLEDGE SITUATION

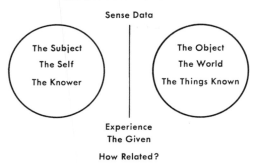

critical or representative realism, intuitionism, pragmatism, phenomenalism, phenomenological existentialism, and recent analytical theories, which are usually varieties of phenomenalism or realism.

Ideas

Ideas are either

(1) *always* produced (caused) by God directly and *are* things—*epistemological idealism*, e.g., Berkeley; *or*

(2) *always* produced (caused) by God directly to *represent* things by a preestablished harmony; i.e., we get the right ideas in perfect harmony or correspondence with things as they occur or as we experience them—*occasionalism*, e.g., Malebranche; *or*

(3) *always* produced (caused) by things themselves—*causal theory of perception*—ideas represent things that cause them—*sensationalism, representative realism*, e.g., Galileo, Locke; *or*

(4) *sometimes* produced (caused) by things which they represent, e.g., Descartes's *adventitious* ideas, but are also *innate; or*

(5) *never* produced by anything; i.e., they occur from an inner necessity or predisposition to understand things in a certain way, are always *innate*, as in Leibniz's *windowless monads; or*

(6) *in things themselves*, i.e., *in re* as their *form* from which the mind (intellect) abstracts them in getting to know things, *classical realism*, e.g., Aristotle, St. Thomas Aquinas; *or*

(7) *not in things* but the universal possibilities of thought, i.e., universal concepts in terms of which anything *is what it is* (*ante re*), i.e., *conceived* by a mind or soul to be *what it is*, as, e.g., in Plato; *or*

(8) *not in things* but requiring *divine illumination* to grasp since the finite and spatial-temporal mind cannot *per se* grasp the infinite or eternal (i.e., the *universals* as described in 7 above), e.g., St. Augustine, St. Bonaventure, *et al.*

THEORIES OF KNOWLEDGE
Skepticism

Skepticism denies the possibility of a complete or genuine knowledge of an *objective world*, i.e., of a world apart from the knower or his experiences. It may *doubt* the possibility of knowledge of the self as well and confine knowledge to *sense data* and their *associations*, as, e.g., did Hume, who confined knowledge and reality to "the stream of perceptions" as impressions and ideas.

Forms of Skepticism

(1) *Solipsism.* I alone exist because I cannot know a world beyond myself and my ideas. This view leads to the *egocentric predicament* (see p. 14).

(2) *Sensory skepticism.* Sensations are relative and unreliable because they are modifications of the knower and no more a part of the world than is the pinprick a part of the pin.

(3) *Rational skepticism.* The conclusions of reason are contradictory or paradoxical, as, e.g., in *Kant's antinomies* (p. 14) or *Zeno's paradoxes* (p. 14).

(4) *Methodological skepticism.* A systematic but tentative doubt is a prelude to genuine knowledge, as, e.g., in the *Cartesian method* (see Descartes, Part V).

Subjectivism as Subjective Idealism

Subjectivism argues that because knowledge is confined to ideas in the mind of the knower, it is impossible to get beyond these ideas to an *objective* or *material reality* separate from and independent of the knower. *Perceptions* and *things known* are *one* (*epistemological monism*) and can only be known as *ideas in the mind* of the *knower* (*epistemological idealism*). Hence the *world* is in a *knower* or belongs to a *knower*. Even if *ideas* represented an independent reality, as realism contends, one could not possibly know it. "Even if physical objects do exist when no one is observing them, we can have no reason to suppose that they do for no one can observe them existing unobserved" (Stace). "To be is to perceive or to be perceived" (Berkeley, see Part V). The world consists of perceivers and perceptions, minds and ideas.

Berkeley's argument for subjective idealism:

(a) Perceptions do not exist unperceived.
(b) Physical objects are complexes of perceptions.
(c) Therefore, physical objects do not exist unperceived.

Objectivism

Objectivism believes that objects are independent of mind and present their properties directly to the *knower* through *sense data*. *Things known* and *sense data* are *one* (*epistemological realism* as *epistemological monism*).

OBJECTIVISM

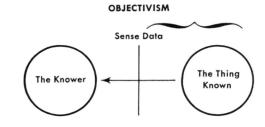

Epistemological realism

(a) ascribes *varying roles to the mind* in knowing;
(b) believes that the *mind knows independent things*—not ideas alone;
(c) believes that *knower* and *things known* are distinct;
(d) believes that the *knower is in the world;* and
(e) teaches that "things known . . . continue to exist unaltered when they are not known" (Montague).
(f) "Even though no one can observe any physical object existing unobserved, we have no good reason to believe that they don't exist unobserved" (Russell).

Forms of Objectivism (as Epistemological Realism)

(1) *Naïve* or *common-sense realism.* Things are perceived directly as they are.

(2) *New realism.* The objective world known is *neutral;* i.e., it consists of mental and material entities and objective relations as well (Moore, Russell, Alexander, Broad, *et al.*). (See Part V and Moore and Russell in "Recent Analytical Theories" below.)

(3) *New materialism.* The objective world known is material (Montague, Woodbridge, *et al.*).

(4) *New (neo) Thomism.* An independently real world is known by independently real minds (Mascall, Copleston, *et al.*).

Forms of Objectivism (as Epistemological Idealism)

For *objective idealism,* the objective world is *mental* but *objective,* i.e., independent of the human *knower* alone, because it belongs to an *absolute knower* or *world mind* (Hegel, Green, Bradley, Bosanquet, Royce, Blanshard, *et al.*).

Note: *Objective idealism* (Hegelianism) differs from *subjective idealism* (Berkeleyanism) in that it teaches an absolute mind (monism) of which finite minds (knowers) are manifestations. *Subjective idealism* (pluralism) teaches many individual minds (knowers).

Critical or Representative Realism

Critical or representative realism (epistemological dualism) ascribes a critical role to *mind* in the formulation of knowledge. Unlike pure objectivism, it distinguishes between *sense data* and the *objects* they represent (epistemological dualism). But the *objects* or *things known* are independent of *mind* or the *knower* in the sense that thought refers to them—not merely to *sense data* or to the *ideas* of the *knower.* Ideas *represent* objects.

CRITICAL OR REPRESENTATIVE REALISM

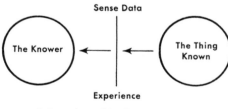

Sense Data

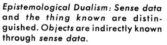

The Knower ← ← The Thing Known

Experience

Epistemological Dualism: Sense data and the thing known are distinguished. Objects are indirectly known through sense data.

Forms of Critical or Representative Realism (Epistemological Dualism)

(1) *Representative realism.* Ideas represent or correspond to the objects of an independent world. Objective or primary qualities of objects elicit subjective or secondary qualities. Together they comprise knowledge (Democritus, Galileo, Kepler, Descartes, Locke, Macintosh, *et al.*).

Descartes's argument for representative realism:

(a) God exists; i.e., the clear and distinct idea we have of God implies his existence just as the idea of a triangle implies three-sidedness (see the *ontological argument,* p. 35).

(b) God by definition is perfect, i.e., benevolent.

(c) A benevolent God would not leave us without a way to know the world.

(d) This way is *reason,* i.e., *intuition* and *deduction.*

(e) If ideas are clear and distinct, they are true.

(f) If ideas are true, they are about what exists.

(g) An external world having none but *primary qualities* is amenable to mathematical analysis and *can* be clearly and distinctly understood.

(h) Therefore the external world has nothing but *primary qualities.*

(2) *Critical realism.* Material objects are known *via* sense data. In Santayana, e.g., knowledge of independently real material things is possible through the joint participation of the *knower* and *things known* in the *essences.* Material things are known indirectly by the act of *animal faith* (Santayana, Lovejoy, Sellars, *et al.*).

Personalism

Personalism (or *personal idealism*) is an epistemological dualism combining elements of objectivism and subjectivism, realism and idealism. In Brightman, e.g., there is the dualism of "situation-experienced and situation-believed-in."

Neo-Thomism

According to Mascall, Maritain, Gilson, Copleston, *et al.*, sense data are the means "through which the intellect grasps in a direct but mediate activity, the intelligible extramental reality, which is the real thing" (Mascall).

Intuitionism

Intuitionism stresses the *immediacy* of knowledge or the self-evident character of certain ideas. Whenever a "whole response" of the knower to the "whole of things" is suggested, *intuition* is usually implied. As the theory of knowledge of *mysticism,* intuitionism teaches the inseparateness of *knower* and *thing known.* "Realism separates object and knower; idealism holds that all objects belong to some knower; mysticism [intuitionism] holds that the objects and the knowers belong to each other . . . they are one" (Hocking). More characteristic of Eastern than Western theories of knowledge, intuitionism seeks knowledge of the *indefinable* or *nonanalyzable.* Yet there may be attempted expression in symbols or poetry. Concerning the communication of knowledge, Lao-tze observed: One who knows does not talk. One who talks does not know.

Forms of Intuitionism

(1) *Platonism.* Intuition or insight *(noesis)* is the goal of the philosopher. The *knower* grasps reality as a whole in terms of the *ideas* and particularly in terms of the highest and most inclusive *idea of the good* (see Plato, Part V).

(2) *Bergsonianism.* This contemporary form of intuitionism views intuition as *the* superior source of knowledge because it places the *knower* in a relationship of identification and intelligent sympathy with the *thing known* (see Bergson, Part V).

(3) *Cartesianism.* This form of rationalism teaches the capacity of mind to intuit *innate ideas.* Descartes believed, e.g., that all knowledge could be deduced from clear, self-evident ideas known by intuition (see Descartes, Part V).

Spinoza made intuition the goal of knowledge as a vision of reality *sub specie aeternitatis* (from the standpoint of eternity). Though not strictly Cartesian, Kant believed that knowledge was possible only because the mind could order *phenomena in space and time*. These he described as the *a priori forms of intuition* or *forms of sensibility* (see Kant, Part V.)

Pragmatism

Pragmatism is primarily a theory of meaning and truth. It stresses the *genetic* and *instrumental* character of knowledge. Pragmatism approaches knowledge in terms of an organism that

(a) adapts to and interacts with its environment;
(b) uses ideas as instruments or plans of action; and
(c) retains ideas that work as true and discards those that fail as false.

Pragmatists emphasize the *experimental method*. Peirce spoke of it as the method of knowledge that is "open to the test of criticism of others." "Knowing is literally something which we do," Dewey argued. It is not something which we come to possess. Pragmatism (i.e., also instrumentalism or experimentalism) is "a behaviorist theory of thinking and knowing" (Dewey).

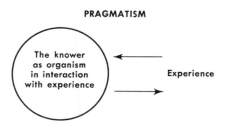

PRAGMATISM

Knowledge is the successful determination or reorganization of experience through what Dewey called a "transaction." Pragmatism pictures an active *organism* developing knowledge from a successful encounter with experience. What is claimed as knowledge must be capable of public confirmation (in Peirce and Dewey).

Forms of Pragmatism

(1) *Radical empiricism.* This form links William James to the tradition of *British empiricism* and in particular to the *pure phenomenalism* of David Hume (see James, Part V).

(2) *Pragmaticism.* This form is associated with Charles Sanders Peirce and by him contrasted with that of James. Whereas James interpreted knowledge and truth in terms of personal needs, verification, or consequences, Peirce emphasized the social and objective nature of knowledge and truth, i.e., the "tough-minded" version of pragmatism (see Peirce, Part V).

(3) *Experimentalism* or *instrumentalism.* John Dewey's form, wherein knowledge is described as *funded experience. Experimental method,* the method of inquiry, is stressed. Like Peirce, Dewey rejected James's individual interpretation for a more socially and scientifically oriented or "tough-minded" pragmatism (see Dewey, Part V).

Phenomenalism

Phenomenalism is the doctrine that *phenomena* and not

things are known. In agreement with *skepticism* and *subjectivism*, phenomenalism denies the possibility of a knowledge of *objective reality*. Only *objective phenomena* are known. Hence knowledge is limited to the totality of *actual* or *possible sense data*, including the sense data of internal experiences, such as feelings, dreams, hallucinations, and fantasies. Objects are *logical constructs* of sense data (e.g., Ayer). They are inferred from sense data.

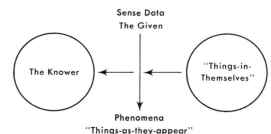

PHENOMENALISM

Phenomenalism differs from *subjectivism* on two points:

(1) The world is all the possible as well as all the actual complexes of sensations and ideas. Perceivability—not actual perception—determines existence. "Matter is the permanent possibility of sensation" (Mill).

(2) What is experienced is not just subjective sensations but *objective sense data,* i.e., *phenomena* which are neither mental (subjectivism) nor material (some forms of objectivism).

Phenomenalism differs from *objectivism* in denying that an objective mental, material, or neutral world is known. Phenomena—sense data—are the sole source and object of knowledge. Some phenomenalists (Renouvier, Shadworth, Hodgson, *et al.*) deny that there is reality behind phenomena. Others (e.g., Kant, Comte, Mill, Ayer) believe that there may be but that it is unknowable. Hence knowledge is limited to objective sense data alone, and physical objects are logical constructs of sense data.

Forms of Phenomenalism

(1) *Pure phenomenalism (Humian skepticism).* (See Hume, Part V, and skepticism, p. 9.)

(2) *Kantianism (critical* or *transcendental idealism).* Knowledge is the joint product of *mind* (knower) and *phenomena* (sense data). Phenomena arise from *noumena* (the ultimately real world of unknowable "things-in-themselves"). Only phenomena (sense data) are knowable as factual or scientific knowledge and then only because the mind (knower) possesses the requisite faculties that make possible the experience and the organization of this knowledge. Things conform to the categories of the mind rather than vice versa as in, e.g., Aristotelian realism. But according to Kant, "concepts without percepts are empty" just as "percepts without concepts are blind."

(3) *Empirical positivism.* This is the form of J. S. Mill, which combines features of Hume's *pure phenomenalism* and the *positivism* of Comte (see Hume and Mill, Part V).

(4) *Logical positivism.* This contemporary form, of A. J. Ayer, holds that the neutral *sense data* are the ultimate units of experience which are given. Mind and matter are both *logical constructs* of actual or possible sense data, not metaphysical entities. Statements about mind (mental state-

ments) or matter (physical object statements) are both fully translatable into sense data or observation statements.

Phenomenology and Existential Phenomenology

See Husserl and Sartre, Part V, and Chart 24 for particulars.

Recent Analytical Theories

See also Chart 23.

The approach of analytical philosophy to the problems of knowledge received its main initial impetus from the ideas and methods of G. E. Moore (1873–1951) and Bertrand Russell (1872–1970), both of whom rejected the dominant idealism of the turn of the century.

"Bradley [objective idealist, see p. 10] argued that everything that common sense [realism] believes in is mere appearance; we [i.e., Russell and Moore] reverted to the opposite extreme and thought that everything is real that common sense, uninfluenced by philosophy or theology, supposes real" (Russell).

The most influential figure of analytical philosophy is Ludwig Wittgenstein (1889–1951), whose early thought in the *Tractatus* (1921) reflected the influence of Russell in his *logical atomism* and *ideal language* approach, but whose later and even more influential *Philosophical Investigations* (1953) reflects the influence of Moore, with its emphasis on common sense and the analysis of ordinary language.

Since Wittgenstein's death in 1951, philosophical analysts have divided generally into

(1) *ideal language* philosophers, who (like Russell, Carnap, or Ayer) have sought to reform and improve knowledge of and language about the world by getting it into logical forms that are free of the imprecision and misleading character of ordinary or natural language; hence emphasis was placed on formal logic and the language of the quantitative sciences as the ideal and correct way of knowing and speaking about the world; and

(2) *ordinary language* philosophers, who (like Moore earlier) took ordinary discourse to be complex and misleading but nonetheless an entirely appropriate way of knowing and speaking of the world. This group divided into two important subgroups: the Cambridge School, where Moore's method and interests were furthered by John Wisdom (1904–   ) in his *conceptual therapy;* and the Oxford School, where Gilbert Ryle (1900–   ) and John Austin (1911–1960) are the leading influences. This school is commonly referred to as *ordinary language* or *linguistic philosophy.*

One recent analytical theory of knowledge is the *phenomenalism* of A. J. Ayer, described above. Moore's and Russell's theory of knowledge are forms of *realism,* as noted above also. Moore's approach to realism is the basis of the *ordinary language* approach to knowledge. Russell's approach to realism is the basis of the *ideal language* approach to knowledge. See *logical atomism* below.

Moore's *epistemological realism* rests on an analysis of beliefs and statements about the world. If, e.g., we are agreed as to what we mean when we speak of seeing a "hand," e.g., then whether we can prove that the hand is really an "external object" is of no consequence, since whether there are really external objects in no way alters facts about hands or the way we speak of them. In other words, if idealists, realists, and phenomenalists speak the same ordinary language and act as though they held the same common-sense beliefs, differences in their philosophical arguments are of no consequence for their knowledge of the world. Moreover, to have sensations *of* something is, according to Moore, "to know something which is as truly and really *not* a part of *my* experience as anything which I can ever know."

The sensation of something, i.e., "knowing" something, is unique and irreducible. Also there are truths of common sense whose certainty is such that to doubt them would be to raise questions about our understanding of what it *means* to know anything at all, since knowing these common-sense truths is the *paradigm,* i.e., the clear-cut example of *what it means to know anything.* Examples of "clear-cut" common-sense truths are

(a) Things exist in space and time.
(b) We can only think and see and feel *where* our bodies are.
(c) Things exist when we are not conscious of them.

For Moore, if some philosopher denies the reality of time, as, e.g., *idealists* like Bradley and McTaggert did, one need only to remind him that he no less than anyone is obliged to acknowledge that he ate his breakfast before his lunch and that he cannot possibly argue that there is anything mistaken about speaking *this* way or believing consequently that time is *real.* We learn to use terms like "real" by referring to simple clear-cut cases just as these.

Russell's *logical atomism* (1918 period) and also the *logical atomism* of Wittgenstein's *Tractatus* (1921) is a descendent of Hume's *atomism of ideas.* Hume believed that philosophers ought to engage in a *psychological* analysis of ideas. Russell, on the other hand, called for a *logical* analysis of ideas. For him, logic is the syntax of an "ideal" or "logically perfect" language. All "ordinary" statements, so far as they are factually meaningful, contain propositions whose structure and relationship to each other follow strict logical rules. Thus Russell holds, as Moore did not, that the model for clear and correct thinking or speaking about the world is to be found in formal logic.

According to logical atomism, the ideal language pictures or mirrors the world just as a map mirrors it with its symbols. There is an identity of structure between the points on the map and points on the ground. An ideal language is like a perfect map. For every proper name, there is a corresponding property. When it is correctly used, it pictures the facts as they are. Wittgenstein's *Tractatus* makes this clear:

(1)   The world is everything that is the case.
(1.1)   The world is the totality of facts, not of things.
(2.1)   We make to ourselves pictures of facts.
(2.11) The picture presents the facts in logical space, the existence and nonexistence of atomic facts.
(2.12) The picture is a model of reality.

As a theory of knowledge, logical atomism holds that the world is organized on a *logical* pattern that can be mirrored by the formal logic that is used to organize propositions about it. The world is the totality of *facts* which can be stated in propositions. Simple unanalyzable propositions like "This is red" *(p)* are *atomic propositions*, and the facts that such propositions state are *atomic facts*.

Facts are simply facts, and their totality is the world; but propositions can be combined as *molecular propositions* by using words like "and" or "or" as, e.g., "This is red or this is orange" *(p* or *q).*

The truth of a *molecular proposition* depends on the truth of its component *atomic propositions* of which it is a *truth-function*. The truth of atomic propositions must be determined empirically. Anything that can be said, can be said in terms of atomic propositions; i.e., whatever is said is either an *atomic statement* (contains an atomic proposition) or a *truth-function* of atomic statements (thesis of extensionality).

The basic theory of knowledge of logical atomism is that the world is composed of atomic facts that are "mirrored" in the atomic and molecular statements of language in such a way that they are true when they correspond to or "picture" the facts (see correspondence theory of truth, p. 7).

In a "logically perfect" language, the words in a proposition would correspond one by one with the components of the corresponding fact. As it turns out, the "logically perfect" language is Russell's mathematical or symbolic logic which he worked out together with A. N. Whitehead in the *Principia Mathematica* and which represents the culmination of ideas originating in Frege, Peano, *et al.* (see pp. 4, 5, 6, 14, and Chart 23). The calculus of the *Principia* "has only syntax and no vocabulary whatsoever. . . . If you add a vocabulary, [you have] a logically perfect language" (Russell).

"The shortest account of *logical atomism* . . . is that the world has the structure of Russell's mathematical logic," according to Urmson. For logical atomism, mathematical logic is the only possible *correct* language. Ordinary or natural languages are mainly misleading stylistic variants. Hence Russell does not, as did Moore, stick to commonsense beliefs but reverts instead to Bradley's distinction between *appearance* and *reality*, except that the distinction for Russell is between the *apparent* logical form of a statement—which often misleads us—and its *real* logical form.

Two main cases of confusion between real (logical) form and apparent (grammatical) form that give rise to nonsense (paradoxes) involve the (1) *theory of types* (cf. Ryle's *category mistake*, p. 46); and the (2) *theory of definite descriptions* (one of the most influential ideas in the analytical theory of knowledge).

(1) *Theory of types.* There is not "one relation of meaning between words and what they stand for, but as many relations of meaning, of a different logical type, as there are logical types among the objects for which there are words" (Russell). Certain paradoxes, like the paradox of Epimenides the Cretan, who asserted that all Cretans are liars (or, e.g., my saying that all Americans are liars), arise from a confusion of expressions of different *logical types*. Thus a linguistic expression is of one logical type (i.e., the assertion that all Cretans are liars), and an expression *about* a linguistic expression (i.e., Epimenides' assertion that all Cretans are liars) is of another logical type. The latter is *metalanguage*—a statement about statements (Carnap) (cf. *metaethics*, pp. 23, 27).

By distinguishing logical types, we are able to identify *apparent* or *grammatical* propositions that are neither true nor false, but meaningless or nonsensical because they are not *real* or *logical* propositions at all, as, e.g., "Socrates is identical." Also we can note that the subject-predicate form of Indo-European languages like Greek or English (*A* is *B*) misleads us into thinking that "every fact has a corresponding form and consists in the possession of a quality by a substance" (Russell), as, e.g., in the metaphysics of Aristotle, Spinoza, Leibniz, Hegel, or Bradley. Russell holds that the predication of attributes and the relating of things are of different *logical types*.

(2) *Theory of definite descriptions.* A definite description is a phrase that describes a particular thing, as, e.g., "*the* so-and-so." By contrast, an indefinite description is of the form "*a* so-and-so."

A confusion arises when one takes *definite descriptions*, like "the present king of France," to have the same *logical function* as names, as, e.g., "The so-and-so is sick." Suppose we say "The present king of France is sick." There is no "present king of France"; yet it is not unintelligible to predicate many things—grammatically—of a nonexistent "present king of France." Thus if the *definite description* "the present king of France" is taken to function as a *name*— a logical type—it must name a nonexistent person and cannot be logically meaningful even though grammatically we can make sense of all sorts of statements about "the present king of France."

Intelligible metaphysical statements about entities whose existence may be doubted are logically suspect, even though grammatically and emotionally they may be quite meaningful, as, e.g., "God is love." Moreover, using any *definite description* as, e.g., "the present king of France," as a *logical name* can lead us into all sorts of metaphysical puzzles and paradoxes. To note the distinction is to preclude many metaphysical problems at the outset of inquiry.

"An important consequence of the theory of descriptions is that it is meaningless to say 'A exists' unless 'A' is (or stands for) a phrase of the form 'the so-and-so.' If the so-and-so exists and x is the so-and-so, to say 'x exists' is nonsense" (Russell). Existence is not a predicate (see also p. 35). To *name* something *is* also to affirm its existence. To give a definite description of something, as, e.g., "the present king of France," does *not* affirm its existence. The idea of definite descriptions enables us to assert that "the round square does not exist without having first to assume that there *is* an object which is both round and square and then denying that there is such an object" (Stebbing).

Some objections to the doctrine of *logical atomism* that language pictures facts are

(1) Linguistic forms may be conventional rather than natural.

(2) Linguistic forms need not and may not resemble facts, i.e., the world.

(3) Ordinary indicative statements need not always refer.

(4) It is uncertain what is meant by the "form" of the facts, i.e., the world.

(5) The form of language may be read into the facts or world.

(6) The world may not comprise a plurality of individual facts *per se*.

(7) Facts depend on how they are interpreted.

── WORDS AND THEIR MEANINGS AS RELATED TO THEORIES OF KNOWLEDGE ──

CONCEPTUAL PRAGMATISM A version of the pragmatic theory of meaning, knowledge, and verification advanced by C. I. Lewis, wherein knowledge is viewed as the joint product of experience and of the activity of thought. Unlike Kant's forms, Lewis's forms of thought are alternative and culturally determined conceptual schemes. They are not the universal and necessary forms of all minds.

CONVENTIONALISM Poincaré's theory of knowledge, wherein it is held that necessary or *a priori* knowledge as it is found in mathematics or logic is conventional, being a choice among a number of possibilities and incapable of validation either rationally or empirically.

DIALECTIC The art of seeking truth through conversation—in Socrates and Plato. For Aristotle, the "process of criticism wherein lies the path to the principles of all inquiries." In Hegel, the essence of the process of reality (see Hegel, Part V).

EGOCENTRIC PREDICAMENT The predicament of the knower confined to his own ideas and incapable of knowing anything else.

EXPERIMENTAL METHOD The method of experimental science (Dewey *et al.*, pp. 5, 7, 8, 11, 41).

FICTIONALISM or FICTIONISM Vaihinger's theory of the "as if," wherein all concepts are viewed as fictions lacking objective truth but useful as instruments of action.

GENETIC THEORY OF KNOWLEDGE Dewey's theory that knowledge is *funded experience,* i.e., the accumulation of *instrumental* ideas (see Dewey, Part V).

INNATE IDEAS Ideas not given in experience which all men possess by virtue of their rational nature (see Descartes, Part V).

KANT'S ANTINOMIES The mutually contradictory ideas of metaphysics which Kant used to illustrate the impossibility of knowing the ultimate nature of the world, as, e.g., whether the world is finite or infinite, etc. (see Kant, Part V).

NOMINALISM The doctrine that universals or general terms like "good" are merely names assigned to particular things which alone are real (William of Ockham *et al.*).

OPERATIONALISM or OPERATIONISM A theory of knowledge advanced by Bridgman, comparable to Dewey's *instrumentalism* in the belief that the meaning of a concept is "synonymous with the corresponding set of operations."

PHYSICALISM Carnap's epistemological realism, wherein he held that "every descriptive term in the language of science is connected with terms designating observable properties of things . . . [which are] *intersubjectively* confirmable by observation." The theory is related to what is characterized by scientific empiricists as *empirical realism,* a form of *objectivism* wherein the world known is "that which is located in space-time and is a link in the chains of causal relations [and is] . . . capable of empirical test" (Carnap).

PROBABILISM The doctrine that certainty is unattainable and that belief and action must rest on probability (see skepticism, p. 9, and fallibilism, p. 4).

PRAGMATICS The study of the functions of language in its psychological and sociological contexts, as, e.g., in Carnap.

RELATIVISM The doctrine that truth varies with circumstances and has no objective criteria or standards (Protagoras *et al.,* Part V).

RELATIVITY, THEORY OF A mathematical theory advanced by Einstein (special theory of relativity, 1905; general theory of relativity, 1914-1916), wherein space and time are no longer considered as absolute but as parts of a four-dimensional space-time continuum and relative to the particular coordinate system of the observer.

SEMANTICS The study of the meanings of terms and expressions, as, e.g., in Carnap or Richards.

SEMIOTIC The general theory of signs and their applications as developed by Peirce and important for *scientific empiricism.*

SENSATIONALISM An early form of empiricism which taught that all knowledge derives from sensations passively received by the knower.

SYMBOLIC (MATHEMATICAL) LOGIC Logic employing special or artificial symbols for the structures of propositions and arguments in the interest of clarity, precision, and the ease of reasoning.

SYNTAX The study of the structural nature of statements and their interrelationships, as, e.g., in Carnap.

TAUTOLOGY In a general sense any statement whose denial would be self-contradictory, as, e.g., "If you're here, you're here" or "All brothers are males" (cf. analytic statements, pp. 3, 4). Strictly speaking, tautologies are compound statements that are true or false by virtue of their form only and regardless of the nature of the content, as, e.g., "either *p* or not-*p*."

VERIFIABILITY PRINCIPLE The central principle of *logical positivism* (logical empiricism, scientific empiricism, etc.) (see pp. 6, 7, 13, 23, 27, 33). "We say that a sentence is factually significant . . . if, and only if, [one] knows how to verify the proposition [meaning] which it purports to express" (Ayer).

ZENO'S PARADOXES The four rational proofs of the impossibility of plurality or of motion advanced by Zeno of Elea and subsequently resolved by mathematical theory.

Part III

The Problem of the World

RELEVANT QUESTIONS

What is the physical world? (Answers state theories of physical reality.)

What is life? (Answers state theories of the origin and nature of living reality.)

What is ultimately real? (Answers state theories of the nature of reality as such, i.e, *ontology*.)

THEORIES OF THE NATURE OF PHYSICAL REALITY

The problem of the nature of physical reality is roughly the problem of *natural science*. Theories associated with general periods of development are the (1) prekinetic Greek theories; (2) medieval theories; (3) classical modern theories; (4) contemporary or relativity theories.

Prekinetic Greek Theories
Monism

In the monist outlook, all things are forms of *one* substance. For example:

(1) Thales: *Water* is the material cause of all things.

(2) Anaximander: The *Boundless* or *Infinite* is the essence of all things.

(3) Anaximenes: All things arise from a condensation or rarefaction of *air*.

(4) Parmenides: *Being* is the one homogeneous and continuous substance.

(5) Heraclitus: *Fire* is the universal flux or becoming of all things and the first principle of reality.

Dualism

In the dualist outlook, all things are forms of *two* substances. Examples:

(1) Pythagoras: The world arises from a *limitation* of the *unlimited*, i.e., an imposition of the numerical forms on space.

(2) Plato: The world consists in *Matter* and the *Ideas* (see Plato, Part V).

Pluralism

In the pluralist outlook, all things are forms of *several* substances. The pluralist theories are of two general kinds:

(1) Quantitative atomism (rudimentary kinetic theory):

(a) Democritus: Reality is *atoms* and *space* (see Democritus, Part V).

(b) Epicurus: Reality is *atoms* and *space* qualified by a kind of spontaneity of atoms; motion is inherent in the atoms.

(2) Qualitative atomism (rudimentary teleology):

(a) Empedocles: There are four elements—earth, water, air, and fire, moved by *love* and *hate*.

(b) Anaxagoras: There are countless elements matching the countless qualities of experience guided by an active element or mind, *nous*.

Teleology

In the teleological outlook, all things have an inherent tendency to fulfill a purpose. In Aristotle, all substances possess *entelechia* (inherent tendencies) toward a *telos* (end) (see Aristotle, Part V).

Medieval Theories

The medieval theories of physical reality, e.g., of St. Augustine and St. Thomas Aquinas, are reformulations of Platonic and Aristotelian theories of physical reality.

Classical Modern Theories
Dynamic Theories

The dynamic theories of Descartes, J. G. Vogt, *et al.* are the forerunners of modern wave theories.

(1) Descartes: Matter is *extension* and *vortices* (see Descartes, Part V).

(2) Vogt: Matter is *modulation* or *vortices* of *ether*, or *ether* and the disturbances of *ether*; there is no empty space.

Kinetic Theories

The theories of Galileo, Newton, Boyle, *et al.* (Chart 12) are the forerunners of modern particle theories. They embrace five principles:

(1) *Kinetic principle.* All physical realities are explainable in terms of *atomic matter in motion* (*materialism* and *reductionism*) (cf. Democritus, Part V).

(2) *Principle of causality.* All occurrences are the necessary consequences of antecedent events.

Taken together, the kinetic principle and the principle of causality comprise *mechanism*—the doctrine that given the mass, position, and velocity of all particles in the universe at any moment, it is theoretically possible to compute the mass, velocity, and position of each particle at any earlier or later moment.

(3) *Principle of uniformity*. Natural laws are the same for all aspects and all locations of physical reality.

(4) *Principle of quantification*. All differences are essentially quantitative and therefore theoretically measurable; science "is written in mathematical language" (Galileo).

(5) *Principle of conservation*. Neither mass nor energy is created or destroyed.

Kinetic theory became Newtonian physics, or what is generally known as *classical physics*.

Contemporary or Relativity Theories

These are the theories associated with Einstein, Planck, Heisenberg, Bohr, Schrödinger, Whitehead, *et al.* Contemporary physics has found that the classical or kinetic approach is adequate only for specific systems moving within the limits of moderate speeds which effect small and generally inconsequential changes. At velocities approaching that of light, changes become considerable.

Some Historical Developments in the Contemporary Theories
The Law of Entropy

This is the Carnot and Clausius Second Law of Thermodynamics, which states that the amount of *available* energy decreases and which raises the question: Is the universe running down?

Radioactivity

From the original research of the Curies, there arose the theory that through nuclear fission or nuclear fusion, mass may be transformed into energy.

The Concept of Mass-Energy

Though others have participated in developing this concept, it was stated in mathematical terms by Einstein:

$$E = mc^2$$

where E = energy, in ergs; m = mass, in grams; c = the velocity of light in centimeters per second = 3×10^{10}, hence $c^2 = 9 \times 10^{20}$. Thus the mass of one shotgun pellet, e.g., approximately equals the total produced by all power stations of the world during 24 hours. In this theory, matter becomes a special state of energy as mass-energy, and space becomes the sum total of the fields of mass-energy, altering with events, relative, and having individual geometries.

Dynamic or Wave Theories of Physical Reality

(1) De Broglie (1922) introduced the concept of "wave-particles."

(2) Schrödinger said that "the electron . . . is a *disturbance* proceeding along the electron orbit in the form of a wave."

(3) Einstein observed that "a moving stone is a changing *field* where the state of greatest intensity travels through space with the velocity of the stone."

Quantum Theory

According to this theory of Planck, the energy emitted in radiation, e.g., in light, occurs in discrete *quanta* but acquires wavelike properties under certain conditions. Light is neither particles nor waves in the classical sense of the terms.

Uncertainty and Complementarity

Heisenberg's *principle of uncertainty* (or indeterminacy) and Bohr's *principle of complementarity*, in contrast with the assumptions of *classical physics*, state that the *position* and *velocity* of atomic physical entities cannot be established simultaneously. "A rigorous space-time description and a rigorous causal sequence for individual processes cannot be realized simultaneously—the one or the other must be sacrificed" (D'Abro).

Theory of Relativity

Einstein's theory of relativity consists of two parts: (1) *special* (or *restricted*) *theory of relativity* (1905); and (2) *general theory of relativity* or *theory of gravitation* (1914–1916).

(1) The *special* theory deals only with objects or systems which either are moving at constant velocity with respect to one another or are not moving at all. Its fundamental postulates are: Ether cannot be detected (though its existence is not denied); hence *all motion is relative,* and *the velocity of light is always constant relative to an observer.* (In *classical* physics, velocity is distance divided by time. In *relativity* physics, distance and time are in terms of the velocity of light.) These postulates result in lengths, speeds, and time being relative to an observer, and the same motion may appear to one observer straight, to another curved, to another looped, and so on. There is no fixed or universal frame of reference, no absolute motion, and straight lines reaching to infinity are nonexistent.

(2) The *general* theory deals with objects or systems which are speeding up or slowing down with respect to one another. In it, Einstein advanced the *principle of equivalence*, wherein he affirmed the equivalence of the effects of gravitation and acceleration (hence the Einstein *theory of gravitation*). This theory was developed into the *unified field theory* on which Einstein was working when he died. He observed that "it is not the charges nor the particles, but the *field in the space* between the charges and the particles which is essential for the description of physical phenomena." The field is curved in content and form. Events occur in it as part of a process. As physical reality, matter (*mass-energy*) is a function of *space-time,* as is also *gravity.* Gravity becomes the phenomenon associated with a distortion of *space-time* and its attempt to "straighten out."

Some Specific Implications of Contemporary Physics

With respect to *mass-energy* (→ = "implies"):
Physical reality is reducible to *energy.*
Energy moving at the speed of light is *radiation.*
Energy concentrated is *mass.*
Mass can be changed (deconcentrated) to *energy* by *radiation.*
No *energy* → no *mass* → no *space* → no *time.*

With respect to motion (↑ = "increases"; ↓ = "decreases"):

Motion ↑ energy ↑ mass ↑ time flow ↓ gravity ↑ curvature of space ↑ metabolism rate ↓ dimension in direction of movement ↓ distances measured in direction of movement ↑ .

In a system moving at 85% of the speed of light, mass would be doubled, but in any given moving system, changes would occur in the same ratio and would not be observable.

WORDS AND THEIR MEANINGS AS RELATED TO THEORIES OF PHYSICAL REALITY

CAUSE A relation between events, processes, or entities in the same time series such that when one occurs, the other invariably follows. When the relation is conceived as *necessary*, the doctrine is *hard determinism*. When the relation is viewed as *constant conjunction*, the doctrine is *soft determinism* or *positivism* (see Hume, Part V, and causality, pp. 5, 29, 30).

CAUSE, MULTIPLE J. S. Mill's doctrine that cause is "the sum total of the conditions positive and negative taken together . . . which being realized, the consequent invariably follows" (see Mill, Part V, and causality, p. 5).

CAUSES, FOUR Aristotle's theory that *cause* is not only *efficient* (as *act* or *push*) but also *material* (as *potential* of matter), *formal* (as directed according to *plan*), and *final* (as initiated by some *purpose* or *end*). This theory of cause comprises a *teleology*, wherein cause is seen in terms of a consequent end (*telos*) aimed at but not yet existent (see Aristotle, Part V, and causality, p. 5).

SPACE, CONCEPTUAL The *ideal* space abstracted from *perceptual* space (see below), having the properties of *unity*, *iso-morphism* (i.e., *homogeneity*), *continuity*, *infinity*, and *three dimensions* (i.e., the objective space of classical physics).

SPACE, PERCEPTUAL The subjective and qualitative sense of the relationship of entities arising from the organization of all perceptions (see Kant, Part V, *re* the doctrine of the subjectivity of space).

SPACE-TIME The *four-dimensional* continuum of *relativity physics*, motionless and changeless, for motion and change are relative to particular physical realities taken in terms of an individual space and time.

TIME, CONCEPTUAL The spatialized or mechanized time of clocks and mechanical counters—one, continuous, and *infinite*, having *one irreversible dimension* (i.e., the *absolute* time of classical physics).

TIME, PERCEPTUAL *Experiential* or "lived through" time, the succession of *specious presents* (units of lived-through presents rather than knife-edged presents), *heteromorphic* (each moment unique), essentially *subjective* but sharable in the group experiences of given cultures (see Bergson, Part V).

THEORIES OF THE ORIGIN AND NATURE OF LIVING REALITY
Life Defined

Life is present in *organisms* capable of some or all of the following:

(1) response to stimuli;
(2) reproduction;
(3) metabolism;
(4) environmental adaptation;
(5) self-maintenance;
(6) self-protection.

Theories of the Origin of Life, or the Monogenetic Assumption

(1) Divine creation (Biblical *supernaturalism*, Biblical *theism*).

(2) Interstellar origin (Anaxagoras, Arrhenius, Helmholtz, Lord Kelvin, *et al.*).

(3) *Hylozoism, animism*. All nature is alive (primitivism, pre-Socratic Milesian philosophy, *et al.*).

(4) Evolution from inorganic matter (now the most widely held view; originally in Anaximander, Lucretius, *et al.*).

The Hypothesis of Biological Evolution

The doctrine that the many complex organisms now existent descended or evolved from relatively fewer and simpler organisms was anticipated in Anaximander, Empedocles, Aristotle, Lucretius, Goethe, Erasmus, Darwin, *et al.* It is considered to be supported by the evidence of fossil remains, geographical distribution, comparative anatomy, embryology, vestigial remains, and artificial breeding "back" to "ancestral" forms.

Theories of the Nature of Evolution

(1) *Mechanism*. Evolution is the product of continu-ous physico-chemical actions (Hobbes, Lamettrie, Holbach, Vogt, Büchner, Haeckel, Loeb, Herrick, T. H. Huxley, Spencer, Weiss, *et al.*). A living organism is defined as a complex system of physico-chemical mechanisms.

(2) *Vitalism*. Evolution is the product of an ever-present and inherent urge—*entelechy*—in all things (Aristotle, Driesch, Schopenhauer, Bergson, Aurobindo [Hindu], Lecomte du Noüy, Haldane, William McDougall, *et al.*) (see Aristotle, Schopenhauer, and Bergson, Part V).

(3) *Emergentism*. Evolution is the emerging of new levels of reality in the manner of matter → life → mind → God (Alexander, Whitehead, L. Morgan, Boodin, Chardin, *et al.*) (see theories of mind, p. 18, and Whitehead and Alexander, Part V).

Modern Hypotheses of Evolution

(1) Lamarck (1744–1829) taught the doctrine of the inheritance or *transmission of acquired characters*. Influence of environmental factors is stressed. Question: Does bodily modification affect germ cells?

(2) Herbert Spencer (1820–1903) taught the doctrine of *cosmic evolution* as well as *biological evolution*. The world is a vast evolutionary process in all aspects from *cosmology* to *culture*. Biological evolution is a reorganization of matter from the more simple (*homogeneous*) to the more complex (*heterogeneous*) (see Spencer, Part V).

(3) Charles Darwin (1809–1882) taught that the biological character of offspring is the same as that with which parents *started* not ended, except for *variations* in body cells. Hereditary factors are stressed. Darwin advanced the principle of *natural selection*:

(a) *Proliferation of species*. Each species tends to increase geometrically.
(b) *Variation*. Each generation produces differences of structure and function in organisms.

(c) *Struggle for existence.* Life reproduces in a greater number than can be sustained.

(d) *Survival of the fittest.* Better-adapted organisms survive, less-adapted perish. Evolution is *eliminative* rather than creative (suggested in Empedocles).

(e) *Heredity.* Surviving organisms transmit their traits to offspring.

(4) August Weismann (neo-Darwinianism) believed that heredity depends on the transmission of *germ cells* which *vary* but are not affected by changes in *body cells.*

(5) Hugo De Vries (the mutation theory, 1900) contended that variations in *germ cells* may be large and sudden and may be inherited by or transmitted to offspring. The principle of *natural selection* holds.

(6) Mendel developed the laws of heredity, *genetics.*

(7) T. H. Morgan elaborated the *gene theory.*

THEORIES OF MIND

The problem of mind and its relation to body is one of the great problems of philosophy. Taken broadly, it includes consideration of all the ways in which phenomena normally identified as mental or associated with mind are explained. It includes such characterizations of the mental as *thinking substance, soul stuff, self, ego, consciousness,* or simply "nature grown intelligent," as Dewey put it. As meant here, mind includes all activities of

(a) *conation,* such as desiring and willing;

(b) *adaptive behavior,* such as reasoning and problem solving; and

(c) *consciousness,* such as simple awareness, self-consciousness. Consciousness is denied by some schools (*behaviorism*) or supplemented by others with *unconsciousness* (*depth psychologies*).

The basic theories of mind are summarized in Charts 3, 15, and 16. In the charts, it will be well to note that contemporary psychologies are not clearly delineated into well-defined schools but often exhibit strong eclectic tendencies. The charts provide only general orientation. It is also important to note that no attempt has been made to distinguish the so-called "scientific" from "prescientific" or "nonscientific" theories of mind, either with respect to the existence or nonexistence of mind or with respect to any particular mind-body theory. It is to be noted, however, that mind has, in general, been viewed progressively as "soul," "substance," and "behavior." Contemporary thought tends to interpret mind in terms of what it does rather than what it is. Hence the term "behavior" is preferred by most psychologies. Yet it would be inimical to the spirit of philosophy to assume the finality of any particular theory of mind, notwithstanding the preponderance of evidence that might be mustered in support of it from any particular school of psychology.

── WORDS AND THEIR MEANINGS AS RELATED TO THEORIES OF MIND ──

ASSOCIATIONISM The theory that mind and its contents may be reduced to simple, discrete experiences that combine to form all aspects of the life of mind (see Hume, Part V).

BEHAVIORISM The theory that all mental activity may be reduced to implicit behavior (Watson).

DEPTH PSYCHOLOGY Any of the psychologies deriving from Freudian *psychoanalysis.*

DOUBLE-ASPECT THEORY OF MIND The theory that body and mind are manifestations of a more fundamental reality (see Spinoza, Part V).

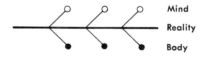

EMERGENTISM The theory that through evolution new realities such as mind form which cannot be reduced to lower levels (see Alexander, Part V).

FACULTY PSYCHOLOGY The theory that mind comprises the unity of a number of faculties: sensibility, intelligence, etc. (Wolff).

FUNCTIONAL PSYCHOLOGY The psychology of *pragmatism* and *instrumentalism,* wherein mind is interpreted biologically in terms of behavior and adaptation to the environment.

GESTALT PSYCHOLOGY A holistic form of structural psychology which opposes all atomistic approaches to mind and which studies behavior in terms of the *Gestalt,* the structure of the whole.

HOLISM Theories of mind, such as those of *Gestalt psychology* and *emergentism,* which deal with mind in terms of its total organization and behavior.

INTERACTIONISM The theory that mind and body are separate realities that mutually influence each other (see Descartes, Part V).

MONAD A unit of metaphysical reality—spiritual for Leibniz—capable of entering into relations that comprise the world.

OCCASIONALISM The theory that mind and body are separate realities which do not interact but that events occur in one as they occur in the other according as God wills their occurrence (Malebranche) (cf. parallelism below).

PANPSYCHISM The theory that all material entities possess a degree of mind (Lotze).

PARALLELISM The theory that mind and body are separate realities which do not interact but that events in each accompany events in the other (according to a *preestablished harmony* in Leibniz, Part V).

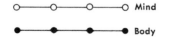

PHENOMENOLOGY The philosophy that attempts to analyze phenomena as contents of experience without reference to causes or metaphysical presuppositions (Husserl) (see Chart 24 and Husserl, Part V).

SELF The person, subject, ego, or knower.

THEORIES OF THE NATURE OF ULTIMATE REALITY

"What is really real?" is a question that has arisen in the minds of reflective men of all ages and of all cultures. An early Greek philosopher named Thales (6th century B.C.) declared that the world was made of water. Anaximenes (also 6th century B.C.) argued that it was air. These rather crude responses to the question of reality posed obvious difficulties which could be resolved only by the introduction of new problems. The answer to the question of reality assumed various forms, e.g., that it is spiritual or that it is material. Some philosophers associated reality with that which changes; others, with that which is changeless. A typical answer was that reality was unknowable. In various ways, the responses were motivated by religious or scientific interests or an interest in speculation for its own sake.

Monism, Pluralism, and Dualism

A basic distinction may be drawn between those who stress the unity or interrelatedness of reality and those who find an essential duality or plurality. The view that reality is fundamentally one as process, structure, substance, or ground is called *monism*. In the ancient world, monism characterized the philosophy of Parmenides (6th-5th century B.C.). Parmenides taught that all is being. Being fills all space and thought. Experience of change and plurality is possible only because there is an abiding and changeless being which makes this experience possible. Change is apparent only to the senses. In reality there is only being; change is illusory. This was an ancient form of monism. Modern monism is illustrated in the philosophy of Hegel (1770–1831), whose *idealism* pictured the world as the the manifestation or unfolding of an all-inclusive or absolute spirit realizing itself in time.

Modern philosophy exhibits *pluralistic* tendencies, however. This emphasis can be traced in part to the ancient Greek philosophy of Democritus (c. 460–360 B.C.). Democritus taught that reality consists in an infinite number of material atoms occupying and rearranging themselves in an infinite space. He attributed the permanence of Parmenides's being to the atoms, and explained change by referring to the rearranging tendency of these atoms as they engage in the process of becoming particular things. A strikingly modern theory, his atomic materialism accounted for the plurality of experiences and things but left many questions unanswered. Pluralistic explanations tend to encourage belief in a flexible and incomplete reality, whereas monistic explanations are generally those of the great system-builders, who would link all of reality together in an interrelated and logical whole.

A third view arises from a strong tendency to explain reality in terms of *opposites*. Indeed, both monistic and pluralistic explanations of reality use contrasting distinctions. Hegel, e.g., wrote of a fundamental opposition and synthesis of theses and antitheses; Democritus spoke of the distinction between material atoms and empty space. In the earliest speculations, philosophers noted the role of opposites in thought and experience—the affirmative and the negative, the good and the evil, being and nonbeing, etc. When these polarities of thought and experience were ascribed to reality or became embodied in explanations of reality, *dualism* developed.

The early modern philosopher Descartes (1596–1650) described the created world as a duality of extended or space-occupying substance and unextended or thinking substance which comprised mind in man. Bergson (1859–1941) distinguished a *dualism* between that which is created and that which creates in the cosmic process. His dualism embraced such distinctions as space and duration, matter and vital impulse. Plato (427–347 B.C.) distinguished an eternal, unchanging, and perfect realm of the Ideas or Forms of things from the changing realm of their embodiment in the phenomena of experience. Yet Plato could be interpreted as a monist as well as a dualist, in the sense that all the Ideas participate in the highest and most all-inclusive of Ideas, the transcendent Idea of the Good. He could also be interpreted as a pluralist for the reason that there are many independently real Ideas which comprise reality. In other words, categories like *monism, dualism,* or *pluralism* are essentially convenient ways of identifying the emphasis in a particular theory of reality, some theories being more distinctly one than another.

Idealism, Realism, and Pragmatism

Speculation about the nature of reality develops more or less in terms of the opposites of dualism, the pluralities of pluralism, or the oneness of monism. Furthermore, speculation about reality has emphasized either the role of the mental in describing or interpreting reality or, on the other hand, elements other than mind or consciousness, such as matter. As a result, certain traditional metaphysical distinctions arose, such as *idealism* and *realism*.

The idealist stresses the role of mind. He tends to argue: "The world is my world or the world of some mind." He insists that only a knowable reality can concern the philosopher and that this reality must therefore relate to ideas, to consciousness, or to the processes of thought. In other words, a material reality, e.g., could be known only through ideas, and one could never know whether his ideas about that reality accurately portrayed it.

His realist opponent answers, however: "I am in the world; the world is not in me." Or, with Whitehead, he might say: "I am in the world, and the world is in me." In any event, he would insist that reality does not depend on mind, that knowing has for its object a world independent of mind, and that reality presents itself to minds.

Realists tend to separate the world and its objects from knowers or minds. *Idealists* stress the intimate relationship which holds between knowers and things known. *Pragmatists,* differing with both, rejected the traditional knower and thing-known distinction altogether and as in James, e.g., held for a reality of "pure experience" in which all relations are found but in which there is no duality of consciousness and content, thought and thing.

Mysticism, Materialism, and Supernaturalism

Some philosophers have attempted to resolve the problem of reality by invoking the answer of *mysticism*. Though insisting on the oneness of reality, mysticism attempts to transcend the usual metaphysical distinctions of monism, dualism, and pluralism for the reason that it believes *ultimate reality* to be ineffable. Mysticism attempts to identify the subject with its world. Interest lies in the experience of a union with the ineffable rather than in knowledge of it in the usual sense.

Straightforward *materialists* simply point to matter or energy as the ultimate substance of reality, and *supernaturalists* speak of a God "in whom we live and move and have our being"—a God who is wholly transcendent but whose thought and whose will create, sustain, redeem, and perfect existence.

Positivism and Linguistic Analysis

See Chart 23.

Existentialism and Phenomenology

See Chart 24.

Marxism and Revolutionary Philosophy

Although all theories of the world attempt to explain the world, the Marxist and the social revolutionary see theory primarily as an instrument of social change rather than as an instrument of rational reflection. Like pragmatists, they reject *intellectualistic* approaches to reality or the world.

Marxism and revolutionary philosophy uniformly reject the social and economic institutions of the recent past. These are characterized by such general labels like "capitalism" or "the establishment." Since social ills and the nature of man—including his world—are largely the products of the established system of values and of the "power structure" in which man lives, that world must be altered in the direction of "humanizing" existence.

Although many Marxists, Communists, and social revolutionaries of various kinds picture the world along the lines of a *mechanistic* materialism, knowledgeable revolutionaries make it clear that it is *dialectical* materialism that interests them. Dialectical materialism calls for the alteration of the world in the direction of explicitly human goals. Although man is a product of his circumstances, he can alter them in the direction of a more humane existence. For these thinkers, capitalism is a phase of historical and cultural evolution that can and ought to be surpassed. Traditional philosophical issues, such as the nature of reality, knowledge, morality, and religion, are interpreted primarily in terms related to historical situations, and to concrete human aspirations (see Marx and Merleau-Ponty, Part V, and Chart 24).

Distinctions and Relations among the Theories

Though monistic and dualistic explanations tend to be idealistic, mystic, or supernaturalistic in emphasis and pluralistic explanations tend to be realistic, these tendencies are by no means necessary. The metaphysics of personalism, e.g., is distinctly pluralistic, and Catholic pluralistic realism (neo-Aristotelianism) embraces supernaturalism as well.

An arbitrary classification is also drawn along the lines of monism, dualism, and pluralism. One might also separate theories of reality into the naturalistic and the non-naturalistic. In this case, the former would stress the view that the nature experienced in phenomena is the extent of any knowable reality, whereas the latter would emphasize the inadequacy of such a view. All labels and distinctions are unavoidably arbitrary and must therefore be used with reservations.

"The history of philosophy is the continuous recurrence and resuscitation of certain well-defined points of view, such as *empiricism, rationalism* [as theories of knowledge], *mysticism, realism, idealism,* etc. [as theories or reality]; in these the mind seems to have achieved a final insight into the nature of things, in the sense that they represent permanent possibilities of explaining the universe" (Demos, *Plato Selections*).

In the charts of theories of reality, care should be exercised not to identify this or that philosopher too closely with any particular theory of reality. Particular philosophers or philosophies vary widely in their doctrines, and their antecedent and subsequent influences need not be congruent. The user of these charts will find overlapping and repetition, and certain key figures will appear on many charts because of their extensive influence. The charts should be used for orientation and as guides to investigation rather than as substitutes for study in original or secondary sources.

Summaries of the particular theories of reality advanced by some representative and important philosophers are to be found in Part V. These comprise a few of the important answers to the question of the nature of ultimate reality. Where these are available, the philosopher's name appears in red on the chart.

WORDS AND THEIR MEANINGS AS RELATED TO THEORIES OF THE NATURE OF ULTIMATE REALITY

ABSOLUTE In *metaphysics,* the highest or most all-encompassing reality, i.e., the Unconditioned, God, Unmoved Mover, World Ground, Being, the Good, *Logos,* One, Substance, in Chinese thought *Tao* (Way), in Indian thought *Brahman* (see Aristotle, Plato, Spinoza, and Hegel, Part V).

BECOMING The process of actualizing potential. It is usually thought of as an activity or movement.

BEING That-which is, *to-on* (Gr.), *ens* (Lat.). In Plato, class concepts or the intelligible universal characteristics of things, the Ideas or Forms (see Plato, Part V). In Aristotle and *scholasticism,* particular existing and developing things (*ens reale*—real being) and rational or conceptual being (*ens rationis*), i.e., true statements that have a mental existence as contents of minds (see Aristotle, Part V). In Heidegger and in *existentialism* generally, distinguished as *being,* i.e., the *thing* as is (*l'étant,* Fr.; *das Seiende,* Ger.); and *Being,* i.e., the *to-be* of whatever is (*l'être,* Fr.; *das Sein,* Ger.) (see Heidegger and Sartre, Part V).

COSMOLOGY The study of the origin and structure of the universe. Though more specific in subject matter than *ontology, metaphysics,* or *natural science,* it cannot be sharply distinguished from them.

ESSENCE *What* a thing is. For Greek philosophy, it means *substance (ousia),* that which is not apparent but is the really real about things—what can be *conceived,* what is *universal* (see *substance* below). In Plato, the Forms or Ideas (see Plato, Part V). In Santayana, a similar but modified meaning (see Santayana, Part V). For *essence* in Husserl, see Husserl, Part V. See also St. Thomas Aquinas, Part V; and for *essence* in existentialist philosophy, see Kierkegaard, Sartre, and Heidegger, Part V, and Chart 24.

EXISTENCE The assertion *that* a thing is, not what it is as a concept of essence. For *existentialism,* existence is *conscious-* ness and precedes essence for man, who finds himself existing and *then* becomes essence by choice and act (see Kierkegaard, Heidegger, and Sartre, Part V, and Chart 24).

METAPHYSICS The theory of *first principles* or, as synonymous with *ontology,* the theory of being as such. It is often made a broader term than ontology, by including *epistemology* (see p. 3). Originally it was an arbitrary title given to a collection of Aristotle's works on first principles that literally came after his physics, i.e., *meta ta physika* (Gr.). For Aristotle, theory of first principles included both ontology and epistemology.

ONTOLOGY The theory of being as such, i.e., of ultimate reality (Gr. *on* being + *logos,* theory).

SUBSTANCE That which makes a thing what it is and not something else, i.e., *essence* in Greek philosophy (*ousia*). St. Augustine writes that "essence (*ousia* in Greek) usually means nothing else than substance in . . . Latin." In Aristotle, primary substance (*substantia prima* in the Latin translations) is the *inherent essence* or *cause* of a *particular* thing, i.e., the unity of its *form* and *matter* (see Aristotle, Part V). In *scholasticism,* substance is that which exists and persists independent of any other being (see St. Thomas Aquinas, Part V). Similarly in *Cartesianism* (see Descartes, Part V), substance is that which exists independent of any other being. *Infinite substance* is God; *finite substance, mind* and *matter.* In Spinoza (see Part V), there is only *infinite substance* (God) and its *modes.* In *Kantianism* (see Kant, Part V), substance becomes a subjective concept of the mind arising from the necessary organizing activity of mind in connection with the data of experience. In *British empiricism,* substance is essentially the systematic or coherent organization of the specific qualities of experience. As such, it does not exist or is unknowable (see Berkeley, Hume, and Mill, Part V).

{ *Part IV* }

The Problem of Values

The study of the theory of values is *axiology* (Gr. *axios,* of like value + *logos,* theory). "Pure *axiology* is the study of values of *all* types" (Urban).

BASIC AXIOLOGICAL QUESTIONS

Is value a quality, a relation, or an attitude?
Is value found or made?
Is value definable? analyzable? reducible? If so, to what?

AXIOLOGY

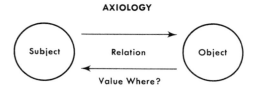

THEORIES OF VALUE

The general theory of value has its origin in the debate between Alexius Meinong and Christian von Ehrenfels during the 1890's concerning the *source of value.* Meinong saw the source of value as *feeling,* or the expectation or possibility of pleasure in an object. Ehrenfels (also Spinoza) saw the source of value in *desire.* The object is endowed with value through actual or possible desire; i.e., an object possesses value because it is desired. In both views, value is the *property of an object—axiological objectivism.*

AXIOLOGICAL OBJECTIVISM

Subject ◄─────────── Object (Value)

Axiological Objectivism or Realism

In this outlook, value judgments are in some sense objective. Values, norms, ideals, etc. are constituents of or reside in objects or in objective reality (as in Alexander); or they are ascribed to objects by desire (as in Spinoza). Value judgments are meaningful, i.e, *true* or *false,* even though they are not verifiable, i.e, not definable in verifiable sensory terms. Values reside in objects as do colors or temperatures. Values are grounded in reality.

Advocates of axiological objectivism include Plato, Aristotle, St. Thomas Aquinas, Maritain, Royce, Urban, Bosanquet, Whitehead, Joad, Spaulding, Alexander, *et al.*

Some Typical Expressions of Axiological Objectivism

Bosanquet (*idealism*): "Value . . . is a certain *quality of objects, bona fide belonging to them,* but especially revealed in their manifestations within the attitude of human minds." Knowing and evaluating are inseparable. (Also Bradley, Windelband, Rickert, and most idealistic theory.)

Scheler (*phenomenology*): "Values are essences, i.e., self-subsistent entities which are *emotionally intuited.*" Through emotion and reason we discern values as objectively and directly as through sense perception we perceive the world. (Also Meinong, N. Hartmann, Urban, *et al.*)

C. I. Lewis (*conceptual pragmatism*): Value judgments are subject to the same standards of inquiry and validity as are any cognitive empirical judgments.

G. E. Moore (*intuitionism*): Values (as, e.g., the good) are indefinable, i.e., unanalyzable properties not reducible to terms other than value terms, but nevertheless may be *factually* predicated of acts or objects.

Axiological Subjectivism

Theories of this outlook reduce value judgments to statements about mental attitudes toward an object or situation. Value judgments are equivalent to statements of *approval* or *disapproval* and as such are *true* or *false.* The statement "*x* has value" means "I like *x*" or "Society likes *x*." Value judgments are therefore analyzable to statements about attitudes, about degrees of approval, about pleasantness, etc. Value has reality only as a state of mind in the subject. Axiological subjectivism tends to endorse the ethical theory of *hedonism,* i.e., the theory that *pleasure is the criterion of value,* and *naturalism,* i.e., the belief that values can be reduced to psychological statements. Values are dependent on and relative to human experience of them; they have no independent reality. Axiological *relativism* is stressed, i.e., the belief that values, including moral values, are relative to culture, circumstances, and other environmental factors.

Advocates of axiological subjectivism include Hume, Perry, Prall, Parker, Santayana, Sartre, *et al.*

Some Typical Expressions of Axiological Subjectivism

Hume (*skepticism*): "*x* has value" means "Most men prefer *x.*"

Sartre (*existentialism*): Values are created by the subject (see Sartre, Part V).

Santayana (*aesthetic hedonism*): Values are indefinable empirical qualities associated with pleasant feelings: "To feel beauty is a better thing than to understand how we come to feel it." "All values are in one sense aesthetic." "*Beauty is pleasure* regarded as the quality of a thing (in experience)." "There is no value apart from appreciation of it."

D. H. Parker (*humanism*): "Values belong . . . to the world of mind. The satisfaction of desire is the real value. . . . A value is always an experience, never a thing or object. . . . We *project* value into the external world, attributing it to the things that serve desire."

Perry (*naturalism*): Value is "any object of any interest" as a relation holding between the interest and the object. The four criteria of value in this relationship are intensity, comprehensiveness, preference, and correctness. Perry approaches the view of axiological relationism (see Perry, Part V).

AXIOLOGICAL SUBJECTIVISM

Subject (Value) ⟶ Object

Axiological Relationism

This outlook proceeds from theories that value is a relation holding between variables or a product of variables in interaction. Values are not private (subjective) but *public*, though not objective in the sense of being independent of interests.

Advocates of axiological relationism include Dewey, Pepper, Ducasse, Lepley, *et al.*

Some Typical Expressions of Axiological Relationism

Dewey (*instrumentalism*): Value is the resolution or harmonious satisfaction of conflicts in the "social or environmental situation," i.e, in the interaction of the individual with his social and physical environment. Value theory is factual, i.e., verifiable, as is any empirical science. Values are "the relation of things as means to the ends or consequences actually reached." Values *qua* values are instrumental.

Pepper (*contextualism*): Value arises in a field having to do with the "quality of events." It relates to a system of personal relations plus a system of impersonal relations.

Ducasse (*humanism*): Value is not an event in the subject nor a quality in the object but a capacity to effect a kind of *relation.*

AXIOLOGICAL RELATIONISM

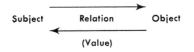

Subject ⟶ Object
Relation
⟵
(Value)

Axiological Nominalism or Skepticism (Emotivism)

Theories of this outlook hold that value judgments are expressions of emotion or attempts to persuade. They are not factual. A science of values—axiology—is impossible.

Historical note on the origin of *emotivism:*

G. E. Moore's doctrine of the *indefinable good.* (But *good* may be *factually* predicated of acts and objects even though *intuited* and not verifiable.)

I. A. Richards's distinction of *factual* and *emotive* meanings.

Emotivism (the value theory of *logical positivism;* see Chart 19 and p. 28): Values are *indefinable* and *emotive,* hence are *factually meaningless.* They do not describe a state of the subject, the object, or a relation.

Advocates of emotivism include Nietzsche, Ayer, Russell, Stevenson, Schlick, Carnap, *et al.*

Some Typical Expressions of Emotivism

Nietzsche (*axiological relativism*): Value judgments are *expressions of feelings* and *custom* rather than statements of fact.

Ayer (*logical positivism*): Value judgments serve an *expressive function,* giving vent to feelings and, as statements, are emotive or noncognitive, i.e., *factually meaningless.*

Stevenson (*logical empiricism*): Value judgments serve a primarily *persuasive function.* Since value judgments are emotive and not subject to error as true or false, persuasion is needed to evoke their acceptance.

ETHICAL THEORY

Values claim a priority with respect to some aspect of human experience. This is their nature, for they demand of us a certain degree of side-taking. Moral values enjoy priority over other values. They are "unlimited priorities for action"; i.e., "So far as action goes, moral values take precedence over all other values. . . . Thus a person may say that the good life is the life devoted to aesthetic enjoyment. Such a statement asserts that aesthetic values have the highest *moral* value" (Mothershead). Because of their relative importance, moral values will receive the bulk of attention.

The Normative-Metaethical Distinction

Ethical theory must be distinguished as *normative* or *metaethical* whereby an attempt may be made either

(a) to identify the universal principle(s) of morality to which all men ought to appeal to guide or to justify their behavior, i.e., an *ideal* or *true* code of morality (*normative ethics*); or

(b) to analyze or describe the way or ways in which moral judgments are actually used (*metaethics*).

Metaethics concerns itself with questions of meaning, truth, and method. It is about words, statements, judgments, etc., that is *moral language.* By contrast, *normative ethics* is about right and wrong acts or the *good life itself.*

Normative ethics may be distinguished as *teleological* or *deontological* or varying combinations of both (see notes below).

Metaethics may be distinguished as *cognitivist* or *noncognitivist* (see "Metaethical or Analytical Theories of Ethics," pp. 27, 28, 29).

Ethical Theories That Are Teleological and Deontological

Socrates originated the Greek teleological ethics of *eudaemonism* but also spoke of obedience to *duty* and an *inner voice*—a teaching that was subsequently stressed by the *Stoics* and their deontological ethics. But the Stoics were also teleological in their effort to achieve *apatheia* (imperturbability) as the state of perfection.

Christian ethics is both teleological and deontological though the latter predominates. The teleological is expressed in references to the eternal bliss of man in heaven (St. Augustine) or the greatest happiness of the greatest number as God's will (Paley). The deontological is expressed in references to obedience to God's will or to conscience or to goodness as deriving from God's will as good because God says so, or it is His will that it be so, etc. (Ockham, Duns Scotus, Descartes, Kierkegaard, Brunner, *et al.*).

In recent ethical theory, C. D. Broad attempts to reconcile the deontological and teleological by noting that rightness or wrongness of an action in a given situation is a function of its *fittingness and utility in that situation*.

The Ethics of Love, or Judeo-Christian Agapistic Ethics

"Thou shalt love the Lord thy God with all thy heart, and with all thy soul, and with all thy mind. This is the first and great commandment. And the second is like unto it. Thou shalt love thy neighbor as thyself" (Matt. 22: 37–40).

Traditional agapistic ethics stresses *both* love of God, which implies that one ought to obey His commandments, *and* love of neighbor, which obedience to His commandments implements. But this ethic may be a derivative *agapism* since it argues that we *ought* to love God and neighbor because God commands us or because God loves us and we *ought* to imitate Him as well as obey Him. This is what being right means, i.e., *deontological agapism* or simply *act deontology* if what we *ought* to do is fundamental.

Thomist *natural law* ethics also may not derive directly from the law of love and therefore not be a pure agapistic ethic.

Evangelical agapistic ethics stresses the indwelling Christ through whom acts reflect a *supernatural* love that is also always in obedience to Biblical imperatives, i.e., an *authoritarian agapism*. Yet, for those without the indwelling Christ, there is a moral law "written in their hearts" that distinguishes right from wrong (Rom. 2:14–15).

In *nontraditional* agapistic ethics (situation ethics), if one identifies loving God with loving neighbor, as in the ethics of *secular theology*, then either a form of *act deontology* or *situation ethics* (existential ethics) follows (as, e.g., in Fletcher, Gustafson, Tillich, or Lehmann) or some kind of *utilitarianism*, wherein the greatest good for one's neighbor is sought. Clearly one need not promote *God's* good, although "for Christ's sake" may be interpreted as "for neighbor's sake," in which case the law of love becomes or approximates the principle of benevolence.

Pure agapism, i.e., love is the only moral absolute, may be interpreted as

(1) *Act agapism*. One should do the most loving thing in each particular situation, i.e., let love determine one's obligation rather than rules (situationism, religious existentialism, antinomianism).

(2) *Rule agapism*. One should follow rules that are most love-producing or love-embodying.

The usual criticism of *nontraditional agapistic ethics* or *situation ethics* is that they do not account for how love can provide one with a way of telling which act to perform or which rule to follow. Thus the implementation of the injunction to love one's neighbor is not explicit, especially if divine illumination or revelation is already ruled out, as well as any philosophical principle.

THE JUSTIFICATION OF MORALITY
Ethical Egoism

One ought always to further his own interest and ignore the interest of others unless it bears on his own interest. One's own interest that ought to be furthered may be:

(a) the maximization of one's own *pleasure* or *happiness*—*egoistic ethical hedonism*, as in Epicurus; or
(b) the maximization of pleasure or happiness in general—*universalistic ethical hedonism* or *hedonistic utilitarianism*, as in Bentham or Mill or what Plato, e.g., called the mixed life of knowledge, pleasure, and other good things. For Plato, morality pays. "The moral [just] man is always the happy man."

Other ethical egoists are Protagoras and the Greek Sophists generally, Aristotle ("Every man is his own best friend"), Spinoza, and Hobbes, who is also a *psychological egoist*.

Psychological Egoism

This is a pseudo-scientific theory that it is impossible for anyone to act contrary to what he believes to be his best interest. If psychological egoism is true, ethical egoism as an ethical theory is pointless, since no one can help acting in what he believes to be his best interest.

Why Be Moral?

This question asks what *reasons* can be given to *justify* being moral, not what *causes* or *provides incentive* for being moral. Representative answers given are

(1) Morality pays for the individual as, e.g., Plato.
(2) Morality furthers the common interest; i.e., being moral *means* "following rules designed to overrule self-interest whenever it is in the interest of everyone alike that everyone should set aside his interest" (Baier).
(3) Morality is in accordance with God's will. One should obey God's will either because

(a) it is in his interest to do so—to avoid punishment and so on (*egoism*);
(b) he loves God and seeks to implement His perfect love (*agapism*); or
(c) God is sovereign authority and therefore entitled to obedience (*authoritarianism*).

(4) Morality is right. If I acknowledge that an action is *right*, I have my reason, i.e., justification, for doing it. To acknowledge an *obligation* is *also* to acknowledge a reason for fulfilling it. Also to the question "Why *this* act?" the answer is "Because it is right." A self-interested reason for being moral *can't* be given for acting contrary to self-interest. Hence only moral reasons can *justify* morality that happens to be contrary to self-interest (see Kant, p. 25, *re* the moral point of view).

Sartre (*existentialism*): Values are created by the subject (see Sartre, Part V).

Santayana (*aesthetic hedonism*): Values are indefinable empirical qualities associated with pleasant feelings: "To feel beauty is a better thing than to understand how we come to feel it." "All values are in one sense aesthetic." "*Beauty is pleasure* regarded as the quality of a thing (in experience)." "There is no value apart from appreciation of it."

D. H. Parker (*humanism*): "Values belong . . . to the world of mind. The satisfaction of desire is the real value. . . . A value is always an experience, never a thing or object. . . . We *project* value into the external world, attributing it to the things that serve desire."

Perry (*naturalism*): Value is "any object of any interest" as a relation holding between the interest and the object. The four criteria of value in this relationship are intensity, comprehensiveness, preference, and correctness. Perry approaches the view of axiological relationism (see Perry, Part V).

AXIOLOGICAL SUBJECTIVISM

Subject (Value) ⟶ Object

Axiological Relationism

This outlook proceeds from theories that value is a relation holding between variables or a product of variables in interaction. Values are not private (subjective) but *public*, though not objective in the sense of being independent of interests.

Advocates of axiological relationism include Dewey, Pepper, Ducasse, Lepley, *et al.*

Some Typical Expressions of Axiological Relationism

Dewey (*instrumentalism*): Value is the resolution or harmonious satisfaction of conflicts in the "social or environmental situation," i.e, in the interaction of the individual with his social and physical environment. Value theory is factual, i.e., verifiable, as is any empirical science. Values are "the relation of things as means to the ends or consequences actually reached." Values *qua* values are instrumental.

Pepper (*contextualism*): Value arises in a field having to do with the "quality of events." It relates to a system of personal relations plus a system of impersonal relations.

Ducasse (*humanism*): Value is not an event in the subject nor a quality in the object but a capacity to effect a kind of *relation*.

AXIOLOGICAL RELATIONISM

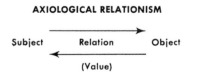

Subject — Relation — Object
(Value)

Axiological Nominalism or Skepticism (Emotivism)

Theories of this outlook hold that value judgments are expressions of emotion or attempts to persuade. They are not factual. A science of values—*axiology*—is impossible.

Historical note on the origin of *emotivism:*

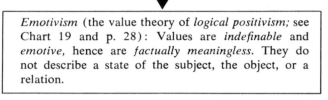

G. E. Moore's doctrine of the *indefinable good*. (But *good* may be *factually* predicated of acts and objects even though *intuited* and not verifiable.)

+

I. A. Richards's distinction of *factual* and *emotive* meanings.

⬇

Emotivism (the value theory of *logical positivism;* see Chart 19 and p. 28): Values are *indefinable* and *emotive*, hence are *factually meaningless*. They do not describe a state of the subject, the object, or a relation.

Advocates of emotivism include Nietzsche, Ayer, Russell, Stevenson, Schlick, Carnap, *et al.*

Some Typical Expressions of Emotivism

Nietzsche *(axiological relativism):* Value judgments are *expressions of feelings* and *custom* rather than statements of fact.

Ayer *(logical positivism):* Value judgments serve an *expressive function*, giving vent to feelings and, as statements, are emotive or noncognitive, i.e., *factually meaningless.*

Stevenson *(logical empiricism):* Value judgments serve a primarily *persuasive function*. Since value judgments are emotive and not subject to error as true or false, persuasion is needed to evoke their acceptance.

ETHICAL THEORY

Values claim a priority with respect to some aspect of human experience. This is their nature, for they demand of us a certain degree of side-taking. Moral values enjoy priority over other values. They are "unlimited priorities for action"; i.e., "So far as action goes, moral values take precedence over all other values. . . . Thus a person may say that the good life is the life devoted to aesthetic enjoyment. Such a statement asserts that aesthetic values have the highest *moral* value" (Mothershead). Because of their relative importance, moral values will receive the bulk of attention.

The Normative-Metaethical Distinction

Ethical theory must be distinguished as *normative* or *metaethical* whereby an attempt may be made either

(a) to identify the universal principle(s) of morality to which all men ought to appeal to guide or to justify their behavior, i.e., an *ideal* or *true* code of morality (*normative ethics*); or

(b) to analyze or describe the way or ways in which moral judgments are actually used (*metaethics*).

Metaethics concerns itself with questions of meaning, truth, and method. It is about words, statements, judgments, etc., that is *moral language*. By contrast, *normative ethics* is about right and wrong acts or the *good life itself*.

Normative ethics may be distinguished as *teleological* or *deontological* or varying combinations of both (see notes below).

Metaethics may be distinguished as *cognitivist* or *noncognitivist* (see "Metaethical or Analytical Theories of Ethics," pp. 27, 28, 29).

The Teleological-Deontological Distinction

The distinction between *teleological* and *deontological* ethical theory must take into consideration the following facts:

(1) The division is made with regard to *degrees of emphasis* rather than on the basis of mutual exclusion.

(2) Elements of *both* the teleological and the deontological are likely to be found in any *particular* ethical theory.

(3) There are marked differences of interpretation by different philosophers of each other's ethical theory; e.g., both G. E. Moore and Stace view Kant as naturalistic, but for different reasons. In this book, Kantian *formalism* is included among the *deontological* and generally *nonnaturalistic* theories.

(4) The interpretation is a broad one that includes most of *ethical formalism* and *ethical intuitionism* under the *deontological* and all instances of naturalistic ethics, e.g., *hedonism, utilitarianism*, etc., under the *teleological*.

Differences between the two kinds of ethical theory are suggested by answers to the question: What is there about an action that makes it right?

Teleological theory answers: the *goodness* of the *consequences,* the *moral values* that result (Bentham).

Deontological theory answers differently, according to whether it is *formal* or *intuitionistic*.

Formal theory answers: the nature of the *goodness* of *motives* for the action or the way we go about the action, as, e.g., in *obedience* to a sense of *duty* (Kant).

Intuitionistic theory answers: the *indefinable appropriateness* of an action in a particular situation (Ross).

Teleological Ethical Theory
Basic Beliefs

Ethical theory is concerned primarily with *ends* or the *good* rather than with moral obligation as such.

Considerations of moral *value* have priority over considerations of moral obligation.

Concepts of obligation, such as *duty, ought,* or *right,* are definable in terms of concepts of *value*.

Rightness is dependent on or connected in some way with the *goodness* (or *value*) of *action* or *consequences*.

The statement "*x* is a right action" means "*x* is likely to produce at least as *good consequences* as any other possible action."

Teleological theories tend to advance one *a priori intrinsic good* as a *moral standard,* as, e.g., *happiness*.

When teleological theory is *naturalistic:*

(1) Ethical judgments are *reducible* or *analyzable* to *nonethical* or *descriptive terms,* as in Spinoza, Hume, Mill, *et al.;* or

(2) Ethical judgments are in terms of *this-worldly ends* or *goods* as opposed to *spiritual* or *otherworldly ends* or *goods*.

Naturalistic ethics may be neither *teleological* nor *deontological,* as, e.g., in *emotivism* (Ayer *et al.*), wherein ethics is viewed as an empirical science of interests, motivations, and other axiological data. In this view, ethics becomes a branch of psychology or sociology, a study of "what people want and how to get it" or "what is" rather than "what ought to be," *descriptive* rather than *normative*.

Some Examples of Teleological Ethical Theory

Plato and Aristotle (Greek *eudaemonism*): Good is pleasure as "well-being," or the fulfillment of one's end.

Epicurus *(egoistic hedonism):* Good is pleasure or the absence of pain. By pleasure, Epicurus meant primarily the pleasures of the mind.

Bentham and Mill *(hedonistic utilitarianism* or *universalistic hedonism):* Good is the greatest happiness of the greatest number.

Paley *(theological utilitarianism):* Good is that which concurs with the will of God, who seeks the greatest happiness of man.

Moore *(ideal utilitarianism):* Good is indefinable but is related to the "ideal" rather than to "pleasure" in consequences. *Right* must be defined in terms of *good;* the latter is indefinable.

Sidgwick *(utilitarian intuitionism):* Good is happiness, but it cannot be defined in terms of a positive balance of happiness.

Spinoza and Spencer *(evolutionary utilitarianism):* "To be virtuous means to perform the specific activities of the species to which you belong efficiently" (Spinoza). "Better conduct is evolutionarily later and more complex conduct" (Spencer).

Hume *(subjective hedonism):* Good is reducible to the mental *attitude of approval* in all or most of the social group (on some interpretations).

Dewey *(instrumentalism):* Good is *that which works* in terms of both personal satisfactions and the resolution of group tensions.

Perry *(naturalism):* "Good is any object of any interest" —a *relational attitude*.

Scheler, N. Hartmann, Meinong *(axiological intuitionism* —phenomenological ethics): Good as such is directly perceived by an emotional *intuition*.

Act and Rule Teleology

Important forms of teleological ethical theory are *act utilitarianism* (traditional utilitarianism) and *rule utilitarianism* (recent utilitarianism).

According to *act* utilitarianism (Bentham, J. S. Mill as applied to individual acts, G. E. Moore), one must ask "What effect will *my* doing *this* act in *this* situation have on the production of good and the elimination of evil?" For example, "As a rule, telling the truth may generally produce the best consequences; but if this is not so in *this* situation, then I ought not to tell the truth." In other words: "Perform the *act* that will produce the most good." The principle of utility is applied to *acts*.

According to *rule* utilitarianism (J. S. Mill as applied to laws of conduct), one must ask "What effect will *everyone's* following *this* rule have on the production of good and the elimination of evil?" For example, "As a *rule, always* telling the truth produces the best consequences, even though it might not in these particular circumstances." It is argued that the most useful rules should be followed on the grounds that following them is *most likely* to produce the best results. If there are exceptions, these are built into the rule. In other words: "Act according to the *rule* whose adoption will produce the most good." The principle of utility is applied to *rules*.

Deontological Ethical Theory
Basic Beliefs

Ethical theory is concerned primarily with *moral obligation*—the *right*—rather than ends or consequences.

Moral obligation relates to *duty*, the *ought*, rightness, or "fittingness."

Moral obligation involves a necessity of doing an act; i.e., it is *categorical*. "You ought to do *x*." "I am obliged to do *x*." "It is our duty to do *x*." (*Duty* is the necessity of acting from respect for the moral law—Kant.)

Considerations of moral *obligation* have priority over considerations of moral *value*.

Concepts of moral value (the *good*, etc.) are definable in terms of *moral obligation* or *rational fittingness* which are themselves underived, i.e., unanalyzable (Reid, Ross).

Deontological ethics stresses the *self-evident* nature of the *right* as revealed to *reason, intuition,* or *moral sense*.

"*x* is intrinsically *good*" means "It is fitting or incumbent that every *rational* being desire *x*."

Ethics is an autonomous discipline deriving from neither science nor metaphysics. It is *deontological*.

Freedom is postulated as the necessary condition of moral choice.

As *ethical intuitionism*, deontological ethics stresses the objectivity of moral rightness or goodness, i.e., *axiological objectivism* (see p. 22), and the nonnaturalistic, i.e., irreducible character, of moral judgments.

A deontologist contends that it is possible for an action or rule of action to be morally right or obligatory even if it does not happen to lead to the best consequences, as, e.g., in Kant, where an act may be morally right—done *in accordance with duty*, i.e., the *categorical imperative*—and the agent morally good, i.e., *he acts from duty*, with a *good will*—yet lead to bad consequences, e.g., it makes the agent or others unhappy. This is sometimes called the *moral point of view*, wherein one does what is right because it is right and regardless of whether it happens to be in his interest to do so (principle of impartiality).

Some Examples of Deontological Ethical Theory

Epictetus (*Stoicism*): Right is *resignation* to *duty* and indifference to consequences.

St. Paul (*Christian ethics*): Right is *obedience to God's will* (but see below, p. 26, concerning *agapistic* ethics).

Kant (*formalism*): Right is the *rational willing* of one's *duty for duty's sake*.

Royce (*idealism*): Right is *loyalty to loyalty* for its own sake.

Clarke, Cumberland, Joseph Butler, Price, Reid (*Cambridge Platonism* and *moral-sense intuitionism*): Right is the indefinable moral *duty* intuited by a common *moral sense*. "Everyone may find within himself the rule of right, and obligations to follow it" (Butler).

Act and Rule Deontology

Deontological ethical theory may be distinguished as *act deontology* or *rule deontology*.

Act deontology. "In this *situation* I should do so-and-so, or it is my *duty* to do so-and-so," as, e.g., in Prichard, Car-

ritt, Aristotle, Joseph Butler, and contemporary existential moralists, such as Barth, Brunner, Fletcher, Lehmann, Gustafson, the Niebuhrs, Robinson, Tillich, Sartre, *et al.*, for whom the *situation determines* one's *moral duty*, although one must *freely decide* to meet his obligation. Rules based on particular cases may be allowed to serve as guidelines for decision but never allowed to prescribe decisions in particular situations. In its *existential* form, act deontology is one kind of *situational* or *contextual ethics*.

Criticisms of *act deontology* and *situation ethics* contend that we cannot do without rules because

(1) Moral situations are usually routine in character rather than uniquely new situations requiring "decisions of principle" (Hare) (*re* moral choosing).

(2) When one makes a moral judgment in a particular situation, one implicitly commits himself to making the same judgment in any similar situation (*re* moral judging).

(3) Moral judgments are justified by *reasons*, and reasons cannot apply to particular cases only. If the reasons apply in *this* case, then they apply in all similar cases (*re* moral reasoning).

(4) Moral *learning* is by way of the use of *principles*. "To learn to do anything is never to learn to do an individual act; it is always to learn to do acts of a certain kind in a certain kind of situation, and this is to learn a principle" (Hare) (*re* moral learning).

Rule deontology. Standards of right and wrong acts are *rules*, as, e.g., "We ought always to tell the truth," as in Clark, Richard Price, Reid, Ross, Kant, and in some cases Butler, who also opts for act deontology (see above).

Criticisms of *rule deontology* contend that no rule can be framed to fit every situation. Provisions must be made for *conflicts of rules* and *exceptions*. (But exceptions may be embodied in rules, as, e.g., "It is wrong to kill *except* in self-defense," and rules may be ranked according to their priority, as, e.g., "One ought to keep promises *except* when life may be endangered.")

Four General Types of Deontological Theory

(1) Butler (*moral-conscience theories*): Right actions in *specific* situations can be immediately discerned or finally settled by a reflective principle of *conscience*. (Cf. Sidgwick: Moral sense is able to note by inspection that certain types of action are necessarily right or wrong without regard to consequences.)

(2) Ross (*deontological intuitionism*): Certain types of action, as, e.g., keeping promises, are always right unless overridden by other duties, e.g., saving a life, in a particular situation. Moral rules are possible but not deducible from a single principle alone.

(3) Kant (*formalism*): There is a supreme principle or *law* of duty binding on all rational wills as a *universal standard* for the maxims of all moral judgments—the *categorical imperative*. In other words: So act that you could will the maxim or rule of your act to become the maxim or rule of all similar acts in an *ideal world*.

(4) St. Paul (*deontological agapism*): We *ought* to love God and neighbor either (a) because Christ lives within us as the law of love which is perfect freedom; or, if not, then (b) because there is nonetheless a moral law or conscience innate to us that prescribes our duty (see *agapistic* ethics below, p. 26).

Ethical Theories That Are Teleological and Deontological

Socrates originated the Greek teleological ethics of *eudaemonism* but also spoke of obedience to *duty* and an *inner voice*—a teaching that was subsequently stressed by the *Stoics* and their deontological ethics. But the Stoics were also teleological in their effort to achieve *apatheia* (imperturbability) as the state of perfection.

Christian ethics is both teleological and deontological though the latter predominates. The teleological is expressed in references to the eternal bliss of man in heaven (St. Augustine) or the greatest happiness of the greatest number as God's will (Paley). The deontological is expressed in references to obedience to God's will or to conscience or to goodness as deriving from God's will as good because God says so, or it is His will that it be so, etc. (Ockham, Duns Scotus, Descartes, Kierkegaard, Brunner, *et al.*).

In recent ethical theory, C. D. Broad attempts to reconcile the deontological and teleological by noting that rightness or wrongness of an action in a given situation is a function of its *fittingness and utility in that situation.*

The Ethics of Love, or Judeo-Christian Agapistic Ethics

"Thou shalt love the Lord thy God with all thy heart, and with all thy soul, and with all thy mind. This is the first and great commandment. And the second is like unto it. Thou shalt love thy neighbor as thyself" (Matt. 22: 37–40).

Traditional agapistic ethics stresses *both* love of God, which implies that one ought to obey His commandments, *and* love of neighbor, which obedience to His commandments implements. But this ethic may be a derivative *agapism* since it argues that we *ought* to love God and neighbor because God commands us or because God loves us and we *ought* to imitate Him as well as obey Him. This is what being right means, i.e., *deontological agapism* or simply *act deontology* if what we *ought* to do is fundamental.

Thomist *natural law* ethics also may not derive directly from the law of love and therefore not be a pure agapistic ethic.

Evangelical agapistic ethics stresses the indwelling Christ through whom acts reflect a *supernatural* love that is also always in obedience to Biblical imperatives, i.e., an *authoritarian agapism.* Yet, for those without the indwelling Christ, there is a moral law "written in their hearts" that distinguishes right from wrong (Rom. 2:14–15).

In *nontraditional* agapistic ethics (situation ethics), if one identifies loving God with loving neighbor, as in the ethics of *secular theology,* then either a form of *act deontology* or *situation ethics* (existential ethics) follows (as, e.g., in Fletcher, Gustafson, Tillich, or Lehmann) or some kind of *utilitarianism,* wherein the greatest good for one's neighbor is sought. Clearly one need not promote *God's* good, although "for Christ's sake" may be interpreted as "for neighbor's sake," in which case the law of love becomes or approximates the principle of benevolence.

Pure agapism, i.e., love is the only moral absolute, may be interpreted as

(1) *Act agapism.* One should do the most loving thing in each particular situation, i.e., let love determine one's obligation rather than rules (situationism, religious existentialism, antinomianism).

(2) *Rule agapism.* One should follow rules that are most love-producing or love-embodying.

The usual criticism of *nontraditional agapistic ethics* or *situation ethics* is that they do not account for how love can provide one with a way of telling which act to perform or which rule to follow. Thus the implementation of the injunction to love one's neighbor is not explicit, especially if divine illumination or revelation is already ruled out, as well as any philosophical principle.

THE JUSTIFICATION OF MORALITY
Ethical Egoism

One ought always to further his own interest and ignore the interest of others unless it bears on his own interest. One's own interest that ought to be furthered may be:

(a) the maximization of one's own *pleasure* or *happiness*— *egoistic ethical hedonism,* as in Epicurus; or
(b) the maximization of pleasure or happiness in general— *universalistic ethical hedonism* or *hedonistic utilitarianism,* as in Bentham or Mill or what Plato, e.g., called the mixed life of knowledge, pleasure, and other good things. For Plato, morality pays. "The moral [just] man is always the happy man."

Other ethical egoists are Protagoras and the Greek Sophists generally, Aristotle ("Every man is his own best friend"), Spinoza, and Hobbes, who is also a *psychological egoist.*

Psychological Egoism

This is a pseudo-scientific theory that it is impossible for anyone to act contrary to what he believes to be his best interest. If psychological egoism is true, ethical egoism as an ethical theory is pointless, since no one can help acting in what he believes to be his best interest.

Why Be Moral?

This question asks what *reasons* can be given to *justify* being moral, not what *causes* or *provides incentive* for being moral. Representative answers given are

(1) Morality pays for the individual as, e.g., Plato.
(2) Morality furthers the common interest; i.e., being moral *means* "following rules designed to overrule self-interest whenever it is in the interest of everyone alike that everyone should set aside his interest" (Baier).
(3) Morality is in accordance with God's will. One should obey God's will either because

(a) it is in his interest to do so—to avoid punishment and so on *(egoism);*
(b) he loves God and seeks to implement His perfect love *(agapism);* or
(c) God is sovereign authority and therefore entitled to obedience *(authoritarianism).*

(4) Morality is right. If I acknowledge that an action is *right,* I have my reason, i.e., justification, for doing it. To acknowledge an *obligation* is *also* to acknowledge a reason for fulfilling it. Also to the question "Why *this* act?" the answer is "Because it is right." A self-interested reason for being moral *can't* be given for acting contrary to self-interest. Hence only moral reasons can *justify* morality that happens to be contrary to self-interest (see Kant, p. 25, *re* the moral point of view).

METAETHICAL OR ANALYTICAL THEORIES OF ETHICS

This section outlines theories about the nature of moral words and discourse, as, e.g., in Moore, for whom "good" is the name of a nonempirical, indefinable quality of *good* things, or, e.g., in Stevenson, for whom moral statements are both expressions of approval and also attempts to influence attitudes or behavior.

Metaethics is the *study of moral statements* or *moral judgments* as contrasted with *normative ethics,* which is the study of *right and wrong or good and bad,* i.e., how behavior ought to be. Metaethics is concerned with the use of moral language and is *descriptive* and *analytical* rather than *prescriptive* and *substantive.*

Cognitivist and Noncognitivist Theories

Metaethical theories may be divided into two general kinds:

(1) *cognitivist*—those that hold that ethical terms and statements are *informative;* and

(2) *noncognitivist*—those that deny that ethical terms are informative or deny that they are *primarily* informative.

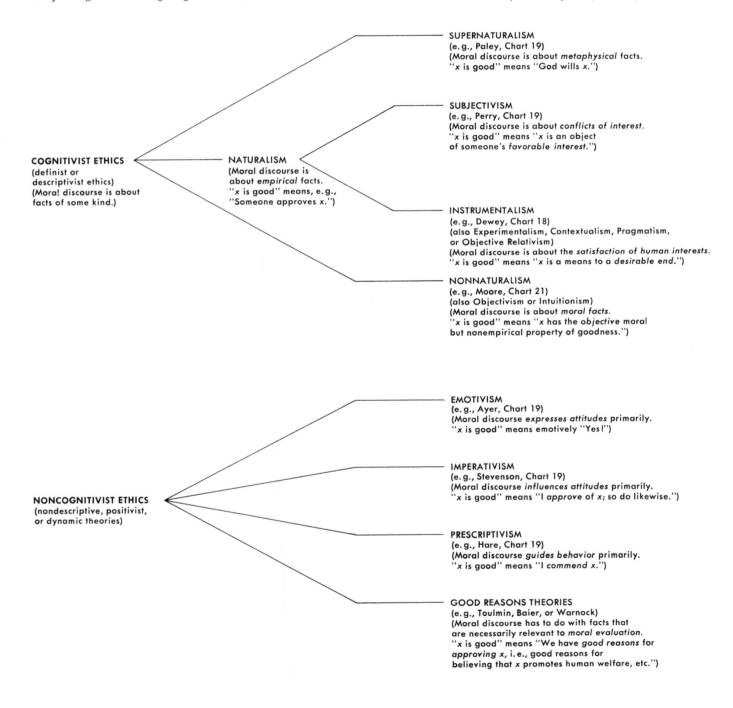

COGNITIVIST ETHICS
(definist or
descriptivist ethics)
(Moral discourse is about
facts of some kind.)

NATURALISM
(Moral discourse is
about *empirical* facts.
"x is good" means, e.g.,
"Someone approves x.")

SUPERNATURALISM
(e.g., Paley, Chart 19)
(Moral discourse is about *metaphysical* facts.
"x is good" means "God wills x.")

SUBJECTIVISM
(e.g., Perry, Chart 19)
(Moral discourse is about *conflicts of interest.*
"x is good" means "x is an object
of someone's *favorable interest.*")

INSTRUMENTALISM
(e.g., Dewey, Chart 18)
(also Experimentalism, Contextualism, Pragmatism,
or Objective Relativism)
(Moral discourse is about the *satisfaction of human interests.*
"x is good" means "x is a means to a *desirable end.*")

NONNATURALISM
(e.g., Moore, Chart 21)
(also Objectivism or Intuitionism)
(Moral discourse is about *moral facts.*
"x is good" means "x has the *objective moral*
but nonempirical property of goodness.")

NONCOGNITIVIST ETHICS
(nondescriptive, positivist,
or dynamic theories)

EMOTIVISM
(e.g., Ayer, Chart 19)
(Moral discourse *expresses attitudes* primarily.
"x is good" means emotively "Yes!")

IMPERATIVISM
(e.g., Stevenson, Chart 19)
(Moral discourse *influences attitudes* primarily.
"x is good" means "I approve of x; so do likewise.")

PRESCRIPTIVISM
(e.g., Hare, Chart 19)
(Moral discourse *guides behavior* primarily.
"x is good" means "I commend x.")

GOOD REASONS THEORIES
(e.g., Toulmin, Baier, or Warnock)
(Moral discourse has to do with facts that
are necessarily relevant to *moral evaluation.*
"x is good" means "We have *good reasons* for
approving x, i.e., good reasons for
believing that x promotes human welfare, etc.")

The Naturalistic-Fallacy Argument

The *naturalistic fallacy* is G. E. Moore's name for the attempt in metaethical theory to define the *ethical* (nonnatural) in *nonethical* (natural) terms, as, e.g., to define the good as pleasure (naturalistic ethics) or the good as what God approves (metaphysical ethics) (see Moore, Part V). Generally it is the weapon used by intuitionist ethics against all forms of nonintuitionist ethics, which, intuitionists say, attribute what is true of part of a whole, e.g., $a + b + c$ (nonethical properties) + good (ethical property) to the whole of which it is a part, e.g., $a + b + c = $ good.

Moore applies the *open-question test*, e.g., "This gives me pleasure, but is it good?" cannot mean "This gives me pleasure, but is it pleasure?" Those who invoke the naturalistic-fallacy argument assume (from Hume) that the "ought" cannot be derived from the "is." *Noncognitivist* or *emotivist* metaethics share Moore's use of the naturalistic-fallacy argument but for different reasons. For them, ethical terms cannot be defined in nonethical terms (pleasure, etc.) because they don't refer to anything. Rather their use is said to be *rhetorical* (persuasive, etc.) rather than *referential* (see noncognitivist ethics, p. 27). Thus both *intuitionist* (e.g., Moore) and *noncognitivist* or *emotivist* (e.g., Ayer) theories are *nondefinist* theories, and *naturalistic* (e.g., J. S. Mill) and *metaphysical* (e.g., Plato) are *definist* theories.

Opponents of the naturalistic-fallacy argument (e.g., Perry and Frankena) deny that the naturalistic fallacy is a *logical* fallacy if suppressed (unstated) premises are added, as, e.g., in the Epicurean inference from *psychological hedonism* (the claim that *as a matter of fact* all men seek pleasure) to *ethical hedonism* (the claim that men *ought* to seek pleasure or that pleasure is *intrinsically good*) (Frankena):

(a) Pleasure is sought by all men (what *is* the case).
(b) What is sought by all men is good (by *definition*).
(c) Therefore, pleasure is good (i.e., *ought* to be sought).

Thus Frankena, e.g., claims that Moore begs the question by assuming what he is trying to prove, i.e., the indefinability of the good. According to Frankena, "the naturalistic fallacy . . . is a fallacy, not because it is naturalistic or confuses a nonnatural quality with a natural one, but solely because it involves the *definist fallacy* . . . [which] is the process of confusing or identifying two properties, of defining one property by another, or of substituting one property for another. . . . The fallacy is always simply that *two properties are being treated as one,* and it is irrelevant . . . that one of them is natural or non-ethical and the other non-natural or ethical."

Opponents of Moore's naturalistic-fallacy argument or theory that "good is a nonnatural property" argue that to speak of something as, e.g., pleasant, i.e., nonethical, *and* good, i.e., ethical, is to refer to the *same* and not to different things. Thus there is no *definist fallacy*. One can use "pleasant" and "good" to mean, i.e., refer to, the same thing. Moreover, "if Moore's motto [or the definist fallacy] rules out any definitions . . . of 'good,' then *it rules out all definitions of any term whatever*" (Frankena).

Definist (i.e., naturalistic or metaphysical) ethics holds that certain propositions involving ethical terms are analytic (true by definition), as, e.g., "All objects of desire are good" (Perry). Intuitionist ethics hold that these statements are synthetic (informative, are about facts of some kind, etc.). *They* claim that *unique ethical properties* are intuited when ethical terms are used ($a + b + c + $ good). Definists, on the other hand, deny any such intuition and claim that the ethical terms, as, e.g., "good" or "right," refer only to nonethical properties as such. To say that x is a good student, e.g., is to refer specifically to some or all of certain characteristics, like lively interest, good attendance, cooperative attitude, excellent comprehension, etc., and not to anything *in addition* to these.

ETHICAL RELATIVISM

Relativism in ethical theory denies the existence of universal moral standards, as, e.g., it would deny Plato's claim that there is an absolute and universal Good.

Sociological Relativism

Sociological or *cultural* relativism holds that *as a matter of fact* moral beliefs are not the same in different cultural groups. What is thought to be right in one culture is not necessarily thought to be right in another culture.

Ethical Relativism

Ethical relativism holds that all moral beliefs are *true*. There is no universal or absolute standard of right and wrong. What is thought to be right in one culture, as, e.g., kindness, *is* right but need not *be* right in another culture. "Whatever is, is right."

Metaethical Relativism

Metaethical relativism holds that when there is moral disagreement, both views may be correct, as, e.g.,

(1) "x is right" *means* "What I *think* is right." (Objection: "What I think is right" = "What I think is what I think. . . .")
(2) "x is right" *means* "What I *approve*." (Objection: There could be no opposing moral judgments since if one person approved and another disapproved, neither would contradict the other. They would not be referring to the same thing.)
(3) "x is right" is *true* for you. "x is wrong" is *true* for me. (Objection: Statements are true or false, period. A confusion arises at the point of thinking that the above statements are like saying that it is true that *you like* strawberries, but it is also true that *I don't like* them.)

Methodological Relativism

Methodological relativism holds that there is no *rational* way of settling moral disputes. Nothing can be proved in ethics. No particular moral judgment is implied by any facts or set of facts.

FREEDOM AND RESPONSIBILITY

"The principle of morality and the freedom of the will are two of the most important matters to be dealt with by a moral philosophy" (Castell). If moral judgments are devoid of *standards* of judgment, there is no point in inquiring whether men should choose one or another course of action. On the other hand, if men cannot choose their courses of action, there is little point in attempting to establish standards of judgment. Nor can responsibility be ascribed

FREEDOM AND RESPONSIBILITY SPECTRUM

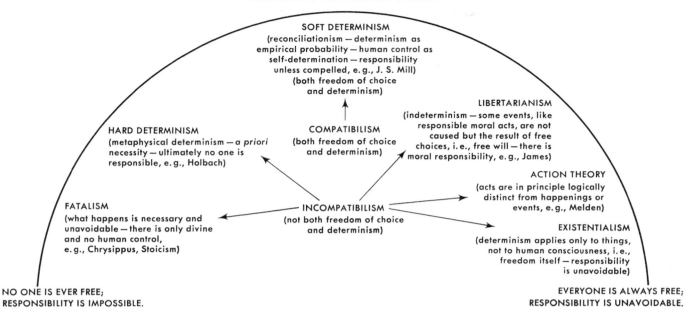

NO ONE IS EVER FREE;
RESPONSIBILITY IS IMPOSSIBLE.

EVERYONE IS ALWAYS FREE;
RESPONSIBILITY IS UNAVOIDABLE.

or praise or blame justified, since these presuppose alternative courses of action unless they are confined in their use to the altering of behavior rather than the making of moral judgments.

Moral judgments in everyday life—"He *can* do it," "He did it *voluntarily*," "He is *responsible*"—are embedded in specific contexts of use, and mark genuine distinctions within these contexts. They *do* function in ordinary moral language. The problem is to analyze out, and to account for, that function. Aristotle, e.g., noted that a person is responsible for his act unless he is ignorant or compelled.

Metaethical and Metaphysical Issues

The *metaethical* (i.e., logical) issue has to do with what it *means* to say of an act or a decision that it was free (voluntary), determined (caused), responsible (accountable), unavoidable (compelled), etc. For example, "Being determined doesn't necessarily mean or even simply mean being compelled."

The *metaphysical* (i.e., substantive) issue has to do with questions like "Given everything as it is, could anyone ever act other than he does?" "Are there genuine alternatives?" "Are such things as choosing, deciding, or acting events and, like all events, caused?" "Are praise and blame justified?"

Determinism

Determinism is the belief that

(1) Everything that happens has a cause.
(2) For every event in the universe, there is a set of conditions such that if the conditions were repeated, the event would be repeated.
(3) All events (facts, states, etc.) are *lawful* in the sense, roughly, that for any event *e*, there is a distinct event *d* plus a (causal) law which asserts, "whenever *d*, then *e*."

Fatalism

Fatalism (e.g., Stoicism) is the belief that events are predetermined by a cosmic purpose, plan, or will:

(1) Whatever is foreordained will occur no matter what.
(2) Human control is limited to attitude, as, e.g., resignation to the will of God, etc.
(3) Nothing happens by accident or chance.

Hard Determinism

Hard (metaphysical) determinism (Holbach, Spinoza, Darrow) holds the following:

(1) Causality is a necessary or *a priori truth* about the world.
(2) Nothing happens for which there is no *sufficient reason*.
(3) The world is a *mechanism*.
(4) The cause of moral choices is settled early and is independent of character. Even choices to alter nonhuman conditions are themselves already determined by antecedent conditions. They can't be other than they are.
(5) *Incompatibilism* is true—either determinism or indeterminism (not both). Since determinism is true, no acts are, in the final analysis, avoidable. Hence responsibility is a matter of good fortune rather than good character or free choice.

Soft Determinism

Soft determinism (reconciliationism) (Hume, Mill, Moore, Nowell-Smith, Schlick, Ayer, Hook) contends that

(1) Causality is a descriptive and therefore empirical generalization about the world or a useful assumption for scientific investigation. It is not *a priori* or prescriptive.
(2) Causality is not compulsion, although compulsion is one kind of causality.
(3) The question is not whether moral choices are caused but how.
(4) Free choices and acts are uncompelled choices and acts consciously determined by interests, goals, etc., by the *self* or one's character.
(5) There can be no freedom, i.e., self-determination, without determinism (compatibilism).

(6) Responsibility is related to the degree of conscious self-determination or control by the individual.

(7) Avoidable acts are free; unavoidable (inadvertent, etc.) acts are not free.

(8) Unlike hard determinism, the cause of moral choices is settled later and by human character.

(9) Responsibility is limited to what a person will choose, given the kind of person he is. The agent is responsible, e.g., to the extent that he could have been a different kind of person.

(10) Praise, blame, reward, and punishment are justified only to the extent that they change a person or his behavior.

(11) Freedom is the possession of the requisite power to act and the *absense of interference* at any of these points:

possible desires → actual desires → decisions → acts

Libertarianism

Libertarianism (*indeterminism*) (St. Augustine, St. Thomas Aquinas, Descartes, Kant, James, Campbell) is the belief that

(1) Not all events, as, e.g., moral choices, are caused (indeterminism).

(2) The self is an agent with *free will* which transcends formed character and can act contrary to character or inclination in making moral choices.

(3) A person is free if and only if he could have acted or chosen differently. This could not be the case if determinism were true (incompatibilism).

(4) Determinism applies only to the person as *observed,* i.e., as empirical phenomena subject to laws, not to the *self.*

(5) Conscious or rational choice (act) and "being caused by *x*" are different things.

(6) Responsibility is possible either by acting according to inclinations that happen to be good *or* by acting contrary to inclinations that are not, as, e.g., in cases of moral temptation.

(7) *Free will* is a necessary condition of responsibility.

Action Theory

Action theory (Melden, P. Taylor, MacIntyre) may be summarized as follows:

(1) A *logical* distinction is made between an action, i.e., what is *intentionally done,* and what *inadvertently happens.* Actions are different in principle.

(2) Causal explanations apply to what happens—not to moral choices as actions. Actions are not definable in terms of happenings or their relations. Determinism has no bearing on actions for logical—not factual—reasons.

(3) To choose, decide, or act is to settle a matter according to *reasons,* not *causes.*

(4) Deterministic accounts of moral choices do violence to the ordinary uses of moral language.

(5) Whereas the libertarian argues that there are *in fact* uncaused acts, action theory argues *a priori* that *acts* are in principle uncaused.

Existentialism

Existentialism (Sartre; see also Chart 3 and Part V) argues that

(1) Consciousness transcends and gives meaning to the world of which it is conscious. "The environment can only act on the subject to the extent that he understands it; that is, transforms it into a situation . . . upon which value [e.g., causality] is imposed."

(2) Consciousness is *nothingness,* hence undetermined, i.e., *freedom.* It arises in the act of intending, i.e., giving meaning, e.g., causality, to the world—being-in-itself. "The act is the expression of freedom." "To act is to modify . . . the world."

(3) Moral decisions are analogous to the creative decisions of artists in concrete situations. In moral decisions, *freedom* is exercised. One becomes *being-for-itself.* "The refusal of freedom can be conceived only as an attempt to apprehend oneself as being-in-itself. . . . Human reality may be defined as a being such that in its being its *freedom* is at stake because human reality perpetually tries to refuse to recognize its freedom."

(4) Responsibility is absolute. Man has no excuse.

Excusing Conditions

Excusing conditions are conditions for exoneration from blame, as, e.g., "He couldn't help doing what he did." The conditions are

(1) *ignorance* if unavoidable;

(2) *compulsion* if beyond one's control, including the demands of *good reasons,* as, e.g., "I could have let him shoot me, but saving my life was a good reason to acquiesce"; and

(3) *trying* if unsuccessful, as, e.g., "He tried to do the right thing but failed."

Note that avoidable ignorance, lack of good reasons, failure to try, etc. would not provide excusing conditions.

Trying

Trying is defined as making the requisite effort. Some concepts of freedom and responsibility are defined in terms of *trying,* as, e.g., "He was free (or responsible)" = "He could have done *x if he had tried*" or "He *can* do *x*" = "He *can* do *x if he tries.*"

But again, is "trying" itself caused no less than "choosing," "deciding," "acting" (determinism), or is it uncaused or simply something different? "Effort of will as we experience it, is an unique phenomenon incapable of being analyzed in terms of anything but itself" (Campbell) (libertarianism, action theory, and existentialism).

Trying is not taken to mean something that doesn't exist if determinism is true. It is taken to be what freedom means for *soft determinism,* e.g., since it refers to what the *person does* to cause what he is doing.

THEORIES OF ART

The study of theories of art is *aesthetics* (Gr. *aesthetikos,* perceptive), which is the systematic study of the nature of of beauty and the arts in the *normative* and *descriptive* sense. A contemporary trend tends to disassociate *beauty* and *art* because of variations in views concerning the nature of beauty and the role of the art which exemplifies it; e.g., art may be interpreted as portraying the ugly as well as the beautiful.

Art has been defined in different terms which are not mutually exclusive but illustrate varying points of view. These are listed below.

As Imitation

(Plato, Aristotle, Leonardo da Vinci, Kant, *et al.*)

For Plato, art was an imitation of appearances, hence a secondhand copy of reality (see Plato, Part V). Aristotle modified this view to suggest that the artist attempts to reproduce the ideal or real, i.e., the *form* in appearances or particulars.

As Pleasure

(Santayana)

"Beauty is pleasure regarded as the quality of a thing." Though *subjective,* beauty possesses *intrinsic value* as the *ultimate good of life.* It tends to become *objectified* as a quality of things themselves.

As Play

(Kant, Schiller, Spencer, Lange, Groos, *et al.*)

Art is view as the creative expression of man's excess energy. Play is the art of the child; art is the play of adults.

As Escape

(Lange, Schopenhauer, Nietzsche, Vaihinger, *et al.*)

For Lange, man escapes from the world of everyday cares to a world of ideals through art. Art may serve as an opiate. For Schopenhauer, art—and particularly music— is the means of escape from the clutches of the irrational cosmic *will* at the root of reality (see Schopenhauer, Part V).

As Insight

(Plato, Schopenhauer, Croce, Alexander, *et al.*)

This theory of art sees it as a means of insight into reality. Schopenhauer viewed art as insight into the *ideas* by which the irrational cosmic *will* objectifies itself as the world. For him, music gives direct insight into the nature of the *will* itself. For Croce, art is intuition into the reality of spirit. It is also an *expression* of that reality.

As Empathy

(Titchener, Lotze, Lipps, *et al.*)

The psychologist E. B. Titchener employed the term *empathy* in connection with art. For Lipps, this was *Einfühlung*—"feeling into." According to this theory, art is the attempt to reproduce the experience of certain objects or actions through a cultivation of certain "sympathetic motor attitudes" or "mind sets."

As the Quality of Experience

(Dewey [*Art as Experience,* 1934], Hirn, *et al.*)

According to Dewey, art should "idealize qualities found in *common experiences,*" i.e., highlight the ordinary experiences of everyday life. For Hirn, art is also the social sharing of man's best experiences. It serves to stimulate social values and comprises a vital part of "the pursuit of social resonance."

As Communication

(Tolstoy [*What Is Art*], McMahon, Ducasse, *et al.*)

Ducasse describes art as "the language of feeling, mood, sentiment, and emotional attitude," to be distinguished from "the language of assertion through which we express facts." Tolstoy also believed art to be the means of communicating feelings, but he saw as well a moral function for art, in that it must communicate a love and understanding which can bind men together. For him, "art is a human activity consisting in handing on to others feelings we have lived through."

As Expression

(Tolstoy, Croce, Santayana, Parker, *et al.*)

Parker sees art as the imaginative expression of a wish. Croce gives art the noble status of expressing the life of reality (*spirit*). For Tolstoy, art expresses as well as communicates feeling. The criterion of its effectiveness is its capacity to evoke or communicate similar feelings in others.

THE PHILOSOPHY OF RELIGION

The problem of values encompasses religious as well as ethical and aesthetic values. For some, the source of value is essentially religious. Others insist that values are strictly a human concern, having no necessary relationship to religion or to a *Supreme Being.*

Philosophy of religion centers on the *problem of God,* i.e., the *theological* problem. This problem involves such questions as the *existence* or *nonexistence* of God and the *nature* of God. There is further the problem of knowledge of God. Such questions arise as: Is *natural theology* possible, or must God disclose Himself through *revelation,* as in *supernatural theology?*

Other problems have to do with the relation of God to the world. Is God identical or coextensive with the world, as in Spinoza's *pantheism* (see pp. 32, 38, 47), or *transcendent* as a Creator apart from the world, as in St. Augustine's *supernaturalism* and *theism* (see pp. 32, 38, 40)? Moreover, is Deity *omnipotent* (all-powerful), as St. Augustine also believed, or *limited,* as Plato and the American philosophers Brightman and James believed (see pp. 32, 33, 38, 43)?

One could inquire concerning the goodness and general character of Deity and why, e.g., evil exists in the world; or one could conclude, as have some, that evil is illusory but ask why the illusion is permitted to plague man. The nature of God as *Supreme Being* (St. Augustine), *Supreme Person* (Brightman), *Supreme Process* (Whitehead), *Supreme Idea, Reason,* or *Mind* (Hegel), or *Being Itself* (Tillich) might be examined. Then there is the question of religious language. Is it informative? moral? symbolic? all of these?

Finally, proofs of God's existence have traditionally occupied the attention of philosophy of religion. As a general observation, one could note that *Roman Catholic* philosophy of religion (as *neo-Thomism*) generally exhibits more confidence in the capacity of philosophy of religion to establish God's existence than has *Protestant* philosophy of religion. *Secular* or nonreligiously oriented philosophy of religion (as, e.g., *humanism*) has been generally *agnostic* (don't know) about God or has categorically denied the evidence or need for God's existence or both (*skepticism* and *atheism*).

Religion has been variously defined, depending on the particular philosophy of religion advancing the definition. Literally the word "religion" derives from the Latin *religio,* meaning "to bind together" that which might otherwise fall apart. Most observers will agree that religion works for personal and social integration of values and for a general orientation of personal human existence. Some equate religion with ignorance or with primitive modes of thought.

Characteristic Theories of Religion and God
Generally Positive Definitions of Religion

(1) Oman (*theism*): Religion is that which deals with the "unseen environment of absolute worth which demands worship."

(2) Tillich (*religious existentialism*): "Religion is man's response to ultimate concerns in terms of the ultimate."

(3) Schleiermacher (*liberalism*): "Religion is a feeling of creaturely dependence on God."

(4) Bewkes (*liberalism*): Religion is that which "adds strength to frailty, fulfillment to frustration, wholeness to incompleteness."

(5) Brightman (*personalism*): "Religion is concern about experiences which are regarded as of supreme value."

(6) James (*empirical theism*): "Religion is man's response to an undifferentiated sense of reality, to the 'more'."

(7) Fromm (*neo-Freudianism*): "Religion is any system of thought and action shared by a group which gives the individual a frame of orientation and an object of devotion."

(8) Malinowski (*cultural anthropology*): Religion and the concept of God fulfill certain specific *functional* needs of individuals and groups.

(9) Royce (*absolute idealism*): "Religion is devotion to a moral code reinforced by beliefs about the nature of things."

(10) Barth (*neo-orthodoxy*): Religion is man striving to make himself righteous before that which he recognizes as ultimate and decisive.

Generally Negative Definitions of Religion

(1) Feuerbach (*materialism*): Religion is a purely psychological phenomenon. It is "the childlike condition of humanity." Consciousness of God is "self-consciousness, and knowledge of God is self-knowledge."

(2) Freud (*Freudianism*): "Religion is a childhood neurosis and God is a father projection."

(3) Durkheim (*sociological positivism*): Religion is an aspect of *totemism* for which God becomes the expression of a deification of the group.

(4) Lucretius (*Epicureanism*): Religion and concepts of God arise through ignorance and fear. If there be god(s), they are far off and indifferent.

(5) Tylor (*cultural anthropology*): Religion is an attempt to give prescientific explanations of the mysteries of life.

(6) Santayana (*aesthetic humanism*): Religion is an expression of aesthetic value as are poetry and myth. God is the highest *symbol* of man's highest ideals.

SPECTRUM OF CONTEMPORARY RELIGIOUS ALTERNATIVES

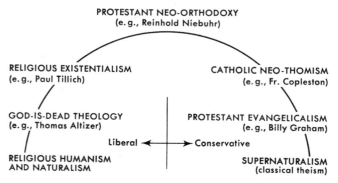

PROTESTANT NEO-ORTHODOXY
(e.g., Reinhold Niebuhr)

RELIGIOUS EXISTENTIALISM
(e.g., Paul Tillich)

CATHOLIC NEO-THOMISM
(e.g., Fr. Copleston)

GOD-IS-DEAD THEOLOGY
(e.g., Thomas Altizer)

PROTESTANT EVANGELICALISM
(e.g., Billy Graham)

Liberal ◄——— ——► Conservative

RELIGIOUS HUMANISM
AND NATURALISM

SUPERNATURALISM
(classical theism)

SPECTRUM OF CONTEMPORARY BELIEFS ABOUT GOD

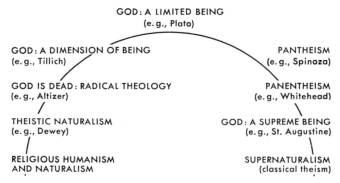

GOD: A LIMITED BEING
(e.g., Plato)

GOD: A DIMENSION OF BEING
(e.g., Tillich)

PANTHEISM
(e.g., Spinoza)

GOD IS DEAD: RADICAL THEOLOGY
(e.g., Altizer)

PANENTHEISM
(e.g., Whitehead)

THEISTIC NATURALISM
(e.g., Dewey)

GOD: A SUPREME BEING
(e.g., St. Augustine)

RELIGIOUS HUMANISM
AND NATURALISM

SUPERNATURALISM
(classical theism)

Contemporary Philosophies of Religion
Neo-Thomism (Neo-Scholasticism)

(Maritain, Gilson, Grabmann, Copleston, *et al.*)

(1) Restates the philosophy of religion of St. Thomas Aquinas (see Part V).

(2) Religious knowledge is a product of *reason* completed by *revelation*.

(3) Stresses *natural theology* and *theism*.

(4) Teaches that *God* possesses all the qualities of *perfection*.

(5) The *Bible* as interpreted by the *Church* is *authoritative*.

Protestant Evangelicalism (Fundamentalism)

(Henry, Carnell, Machen, Montgomery, van Til, *et al.*)

(1) Stresses *supernaturalism, theism,* and *personal regeneration*.

(2) The *Bible* is the *supreme authority* as the verbally inspired *Word of God*.

(3) Certain doctrines, as, e.g., the *virgin birth* and the *divinity* of Jesus, are the necessary conditions of *orthodox* belief.

Protestant Neo-Orthodoxy

(Barth, Brunner, the Niebuhrs, *et al.*)

(1) Derives from the *existentialism* of Kierkegaard.

(2) Stresses the *existential* and *psychological* aspects of religion.

(3) Opposes *Biblical literalism, propositional revelation, natural theology,* and all forms of *religious humanism.* "Scripture is only revelation when conjoined with God's Spirit in the present" (Brunner).

(4) Knowledge of God is not grasped by reason but through an act of God's *personal* self-disclosure (*Word of God*).

(5) Reasserts and reinterprets the role of sin in religious understanding and in the problems of the human situation.

Religious Existentialism (Radical Theology)

(Tillich, Buber, Bultmann, Bonhoeffer, Robinson, Pike, Altizer, Dewart, *et al.;* see Tillich, Part V, and Chart 24)

(1) God is a dimension of quality of existence (or being, reality, etc.).

(2) "The ultimate of the act of faith and the ultimate that is meant in the act of faith are one and the same" (Tillich). God is *participation* in the *ground* or *depth* of one's own being.

(3) *Faith* is not a kind of knowledge. Knowing is confined to science.

(4) "Faith is the total and centered act [i.e., *commitment*] of the personal self" (Tillich).

(5) Except for assertions like "God is Being Itself," all assertions about God are *symbolic,* including the assertion "God is dead" (qualified, p. 34). Statements about God are about one's experienced relation to existence (or being), as, e.g, "God exists" means "I experience a depth in my being when I respond to reality with *ultimate concern*" (Tillich) (see also religious language, pp. 34, 48).

Although this kind of religious philosophy comes under different names (*new theology, radical theology, secular theology,* or *religious existentialism*), it is in many respects various forms of *idealism,* as, e.g., in Tillich, Robinson, or Altizer—whose ideas are distinctly Hegelian, as, e.g., in his view that history is God becoming incarnate in the concrete life of man, a God-in-process-of-transforming-the-world.

The secular-sacred dichotomy of traditional theology is rejected since God is a dimension or quality of human being, i.e., *this*-worldliness, hence such characterizations as *secular* theology, *religionless* Christianity, or, in its most radical form, Christian *atheism* (Altizer, Hamilton, *et al.*).

Protestant Liberalism (Modernism)

(Schleiermacher, Rauschenbusch, Case, Mathews, *et al.*)

(1) Includes most Protestant religious philosophies that attempt a reconciliation of science, humanism, and traditional Christianity.

(2) Stresses the ethical teachings of Jesus and a *social gospel.*

(3) God is conceived as man's fellow worker in reforming the world.

(4) Human nature is essentially good.

Mysticism

(Jones, Inge, von Hügel, Otto, *et al.*)

(1) God is the ineffable *One*—transcendent, yet not absolutely Other.

(2) As *Absolute Self,* God is linked to the Real Self of individuals. "The soul finds God in its own depths" (Ruysbroeck).

(3) Knowledge of being "one with God" is directly experienced in *intuition.*

(4) To know God is to understand *that* He is, not *what* He is.

Religious Pragmatism (Empirical Theism)

(James *et al.*)

(1) God is *limited*—one of many "reals" and is known *via* "the will to believe" as a "superhuman consciousness."

(2) Man is conscious of this *more* in the universe which "is on its hither side the subconscious side of our [own] conscious life."

(3) *Natural theology* is inadequate; *experience* and *faith* are primary.

Whiteheadian Philosophy of Religion (Process Theology)

(Whitehead, Hartshorne, Weiman, *et al.*; see Whitehead, Part V)

(1) Teaches a process philosophy and a Platonism

modified by the theory of relativity; three factors are enumerated: formative principle, indeterminate matter, and ideal forms (eternal objects).

(2) God is the principle of *concretion.*

(3) He determines which *forms* will actualize out of limitless possibilities.

(4) *God* and *World* are mutually *interdependent* but *not identical.*

(5) Teaches a *panentheism*—"the view that deity is in some real aspect distinguishable from and independent of any and all relative items, and yet, taken as an actual whole, includes all items" (Hartshorne).

(6) God is *limited* by a "primordial" and "consequent" nature, hence is developing.

Religious Humanism or Naturalism

(Dewey, *Pragmatic Humanism;* Santayana, *Aesthetic Humanism*; Russell and J. Huxley, *Scientific Humanism; et al.*)

(1) These philosophies of religion are *naturalistic; there* is no supernatural, no personal deity, no ground of being.

(2) Religion is viewed as the quest for a more worthwhile life.

(3) The ultimate value is "all the natural forces and conditions—including man and human association—that promote the growth of the ideal and that further its realization" (Dewey). Dewey, e.g., distinguishes the "religious attitude," which he approves, from "religion" as such, which he disapproves. The religious attitude is the "sense of the possibilities of existence and devotion to the cause of these possibilities."

(4) Santayana pictures religion as the "symbolic expression of highest ideals."

(5) Russell urges man to develop his highest ideals and aspirations in the face of cosmic indifference.

(6) Julian Huxley advocates the full implementation of evolution—both biological and cultural—for human good.

(7) Teilhard de Chardin finds the God hypothesis necessary in order to explain the consistent movement of evolution toward the production of ever higher levels of consciousness in what he calls an "irreversibly personalizing universe."

Religious Language

The two main issues concerning religious language are (1) the *nature* of statements about God—factual? symbolic? (2) the *function* of religious language—informative? moral?

For example: *Good* in "God is good" is not *exactly* the same as "Here is a good man." One who says "God is good" does not mean that God is judged good by an independent standard of good, nor does he mean that, like some men, God can resist temptations, etc. What, then, does it mean to say that God loves, God forgives, God cares, etc? Is one giving information about God? Is religious language *cognitive* in some sense either literal or figurative, as traditional and conservative theories hold (e.g., Thomism and evangelicalism)? Is religious language distinctly *noncognitive,* i.e., symbolic, moral, or otherwise, as existential and liberal theories hold (e.g., religious existentialism, mysticism, empiricism, and humanism). The strongest versions of noncognitive theories whose criteria of meaning are verifiability or falsifiability (see pp. 13, 14, 23, 27, 28) hold that religious language is *literally* meaningless but serves an *emotive function*.

Religious language may be (1) informative, (2) moral, (3) symbolic, (4) existential, (5) emotive, or any combination of these.

(1) St. Thomas (*Thomism*): "Good" is applied to God *analogically* (doctrine of analogical predication); i.e., God's goodness *resembles* man's goodness or is the same in some sense, but neither exactly the same (univocal) nor entirely different (equivocal). The perfections of God are known *indirectly* by way of knowing the characteristics of his creatures. The reason is that we know creatures who are in some sense like God before we know God, so that since our knowledge of goodness, e.g., is derived from creatures, the idea of goodness and the word "good" are predicated primarily of creatures and analogically of God, even though goodness itself belongs first to God and is then imperfectly embodied in creatures.

(2) Braithwaite (*religious empiricism*): "The *primary* use of religious assertions is to *announce* allegiance to a set of moral principles." For Christian assertions, this will be the pronouncement of the "intention to follow an agapistic way of life" backed by Christian, i.e., Biblical "stories" or myths (see myths, below). Only as religious statements are about *behavior* are they *cognitive*, i.e., literally meaningful, although Braithwaite substitutes "use" for verifiability. To say, e.g., "Jesus is Lord" is to make the noncognitive pronouncement "I henceforth intend to engage in Christlike behavior."

(3) Tillich (*religious existentialism; see Part V and pp. 32, 33*): Only the statement that God is being itself is non-symbolic. All other religious utterances are symbolic. But "God is being itself" appears to be a definition of God rather than a description of God. Tillich altered his claim to say that the only nonsymbolic statement about God is "the statement that everything we say about God is symbolic." But *this* assertion appears to be about *statements* rather than about God. Tillich's resolution was to say that "God is being itself" is *both* symbolic and nonsymbolic, i.e, a "boundary-line" kind of assertion.

Unlike *signs* which are *made* to refer to something, i.e, as arbitrary conventions, *symbols* "point beyond themselves while also *participating* in that to which they point." *Religious symbols* express man's *ultimate concern*. They "open up levels of reality which otherwise are closed to us," as, e.g., in the creative arts. By his use of the "boundary-line" concept, Tillich tries to say both that religious language "points beyond itself," i.e., has an objective reference, and that it also symbolizes what it itself does as a *religious symbol* for the one who uses it. *Religious symbols* can change according as they fail adequately to express *ultimate* concern. Thus ultimate—as existential—truth can be *re*-mythologized (cf. Bultmann and demythologization, below).

The Problem of Myths in Religious Beliefs

Although popularly conceived as an imaginary and literally false account of events that were supposed to have happened, *myths* in religious beliefs are not understood as *merely* imaginary stories by those concerned with their role in religious belief and language. Some characteristic contemporary theories of myths in religious belief are listed below.

(1) Malinowski (*cultural anthropology*): "Myth . . . is not merely a story told but a reality lived. It is not . . . a fiction such as we read in a novel, but a living reality believed to have once happened . . . and continuing . . . to influence . . . human destiny. . . . Sacred story . . . governs faith and controls conduct."

(2) Braithwaite (*religious empiricism*): Myths are stories that serve to buttress pronouncements which are actually moral pronouncements concerning intentions to live a certain kind of life.

(3) Bultmann (*religious existentialism*): "The real purpose of myth is not to present an objective picture of the world as it is, but to express man's understanding of himself in the world in which he lives. Myth should be interpreted . . . *existentially*." Bultmann's concern is the *demythologization* of Christian truth, i.e., the identification of its existential truth within and the removal of the mythical view of the world in which this truth was set in Biblical accounts as, e.g., belief in *supernaturalism*, a three-storied universe, and so on.

(4) Reinhold Niebuhr (*Protestant neo-orthodoxy*): "The myth of the Fall of Adam universalizes as well as individualizes . . . man's revolt against God. . . . Myth . . . *symbolizes* the consistent Biblical diagnosis of moral and historical evil."

(5) Carnell (*evangelicalism*): Biblical accounts must be distinguished from other primitive accounts of the origin of religious belief and faith, since the former are given under *divine inspiration* and are literally factual although in a *figurative* sort of way.

Arguments for God's Existence and Objections

Arguments for the existence of God reduce to several standard forms. There are numerous arguments that may be advanced in objection to them. The following can only be representative. Philosophy of religion does not always feel obliged to advance an argument in support of the existence of God, as, e.g., for the existential believer who asserts that "God does not exist; He is eternal" (Kierkegaard) or "God does not exist; He is the Ground of existence" (Tillich).

(1) ARGUMENT *from experience:* Religious experience confronts us with a reality for which only theistic explanations are adequate (Trueblood *et al.*). OBJECTION: Suppose we agree that religious experience points to God. By definition, then, an experience of God means God exists. But can one define God into existence?

(2) ARGUMENT *from utility* (moral argument): Belief in God is justified for moral reasons and for the practical needs of everyday living (Kant). Since God's existence cannot be established logically or factually, one may exercise a "will to believe" that consequences justify (James *et al.*). OBJECTION: If belief in ghosts improved human behavior, would ghosts thereby exist?

(3) ARGUMENT *from intuition:* "There is no such thing as a *natural theology*. God is known by revelation . . . by *intuition*—or not at all. . . . No scientific arguments . . . can ever have the slightest tendency either to prove or disprove the existence of God" (Stace). OBJECTION: There is no systematic way of checking intuition, of knowing, e.g., when it is mistaken, or of achieving public agreement on its findings.

(4) ARGUMENT *from consensus:* The only sufficient explanation for the widespread consciousness of God is God

Himself. OBJECTION: The widespread belief that the world was flat does not now persuade us that it was actually flat.

(5) ARGUMENTS *from reason:*

(a) *Ontological argument* (St. Augustine, St. Anselm, and, in modified form, Duns Scotus, Descartes, Leibniz, Spinoza, Royce, Malcolm, Hartshorne, *et al.*).

This is an *a priori* argument that the *very idea of God implies his existence.* OBJECTION: To predicate existence of anything adds nothing to the idea of the thing; e.g., our idea of a mermaid is not altered by saying that it exists (Kant).

By *God* is meant *that than which nothing greater can be thought.* Since that which exists *in fact (in res,* in thing) as well as *in idea (in mente,* in mind) is greater than that which exists *in idea* alone, God must exist. (OR) God would be less perfect as *idea* alone, but He is perfect, hence must exist (first form of St. Anselm's argument). God can also be said not only to exist but also to exist *necessarily,* since God is defined in such a way that it is impossible to conceive of him as *not* existing (second form of St. Anselm's argument).

Descartes's version is that the idea of a perfect God necessarily requires existence as one of God's defining characteristics. Also, only God could be the cause of the idea of God. OBJECTION: Even if existence were included in the *idea of perfection,* it would not follow that existence were actually the case. It would only mean that in order to think perfection, one must also think existence. Only *if* there *were* a God, would he *have* to exist, i.e., exist necessarily.

(b) *Cosmological (or causal) argument* (Plato, Aristotle, St. Augustine, St. Thomas Aquinas, *et al.*).

The argument is from a *First* or *Uncaused Cause* because the infinite regression of causes is impossible or inconceivable. OBJECTION: Even if valid, the causal argument would tell us nothing about the nature of *First Cause.* Moreover, "the principle of causality has no meaning and no criterion for its application save only in the sensible world" (Kant).

(OR) The argument is from *contingency* because all things may be or not be. There must be something that exists as *Necessary Being* so that there may be *contingency.* OBJECTION: If God were *timeless*—outside of time—His relation to the world would not be *causal,* for causality is a relation holding between events in time (Kant).

(c) *Teleological argument* (or argument from design) (Plato, St. Thomas Aquinas, Paley, and many others).

The design of things implies the necessity of a designer. OBJECTIONS: Kant argues that the *teleological* argument leans on the *cosmological* argument which in turn depends on the *ontological* argument (which presupposes that what we are obliged to think is, in some sense, real). The teleological argument is a tenuous argument from analogy. (AND) Facts may be found to support and refute it. Hume argued that if the universe consists of a finite number of particles, random movement in unlimited time would produce the order observed.

(6) The FIVE ARGUMENTS of St. Thomas Aquinas: Though they are not exhaustive or conclusive, the arguments of St. Thomas Aquinas are classic. He infers the existence of God

(a) from movement to an *Unmoved Mover;*
(b) from causation to a *First Cause;*
(c) from the "may be" to the "must be" *(contingency);*
(d) from the "more" to the "most" *(perfection);* and
(e) from design to the designer *(teleology).*

Explanations of Evil and Objections

The problem of evil has perplexed many generations of philosophers. Epicurus is supposed to have given it the classic formulation that follows:

Either God would remove evil out of this world, and cannot; or He can, and will not; or He has not the power nor will; or He has both the power and will. If He has the will, and not the power, this shows weakness, which is contrary to the nature of God. If He has the power, and not the will, this is malignity, and is no less contrary to His nature. If He is neither able nor willing, He is both impotent and malignant, and consequently cannot be God. If He is both willing and able (which alone is consonant to the nature of God), then whence comes evil, or why does He not prevent it?

(1) Evil is the result of man's wickedness. OBJECTIONS: What of nonhuman evils? What of plagues and the like? Are suffering children evil?

(2) Good can come of evil. OBJECTION: Doesn't evil breed more evil?

(3) Evil brings good in the long run. OBJECTION: Men must live in the short run.

(4) Evil is a moral exercise. OBJECTION: For innocent people who suffer?

(5) Evil is undesirable but an unavoidable aspect of the best of possible worlds. OBJECTION: Is not God responsible for the design of the world?

(6) What we call evil is not really evil but good. OBJECTION: "Even if everything we think evil is really good, we still think it an evil, and . . . this error . . . would be at least one evil" (Hospers).

(7) Evil is necessary to highlight the good. OBJECTION: Is not good able to recommend itself?

THE PHILOSOPHY OF EDUCATION

"Education" may refer to

(1) what parents, teachers, and schools do, i.e., the *activity* of educating;

(2) what goes on in the learner, i.e., the *process* of becoming educated;

(3) what the learner gets as the *end product,* i.e., an education; or

(4) what the *discipline* of education is about, i.e., the *study* of 1, 2, and 3 above.

A philosophy *of* education depends on what one has in mind (i.e., 1, 2, 3, or 4 above) when talking about education as well as one's general *metaphysical* position, i.e., the first principles from which one's philosophy of education derives.

Metaphysics includes theories of value *(axiology)* as well as theories of reality *(ontology)* and theories of knowledge *(epistemology).* Those philosophies which advance theories or proposals concerning the nature of reality, knowledge, or value, as, e.g., *idealism,* are metaphysical. Those which do not or at least do not presume to do so, as, e.g., *ordinary language philosophy,* are nonmetaphysical (see pp. 6, 12, 27, 29).

With few exceptions, philosophies of education *do* assume or *do* propose metaphysical positions. This is because the philosophy of education is essentially a *constructive* activity that attempts to provide a systematic understanding of the nature and goals of education (see p. 35). Hence it is to this extent a *normative* discipline. Yet it may also be an *analytical* discipline to the extent that its attention centers on concepts, definitions, distinctions, etc., rather than on the nature and goals of education as such.

Accordingly, philosophies of education may be identified by their general historical and metaphysical approaches as forms of (1) *idealism,* (2) *realism,* and (3) *pragmatism,* or in their more recent expressions as forms of (1) *existentialism,* (2) *Marxism,* and (3) *analytical philosophy* (i.e., *non*metaphysical or *anti*metaphysical philosophy). These are summarized below:

Idealism

Idealistic philosophies of education hold that

(1) *Ultimate reality* is spiritual or is becoming so.

(2) The spiritual contrasts with the material significantly.

(3) The world depends upon mind or a point of view.

(4) The *goal* of education is

(a) the preservation of cultural, social, and spiritual *excellences;*

(b) the promotion of things of the spirit, such as the intellectual life; or

(c) the development of the ideal man and ideal society.

(5) The personal is more important than the factual as such; self-knowledge is more important than world knowledge. "Know thyself" (Socrates). (*Self-realization* is sought by idealists, as it was also by realists like Aristotle.)

(6) *Truth* is objective and discovered, but lies in

(a) the *coherence* or "fittingness" of judgments (Hegel, Blanshard); and

(b) understanding things as they are aided by the *Idea of the Good* (Plato) or *God* (St. Augustine), i.e., the *correspondence* of judgments to facts (see p. 7).

Past idealists in educational theory are Socrates, Plato, St. Augustine, Berkeley, Kant, Hegel, Harris, and Froebel. Recent idealists in educational theory are Bradley, Croce, Gentile, Royce, T. H. Green, T. M. Greene, Hocking, Blanshard, Ulich, Bagley, J. D. Butler, Antz, and Castell.

Realism

Realistic philosophies of education hold that

(1) *Ultimate reality,* though independent of mind, is nonetheless known by minds, as, e.g.,

(a) Descartes, for whom both mind and matter are *created* by a theistic God, who is Substance;

(b) Spinoza, for whom both mind and matter are *aspects* of God, who is Substance (pantheism); and

(c) Whitehead, for whom both mind and matter are *aspects of a creative process* in which God is the principle of *concretion* (panentheism).

(2) The *goal* of education is the transmission of

(a) universal truths that are independent of minds or

points of view—the intellectual emphasis;

(b) knowledge of God as well as knowledge of man and the natural order if there is a God as in St. Thomas Aquinas or Maritain; or

(c) cultural values or excellences. "Education should make one aware of the real world including values and potentialities of life" (Broudy).

(3) *Truth* is objective and discovered.

(4) The *rational man* is the discoverer of objective truth. According to *realism,* idealism is correct in its emphasis on the intellectual but incorrect in believing that the world is dependent on intellect or mind.

Past realists in educational theory are Aristotle, St. Thomas Aquinas, Comenius, Descartes, Spinoza, Locke, Rousseau (qualified), Hobbes, and Pestalozzi. Recent realists in educational theory are Herbart, Broudy, Maritain, Newman, Whitehead, Hutchins, Adler, and Wild.

Pragmatism

Pragmatic philosophies of education hold that

(1) *Ultimate reality* is the general process of experience from which subject (mind) and object (matter) are differentiated as explicit factors. Thought, e.g., is intelligent behavior. There is no spiritual or transempirical reality as such (see pp. 7, 8, 11, 14, 18, 19, 23, 27, 31, 33, 41, 43).

(2) The *goal* of education is

(a) the successful organization and reorganization of experience as adaptation to life, i.e, *science* as an end in itself;

(b) the promotion of the growth of "a life which is fruitful and inherently significant" (Dewey); or

(c) "the process through which the needed [social] transformation may be accomplished" (Dewey) or "that reconstruction or reorganization of experience which adds to the meaning of experience, and which increases ability to direct the course of subsequent experience" (Dewey), i.e., practical adaptation to present needs rather than intellectual excellence alone.

(3) *Knowledge* is

(a) *relative* and *instrumental* rather than universal or representational. "The only use of a knowledge of the past is to equip us for the present" (Dewey);

(b) *experimental problem-solving inquiry,* a practical activity, knowing *how,* rather than knowing *that* or correct intellectual judgment or idea as such; or

(c) initiated in an *indeterminate situation* which is transformed into a *problematic situation* with a specific problem that is resolved through scientific or experimental method (see pp. 5, 6, 7, 8, 11, 14, 43).

(4) *Truth* is a "thing done" (*pragma*tism), a function of practical value, *made to happen,* i.e., brought about rather than discovered to be the case (cf. Plato, where value is a function of truth; see pp. 7, 8).

Although historical precursors of the pragmatic philosophy of education are philosophers like Protagoras, Bacon, and Comte, the pragmatic philosophy of education is relatively recent and perhaps the dominant philosophy of education today. It is found explicitly in the writings of Dewey, for whom *pragmatism* is primarily a theory of meaning and truth (*instrumentalism* or *experimentalism*) and in Kilpatrick, Childs, Counts, Raup, Brubaker, Neff, Bode, Axtelle, Thomas, Bayles, Stanley, Benne, Rugg, Hook, and Brameld, who identified his theory as *reconstructionism*.

Brameld's categories of educational philosophy are

(1) *essentialism*, in which education is seen as the transmission of cultural essentials, as in *idealism* and *realism;*

(2) *perennialism,* in which education is seen as the transmission of perennial or absolute and universal truths, as, e.g., in realists like Maritain or Adler or in those holding for religious absolutes;

(3) *progressivism,* in which education is seen as the process of intelligent problem solving, with emphasis on method, as in Dewey's theory; and

(4) *reconstructionism* (Brameld's own view), in which education is seen to be the source and implementation of new social ends for social reconstruction. Emphasis is on goals as well as on method.

Existentialism

Existentialist philosophies of education hold that

(1) So far as it is meaningful to speak of it, *ultimate reality* is the perspective created by human choice.

(2) The world as such is indifferent, meaningless, and absurd; *but* freedom, i.e., *human existence*, is the possibility of meaningfulness and transcendence. "Man makes himself" (Sartre; see also Chart 24 and pp. 29, 30, 46).

(3) *Human existence* is unique in itself and contrasts both with society and nature generally. Its essence is determined by choice; it is not predetermined, preestablished, or settled.

(4) The *goal* of education is

(a) the amelioration of the human predicament of meaninglessness and responsibility;

(b) the encouragement of the exercise of freedom;

(c) openness to "Being Itself" or possibility as the path to *authenticity;*

(d) experience of the existential truth of authenticity;

(e) personal relevance through action rather than intellectual excellence as such; or

(f) humanistic rather than scientific.

(5) *Truth* is existential rather than propositional or factual. As in pragmatism, it is created—not found, lived—not thought, contextual and relative—not universal or absolute, subjective and particular—not objective or general. But it is not *instrumental* or practical. Rather it is a state of personal orientation.

(6) The educator should encourage conviction and commitment.

(7) The problems of human existence transcend the behavioral sciences.

Existential ideas about education can be found in Kierkegaard, Nietzsche, Sartre, Heidegger, Jaspers, Merleau-Ponty, Marcel, Buber, Tillich, Morris, and Kneller.

Marxism

Marxist philosophies of education hold that

(1) *Ultimate reality* is a dynamic process of natural and cultural change in which mind is an expression of class- or group-consciousness (see p. 20).

(2) The *goal* of education is the conditioning of learners to act on behalf of and as part of the inevitable cultural and social change that leads to the ideal classless society,

i.e., to implement social revolution.

(3) *Truth* is relative to revolutionary needs; it is a product of social consciousness and historical timeliness—not discovered or universal.

(4) Socialism and finally Communism are the ideals which education should implement.

Some Marxist philosophers of education are Marx, Makarenko, and Koralev.

Analytical Theories

Analytical or generally nonmetaphysical philosophies of education hold that

(1) Man is essentially a symbol-using creature of communication.

(2) The *goal* of education is

(a) the effective use and understanding of language— "Languages are forms of life" (Wittgenstein);

(b) the inculcation of, though not uncritical use of, scientific method;

(c) the development of logical sophistication and conceptual clarity;

(d) the improvement of learning as an intrinsic good rather than as a means to some extrinsic good; or

(e) "There is a quality of life embedded in the activities which constitute education" (Peters).

(3) Education is primarily admonitory, but—

(4) Metaphysical neutrality and openness are better than doctrinaire commitment.

(5) The metaphysical claims of both traditionalists and progressives need analysis.

Some analytical educational theorists are Wittgenstein, Feigl, Scheffler, Peters, O'Connor, Lenz, Frankena, Hardie, Stevenson, Steinberg, Hirst, Atkinson, Best, and L. M. Brown.

Philosophical analysts fall into two general groups: (1) those who, like the early Wittgenstein of the *Tractatus*, are positivists or *ideal* language analysts, and (2) those who, like the later Wittgenstein of the *Investigations*, are *ordinary* language analysts. The latter are more kindly disposed toward metaphysics as a legitimate philosophical enterprise but prefer a *descriptive* to a *revisionary* kind of metaphysics (Strawson), wherein the metaphysical categories or categories of reality are ferreted out of the assumptions and forms of language in use (ordinary language) rather than advanced as proposals for improving one's way of looking at things. According to Strawson (Chart 23 and pp. 6, 12, 40), Kant's transcendental metaphysics, e.g., is descriptive, whereas Berkeley's (p. 40) is revisionary.

Logical positivists and empiricists on the other hand, as, e.g., Ayer, whose interest is in the improvement of *ordinary* language, i.e., *ideal* language, explicitly reject all traditional metaphysics for what amounts to a form of *anti*metaphysical empiricism (see Chart 23 and pp. 4, 6, 7, 11, 12, 14, 23, 27, 28, 29, 33, 34). "Philosophy is nothing but logical analysis" (Ayer). Up to now, analytical philosophers have given considerable attention to almost every philosophical problem area except the philosophy of education.

Naturalistic Theories

Educational philosophy may also be viewed generally as *naturalistic* or *nonnaturalistic*.

Naturalistic philosophies of education hold that

(1) *Ultimate reality* is limited to physical nature.
(2) The "spiritual" or "mental" is an aspect or form of the "material," i.e., observable, or it is nothing.
(3) The *goal* of education is

(a) the natural goal of the evolutionary development of man (Pestalozzi);
(b) the social and cultural goals of the materialistic dialectic (Marx);
(c) the uncoerced natural and spontaneous growth of individuals (Rousseau); or
(d) the natural and "balanced growth of individuality" through increasing sensitivity to value, precision of thought, and creativity (Whitehead).

Naturalistic philosophies of education may be forms of

(1) realism (e.g., Aristotle), (2) existentialism (e.g., Nietzsche), (3) Marxism (e.g., Makarenko), (4) analytical philosophy (e.g., Peters), or (5) pragmatism (e.g., Dewey).

Note: A naturalistic philosophy of education may hold either a pragmatic or a realistic theory of knowledge.

Nonnaturalistic Theories

Nonnaturalistic philosophies of education hold that

(1) Physical nature is not *ultimate reality* (e.g., Plato, St. Augustine, Hegel, or Maritain).
(2) The *goal* of education is

(a) the fulfillment of the will of God for man (St. Augustine, St. Thomas Aquinas, or Maritain); or
(b) the realization of the ideal man as spirit (Kant or J. D. Butler).

── WORDS AND THEIR MEANINGS AS RELATED TO THE PROBLEM OF VALUES ──

ALTRUISM The doctrine that it is one's duty to ignore one's own happiness except as it may affect the happiness of others.

ANTHROPOMORPHISM (Gr. *anthropos,* man + *morphe,* shape) The belief that God is like man in at least some respect, as, e.g., "God is a Person" if by "a Person" is meant that God possesses features like a face etc.

ASEITY (Lat. *a se esse,* being from oneself) Self-existence. As applied to the concept of God, it means that God is not dependent either for his existence or for his characteristics upon any reality other than himself and that God is eternal, i.e., without beginning or end. Basic to the notion of God's *necessary* being as contrasted with the contingency of *created* being.

ATHEISM The denial of the existence of God or, as in Sartre, e.g., the belief that the *idea* of God itself is self-contradictory.

DEISM Either the belief in an "absentee" God who sets the world in motion and leaves it alone or the eighteenth-century belief that natural theology alone is adequate.

EUDAEMONISM Greek ethical theory that the aim of right action is personal well-being or happiness as, e.g., in Aristotle (Part V, Chart 17, p. 24).

FORMALISM Any ethical theory in which the basic principles for determining our duties are purely formal as, e.g., in Kant (Part V, Chart 20, pp. 25, 26).

HEDONISM, ALTRUISTIC (Gr. *hedonê,* pleasure) The belief that one ought to sacrifice any amount of personal happiness in order to bring *any* increase of happiness to others.

HENOTHEISM The belief that there are many gods but only one to whom allegiance must be given.

IMMANENTISM The doctrine that God is directly concerned with the world or, as in *radical theology,* e.g., the belief that God *is* the responsible involvement of men in the world or the *ground* of that involvement.

INCARNATION, DOCTRINE OF The embodiment of God or certain attributes of God in finite human life or existence, as, e.g., the *incarnation* of the moral attributes of God in Jesus (*liberalism*) or the *incarnation* of God's *divinity* in Jesus (*evangelicalism*).

INSTRUMENTAL (EXTRINSIC) VALUE Value as a means to another end or value.

INTRINSIC VALUE Value for its own sake and not as a means to an end, as, e.g., happiness in Aristotle.

KERYGMATIC THEOLOGY Rejects natural theology, which attempts to reason from the facts of the world to God, and argues instead that knowledge of God is initiated by God in *revelation,* as, e.g., in Barth.

MELIORISM The doctrine that whatever the state of the world, it may be improved. Associated with *pragmatism* (see James, Part V).

NATURALISM In philosophy of religion, the belief that every aspect of human experience can be adequately accounted for in terms of human existence as a product of biological and cultural evolution.

PANTHEISM The belief that God is identical with the world. One kind of pantheism holds that God's nature is eternally complete and necessary, yet He is constituted of changing, incomplete parts whose possibilities are not yet actualized. Another kind holds that "in the nature of things nothing contingent is granted but all things are determined by the necessity of divine nature for existing and working in a certain way" (Spinoza; see Part V).

PARAPSYCHOLOGY The attempt to establish belief in life after death by means of communication between the living and the dead, as, e.g., psychokinesis and extrasensory perception. Associated, e.g., with the Society for Psychical Research, whose leadership has included philosophers like Bergson, James, Sidgwick, Broad, and Price.

POLYTHEISM The belief that there are many gods holding sway over different aspects of life.

PRINCIPLE OF UTILITY The principle that those acts or rules are right which produce the greatest happiness or greatest good for the greatest number (*utilitarianism,* see p. 24).

SUMMUM BONUM (Lat., the highest good) The ultimate aim of human conduct for those who hold that there is a single and ultimate aim or value in terms of which all values must be defined (see Aristotle, Part V).

THEISM, ABSOLUTE The belief in one personal God (*monotheism*) having all the qualities of perfection, i.e., power (*omnipotence*), goodness (*love*), knowledge (*omniscience*), etc., who is *external* to the world as creator and sustainer but also actively involved and concerned, as, e.g., St. Augustine.

THEISM, LIMITED The belief in a God having goodness but not absolute power, as, e.g., in Plato, James, Brightman, Montague, *et al.* According to Plato, God is the cosmic artist who fashions an uncreated and recalcitrant matter ("receptivity") external to him and according to the Idea of the Good.

THEODICY The attempt to reconcile (explain) the existence of evil in a world ruled by a benevolent deity, as, e.g., in the writings of St. Augustine (ancient), Leibniz (modern), and Toynbee (contemporary).

{Part V}

Philosophers

This section sketches in brief some relevant aspects of the philosophies of the philosophers whose names appear in red on the charts. These men are not necessarily the most important thinkers, nor are the ideas listed necessarily their most important contributions. Rather the information given *supplements* that given elsewhere in this book. For page and chart references to these and other important philosophers, see the Chronology with References.

ALEXANDER, Samuel (1859–1938) *Space, Time, and Deity.*

Theory of mind—emergentism, new realism ▪ Mind evolves from matter and life. ▪ Evolution produces genuine novelties not reducible to the elements of lower levels. ▪ Each emergent has (1) a structure differing from the structure of its constituents and (2) a function peculiar to its level. ▪ The tendency toward emergence is identified as a *nisus* (striving) (cf. Bergson's *élan vital* below). ▪ There is a continuous interaction and interdependence of all the levels, as, e.g., of brain (life) and mind (interactionism, p. 18).

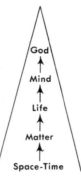

God

Mind

Life

Matter

Space-Time

ARISTOTLE of Stagira (384–322 B.C.) Partial list of works—Logic: *Organon* (instrument). Physics: *Physics*. Metaphysics: *Metaphysica*. Psychology: *De Anima* (on the soul). Ethics: *Nichomachean Ethics*. Politics: *Politics*. Rhetoric: *Rhetoric*. Aesthetics: *Poetics*.

Theory of knowledge—rationalism ▪ Develops logic as a method of knowledge. ▪ Unlike Plato, deems the object of knowledge not the world of ideas but "that relation between idea and phenomenon which shall make conceptual [rational] knowledge able to explain what is perceived" (Windelband). ▪ Combines the scientific rationalism of Democritus with the axiological rationalism of Plato—materialism with idealism. ▪ Ideas or

forms are in things only. ▪ Logic becomes the means of relating the general (i.e., ideas) or being to particulars (i.e., phenomena) given in perceptions. ▪ "The task of science [is] to exhibit [demonstrate] the logical necessity with which the particular insight (of perception) follows from the general insight (of conception)" (Windelband). ▪ The mechanism of deduction is the syllogism, wherein two propositions presumed to be true are given and a third is inferred. ▪ Deduction can demonstrate general principles in particulars but does not establish the general principles themselves or new knowledge. ▪ Aristotle abstracted general principles from particulars by induction or investigation. ▪ "Investigation in Aristotle proceeds from the particular given to perception . . . to the general from which the particular can then be proved and explained" (Windelband). ▪ Aristotle links the concepts of investigation—first principles—to reality as the causes of the particulars. ▪ Unlike contemporary science, Aristotelian science sought the general or metaphysical causes of things. ▪ Contemporary non-Aristotelian induction arrives at probable rather than intuitively certain general principles; certainty rather than probability characterizes Aristotelian science and theory of knowledge.

Theory of reality—teleology, Aristotelianism, vitalism ▪ Reality is that which unfolds in phenomena; it involves matter and form. ▪ Matter is that in which things consist. ▪ Form is that which organizes or directs matter. ▪ Form and matter are inseparable; where there is form, there is matter except that First Cause—the Unmoved Mover—is transcendent pure form. ▪ Together matter and form comprise substance; e.g., man's essence is form; his physical and psychological makeup is matter. ▪ Substance (e.g., man) possesses attributes or universals, as, e.g., redness. ▪ Universals (redness, etc.) are in particular things only—as opposed to Plato. ▪ There are ten categories of reality, of which *substance* is primary because it is "that which is neither predicable of a subject nor present in a subject"; only substance is subject; all other categories, such as, e.g., quality (e.g., redness) or quantity (e.g., *x* inches long), must be predicated of a *substance*. ▪ Categories refer not only to thought and language but to reality as well. ▪ Matter and form are relative; e.g., lumber is the form of wood but the matter of a house. ▪ Matter possesses the potentiality of becoming form. ▪ Form is actuality; e.g., an acorn is the actuality of itself but the potentiality of an oak tree. ▪ Actualization or becoming results from cause. ▪ Causes or factors of change are (1) material—the limitations of matter; (2) formal—the pattern of form acquired; (3) efficient—the force producing change; and (4) final—the end (entelechy) or purpose of actualization. ▪ The Final Cause of all reality is an unchanging, unmoved mover or pure form. ▪ Reality is an eternal but teleological process by which potentiality

ARISTOTELIAN METHOD

GENERAL PRINCIPLES OR CONCEPTS

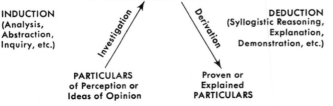

INDUCTION (Analysis, Abstraction, Inquiry, etc.)

Investigation

Derivation

DEDUCTION (Syllogistic Reasoning, Explanation, Demonstration, etc.)

PARTICULARS of Perception or Ideas of Opinion

Proven or Explained PARTICULARS

acquires actuality in the interest of actualizing pure form (reason).

Theory of mind (soul) and ethics—functionalism, eudaemonism ■ Mind (soul) is the "primary actuality of a natural body endowed with life" and related to it as vision is to the eye. ■ The entelechy of the body is the body's inherent nature. ■ Mind is that for which the body as rational being exists. ■ Mind is that which animates the body toward self-realization. ■ The *summum bonum* (highest good) is activity directed to self-realization in terms of the exercise of active or pure reason. ■ Achievement of self-realization produces eudaemonia (well-being).

St. AUGUSTINE (Aurelius Augustinus) (354-430) *Confessions. The City of God. On the Trinity.*

Theory of reality—absolute theism, supernaturalism ■ Reality is God, who is Being. ■ Being is good; non-Being is evil (cf. Plotinus below). ■ God has personality and impersonality, transcendence and immanence, omnipotence and perfect will.■ Hence, "being, knowing, and willing comprise all reality, and in omnipotence, omniscience, and perfect goodness, the deity encompasses the universe" (Windelband). ■ As Being, God gives reality to phenomena. ■ As *Supreme Person* (theism), God exercises perfect will by which the world is created from nothing, sustained, perfected, and consummated. ■ All existence, including space and time, are absolutely dependent on God's will. ■ Reality is twofold (dualism): God as Being, the Good, the Eternal; and His creation as phenomenal, dependent, temporal.

AUSTIN, John L. (1911-1960) Not to be confused with the utilitarian philosopher of jurisprudence John Austin (1790-1859), who founded the English analytical school of jurisprudence. *Philosophical Papers* (compiled by Urmson and Warnock). *How to Do Things with Words* (edited by Urmson).

Theory of language—Oxford School of analysis, linguistic analysis, ordinary language philosophy ■ Even more than Wittgenstein, Austin attempted a careful, detailed, and accurate "description" of the *uses* of language—specifically, uses in concrete, fully realized examples that often are misunderstood or misrepresented in philosophy. ■ Unlike Wittgenstein, Austin did not think that the whole purpose of philosophical analysis was the dissolution of philosophical perplexities. ■ There is something to be learned *from* language as well as *about* language; e.g., the analysis of the concept of moral responsibility can be fruitfully implemented by noting the multiplicity of ordinary idioms used in connection with concrete cases of responsibility. ■ It is not merely of verbal interest that one would want to say of a particular action that it was, e.g., "deliberate" or "accidental," since language is developed to *perform* a vast number of highly important functions (see pp. 6, 12). ■ Hence it is not likely that ordinary idiomatic distinctions are *merely* accidental or arbitrary; their survival in use would suggest their functional importance. ■ Strawson has, e.g., further developed Austin's interest in *descriptive analysis* in the direction of a *descriptive metaphysics*, whereby the structures of language in use are ferreted out for the purpose of identifying basic facts about the world. For his correspondence theory of truth, see p. 7.

AYER, Alfred J. (1910–   ) *Language, Truth and Logic. The Foundations of Empirical Knowledge. The Problem of Knowledge.*

Theory of knowledge—logical positivism, phenomenalism ■ For a statement of Ayer's *phenomenalism* as a theory of knowledge, see pp. 11, 12. ■ For a statement of the nature and development of his *logical positivism*, see Chart 23.

BERGSON, Henri (1859-1941) *Introduction to Metaphysics. Creative Evolution. The Two Sources of Morality and Religion.*

Theory of knowledge—intuitionism ■ "By intuition, I mean instinct that has become . . . self-conscious, capable of reflection upon its object and of enlarging it indefinitely." ■ Intuition transcends intellect or reason, which is merely "a way station between Instinct and Intuition." ■ Intuition is superior as a source of knowledge because it places the knower in a relationship of identification and intelligent sympathy with the object. ■ Intuition is superior because it requires a getting-hold of reality as on-going process. ■ Reason is analytical, piecemeal, static, and external—incapable of grasping the flux of reality.

Theory of reality—vitalism ■ The reality revealed by intuition is the ever-moving stream of time as duration (*durée*). ■ Reality is moved by a vital impulse (*élan vital*) which evolves omni-directionally and with infinite novelty and freedom. ■ There is a dualism of matter (as the created objects of space) and time (as the creating impulse). ■ Matter opposes its mechanism to the freedom of the vital impulse.

BERKELEY, George (Bishop) (1685-1753) *A Treatise Concerning the Principles of Human Knowledge. Three Dialogues Between Hylas and Philonous.*

Theory of knowledge—subjectivism (see p. 9)

Theory of reality—subjective idealism ■ Reality consists in perceivers and their perceptions (*esse est percipi et percipere*).

BERKELEY'S THEORY OF REALITY

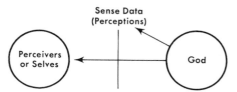

■ Individual perceivers are real but dependent spirits. ■ The supreme perceiver is God, who presents nature as ideas to individual perceivers. ■ Reality is threefold: ideas as mental contents, active individual spirits as finite minds, and God as ultimate spiritual cause.

CARNAP, Rudolf (1891–   ) *Logical Syntax of Language. Philosophy and Logical Syntax. Meaning and Necessity: A Study in Semantics and Modal Logic. Logical Foundations of Probability. The Continuum of Inductive Methods.*

Theory of knowledge—scientific empiricism, physicalism) ■ Important member of the Vienna Circle (see Chart 23 and pp. 6, 7, 12, 14). ■ The basic reports of direct observations, i.e., *protocol statements*, by which the truth of all other empirical statements are tested must, like all other statements of fact, be *intersubjectively verifiable*, i.e., must refer to physical events (physicalism). ■ All scientists investigate the same physical world and although they use different vocabularies, they speak the same language (unity of science and empirical realism). ■ Rejected the earlier Vienna Circle correspondence theory of truth, i.e., Schlick's (see pp. 7, 46) for a revised coherence theory of truth, whereby the criterion of truth is not correspondence with fact but consistency with other statements (see p. 7).

Theory of language—ideal language theory, formalism (see Chart 23 and p. 12) ■ Language can consistently contain the formulation of its own syntax. ■ A sentence is said to be in the *material mode*, i.e., syntactical, when it expresses a verbal statement which is misleadingly made to look as if it were factual, i.e., about the world, e.g., asserting "A rose is a thing" as though asserting "A rose has thorns." ▪ Translation into the *formal mode* makes the verbal character of a statement explicit. ▪ Philosophical, i.e., metaphysical, statements are syntactical, i.e., in the *material mode,* and thereby misleading (see pp. 12, 13).

CHRYSIPPUS (as representative of Stoicism) (282–209 B.C.)

Theory of knowledge—Knowledge arises solely from perceptions. ▪ Class-concepts (ideas) are subjective but are nevertheless shared by all men as a common rationality, hence the existence of common sense and innate ideas. ▪ Truth is that which accords with common sense as the common consent of rational men.

Theory of reality—monism, teleology ▪ Reality is a single, interrelated whole as world-being—a "primitive power"—or vital principle unfolding in the world (see Hegel below). ▪ It is a "purposefully creating and guiding Reason (*logos*) . . . the all-ruling Providence" (Windelband). ▪ Reason (*logos*) is binding on all things as Necessity or Destiny (determinism). ▪ Determinism as necessity is combined with teleology to become providential guidance.

DEMOCRITUS of Abdera (c. 460–360 B.C.)

Theory of knowledge and reality—atomic materialism, mechanism, determinism, representative realism, reductionism ▪ Combines the sensualism of Protagoras and the rationalism of the pre-Socratics. ▪ Perceptions yield opinions; reason gives knowledge of reality. ▪ Reality consists in an infinite number of material atom-forms having primary qualities (form, inertia, etc.) and rearranging themselves in an infinite space. ▪ Reason must abstract knowledge of them from the secondary qualities of perception (color, taste, etc.). ▪ Reason is itself a product of matter in motion. ▪ Mind-atoms are "hit" by images (small copies) of objects, giving rise to perceptions from which scientific knowledge must be abstracted.

DESCARTES, René (1596–1650) *Meditations. Discourse on Method.*

Theory of knowledge—rationalism, intuitionism ▪ Goal of knowledge is certainty. ▪ Certainty derives from (1) intuition—"the natural light of reason" which yields indubitable clarity; and (2) deduction—"all necessary inference from other facts known with certainty" (see pp. 8, 10, 11). ▪ Certainty requires systematic doubt (methodological skepticism, p. 9). ▪ This systematic doubt leads to indubitably clear and necessary first principles from which all necessary and genuine knowledge can be deduced, as, e.g., in the science of geometry. ▪ The Cartesian method invokes four rules as guides in moving from opinion to science: (1) Never accept anything as true unless it is clearly and inescapably so. (2) Analyze or reduce a problem to resolvable parts. (3) Organize particulars into general knowledge. (4) Check for completeness and negative cases.

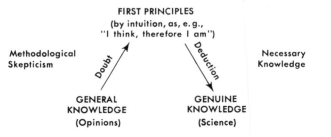

CARTESIAN METHOD

FIRST PRINCIPLES
(by intuition, as, e.g.,
"I think, therefore I am")

Methodological Skepticism   *Doubt*   *Deduction*   Necessary Knowledge

GENERAL KNOWLEDGE (Opinions)   GENUINE KNOWLEDGE (Science)

Theory of reality—dualism ▪ Reality for man is two substances: (1) matter (*res extensa*), i.e., extension in space and time; (2) mind (*res cogitans*), i.e., unextended thinking spirit mirroring the material world. ▪ God is absolute substance, uncreated, unmoved, and perfect—creator of matter and human minds. ▪ As the inner world of consciousness, mind is free and motivated by God. ▪ As the outer world of space, matter constitutes the mechanism of the world machine set in motion by God, who is first cause, and is continued in motion according to inherent and necessary laws of nature (determinism).

DEWEY, John (1859–1952) *How We Think. Reconstruction in Philosophy. Human Nature and Conduct. Art as Experience.*

Theory of knowledge—instrumentalism, experimentalism, pragmatism ▪ Knowing is a "kind of interaction which goes on with the world of experience . . . Knowing is a participant in what is finally known." ▪ Knowledge is hypothetical and predictive, "not final or complete but intermediate and instrumental," because life is a process requiring constant reevaluation of ideas as the instruments of adaptation (cf. James and Peirce below). ▪ "Experimentation enters into the determination of every warranted proposition"; the experimental method is the method of knowledge. ▪ Knowledge is the "funded experience" of the human community, justifying itself in terms that have meaning in future experience.

FREUD, Sigmund (1856–1940) *General Introduction to Psychoanalysis. Civilization and Its Discontents.*

Theory of mind—Freudianism, depth psychology, psychoanalysis, materialism ▪ Mind (self) is conceived as a dynamic unity of three interacting and interrelated components: (1) *id*—the unconscious driving force originally identified with sex instinct but later associated with the opposing drives of *eros* (life instinct) and *arakne* (death instinct); (2) *ego*—the conscious, thinking activity of self, calculatingly selfish in seeking its own satisfactions alone (psychological egoism, p. 26); (3) *superego*—originally the censor or the conscience of the self as an internalized social morality developed entirely in early childhood and as the result of conflict between the *id* (as child) and society. ▪ *Ego* or consciousness (mind in the usual sense) develops from the *id* in its encounter with the social and physical environment.

HEGEL, Georg Wilhelm Friedrich (1770–1831) *Phenomenology of Mind. Science of Logic. Philosophy of History.*

Theory of reality—absolute idealism ▪ Reality is the realization or unfolding of Spirit (*Geist*). ▪ Reality is a process analogous to thought, a dialectic (thesis-antithesis-synthesis) in which Spirit objectifies itself as the world and develops a knowledge of itself in the world. ▪ "Hegel's whole system is built upon the great triad: Idea-Nature-Spirit. The Idea-in-itself [thesis] is that which develops, the dynamic reality of and behind—or before—the world. Its antithesis, Idea-outside-of-itself, namely Space, is Nature. Nature develops . . . into man, in whose consciousness the Idea becomes conscious of itself. This self-consciousness of the Idea is Spirit, the antithesis of Idea and Nature, and the development of this consciousness is *History*. . . . History is . . . 'the autobiography of God' . . . the reality of God" (Hartman). ▪ Through history, i.e., the life of man and his institutions, Spirit achieves its goal of self-consciousness and freedom. ▪ In and through man and his growing self-consciousness and freedom, Spirit achieves its own realization as freedom—the Idea which understands itself. ▪ Parallel with the rational dialectic is the dialectic of events. ▪ From every thesis in thought and event arises a necessary opposition in antithesis. ▪ The opposition is resolved as a synthesis, i.e., a higher reality or truth that incor-

HEGELIAN DIALECTIC

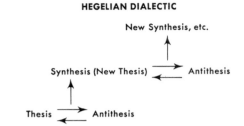

HEGELIAN TRIAD

	Thesis IDEA (Idea-in-Itself)	Antithesis NATURE (Idea-outside-Itself)	Synthesis SPIRIT (Idea-in-and-for-Itself)
Structure: as fundamental manifestation	Logical or Rational Dialectic	Physical Space-Time	Time (as "Lived-Through" Time or Time of Self-Consciousness)
Science: as fundamental discipline	LOGIC	GEOMETRY	HISTORY

porates but transcends the opposition (cf. Marx below). ▪ Spirit is the dialectic process taken as a whole. ▪ "What is rational is real, and what is real is rational." ▪ Particular entities or events are real only as aspects of the life of Spirit.

Theory of mind—Individual minds are the *Absolute Mind (Spirit)* objectifying itself and becoming self-conscious in human self-consciousness. ▪ Mind exists (1) subjectively as knowing and reasoning; (2) objectively as nature and history; (3) and absolutely as the Idea. ▪ The world is not inner reality and outer appearance; the inner is the outer—mind is the body; nature is the absolute objectified in space and time. ▪ Nature is visible Spirit; Spirit is invisible Nature. ▪ Mind evolves as (1) soul, i.e., mind dependent on nature; (2) consciousness, i.e., mind opposed to Nature; (3) Spirit, i.e., mind reconciled with Nature in understanding and knowledge. ▪ The Absolute (1) embodies itself first as the individual, i.e., soul; (2) becomes conscious of itself as other than merely body, i.e., in consciousness; (3) then develops self-consciousness as Spirit. ▪ In self-consciousness, mind combines subject and object and becomes Spirit, i.e., Reality. ▪ In other words, soul and body are annulled by their opposition, but in another sense are preserved by the resulting synthesis as Spirit, at a higher level. Hegel characterized this end by the fortuitous German word *aufgehoben*.

HEIDEGGER, Martin (1889–   ) *Existence and Being. Being and Time. An Introduction to Metaphysics.*

Theory of reality—existential phenomenology, phenomenological ontology, atheism ▪ The fundamental question is "What is the *meaning* of Being?" ▪ Initially, Heidegger is interested in phenomenological analysis of the *Dasein*, i.e., human existence. ▪ Later, it appears to him that *Being* is prior to the *Dasein* and reveals itself in the *Dasein* as an "irruption" of truth, i.e., the meaning of all there is. ▪ The *Dasein*—human "being-in-the-world"—is characterized as a field of relations rather than as an entity alongside of or among other things. ▪ It is characteristically "fallen" or estranged (*Verfallenheit*), the overcoming of which recovers "truth." ▪ Man does not create his world, i.e., give it meaning; rather "it is Being [itself] that creates for itself the ear destined to hear and the words that carry its revelation." ▪ But Being is not God in the traditional theistic sense. ▪ Hei-

degger uses the etymology of the Greek *a-létheia*—"truth" as "the hidden being which reveals itself." ▪ Existential truth is "openness" to existence rather than the intellectual grasp of an idea. ▪ One exists "*in* the truth" rather than "*knows* the truth."

HOBBES, Thomas (1588–1679) *Leviathan. Human Nature. On the Body Politic. On the Citizen. On Body. On Man.*

Theory of reality—naturalism, mechanistic materialism, behaviorism ▪ All that is, is "body." ▪ If there is God, God also is "body." ▪ The *mechanism* that Galileo and Descartes ascribed to the material or *extended* world is also ascribed to the human world. ▪ Nothing whatever is immaterial (naturalism). ▪ All "bodies" are subject to *efficient causes* (mechanistic materialism). ▪ Man is solely "body" subject to forces which move him emotionally as well as physically (behaviorism).

Theory of knowledge—nominalism, rationalism (but also skepticism) ▪ Sensations (*phantasms* or *sense images*) produced by bodily motion together with reason constitute knowledge. ▪ But *reason* is not a "light" illuminating universal truths, as in medieval or Cartesian philosophy, nor is it an activity of a mind in any sense (there is *no mind*). ▪ Rather reason is an *epiphenomenon* of the human body such that certain operations like naming, identifying natural causes, or symbolic references occur. ▪ Although the human understanding can ascribe *general names*, there are *no universals* either as independent entities (as, e.g., Plato's Ideas) or as mental entities (as, e.g., Abélard's concepts) (nominalism). ▪ Thought of any kind arises as an "endeavor" or reaction (response) to outside forces (stimuli) in the form of *phantasms* or *sense images*; thought is the succession of these or their epiphenomena. ▪ Truth consists in the coherence of one's speech and thought as a symbolic system rather than in the correspondence to fact. ▪ Knowledge is the coherent and successful organization of linguistic symbols rather than the intellectual grasp of some objective reality. ▪ The purpose of knowledge is the control of nature, including human nature. ▪ Although a rationalist and determinist, Hobbes showed his *skepticism* in his hesitations about the objectivity of causal demonstrations and in his view—unlike other rationalists—that reason is epiphenomenal rather than metaphysical. There is, e.g., no *cogito*, as in Descartes.

Moral, psychological, and political theory—naturalism, psychological and ethical egoism, authoritarianism, legalism, positivism, epiphenomenalism ▪ Moral approval or disapproval is a function of *endeavors*—desire being the positive endeavor and aversion the negative one. ▪ "That which men desire [i.e., the 'good'] they are also said to *love*: and to *hate* those things for which they have aversion [i.e., the 'evil']." ▪ Without law and order, men are in a *state of nature* where "every one [has] a right to all"; i.e., whatever one desires is the "good" for him. ▪ Because of the contentiousness of men, the state of nature is "solitary, nasty, brutish, and short." ▪ By agreement, men live under laws whereby their right "to all" is surrendered to a *sovereign authority* whose decision determines morality, i.e., whatever is legal, and whose power enforces it. ▪ Right is what the law says, and what the law says is what the sovereign says. ▪ Society and morality arise as the rational alternatives to the state of nature for men who pursue their own interests exclusively (psychological egoism) and who find that their interests are best served with a sovereign authority and strictly enforced laws; without these, there is no society or morality.

HUME, David (1711–1776) *An Enquiry Concerning the Human Understanding.*

Theory of knowledge—skepticism, pure phenomenalism, empiricism ▪ All knowledge derives from perceptions. ▪ Perceptions consist in (1) impressions, i.e., original experiences; (2) ideas, i.e., copies or memories of impressions. ▪ Impressions are (1) prior to and more lively than ideas; (2) sensations of external sense data, i.e., color, etc.; (3) reflections on internal feelings, i.e., emotions; (4) copied by memory or imagination to form simple ideas. ▪ Simple ideas combine to form complex ideas according to the laws of association of ideas: law of resemblance—similar ideas associate; law of contiguity—ideas together in space or time associate; law of causality—the constant conjunction or sequence of ideas suggests causal association. ▪ Valid knowledge consists in ideas reducible to specific impressions. ▪ Ideas like causality, substance, the self, and God cannot be reduced to impressions, hence are convenient grammatical fictions. ▪ We cannot know an external world. ▪ "As no beings are ever present to the mind but perceptions, we can never observe a relation of cause and effect between perceptions and objects."

HUSSERL, Edmund (1859–1938) *Ideas. Cartesian Meditations.*

Theory of knowledge and reality—transcendental phenomenology ▪ Philosophy is a rigorous science (phenomenology) of the structures of meaningful conscious experience of "things themselves" (see Chart 24). ▪ The primary structure is *intentionality*. ▪ Attention is directed to "objects" insofar as they are intended by consciousness, i.e., the "ideal essences" of "things themselves." ▪ These essences are neither ideal (Plato) nor psychological (Hume) realities. ▪ *Transcendental phenomenology* is the descriptive analysis both of the essences intended by consciousness *and* of the consciousness in the act of intending objects, i.e., giving meaning to the world. ▪ The "transcendental ego" is Husserl's name for the constituting intentionality of consciousness; it is concrete rather than formal, as in Kant. ▪ There is only one world—not things-in-themselves and things-as-they-appear, as in Kant. ▪ The object (or world) is not constructed by consciousness under *a priori* categories; it is already tied to consciousness by intentionality in a "Life-World." ▪ The world gives itself to consciousness, which reciprocates by giving meaning. ▪ Nor is consciousness or the transcendental ego a "thinking thing," as in Descartes, which looks "out" at the world; it is immersed in the "Life-World" and becomes aware of itself reflexively in the act of intending the world and reflecting upon it.

JAMES, William (1842–1910) *Pragmatism. A Pluralistic Universe. Essays in Radical Empiricism. The Will to Believe and Other Essays. The Meaning of Truth. The Varieties of Religious Experience.*

Theory of knowledge—pragmatism, radical empiricism ▪ Like the later existentialists, James held that the philosopher's realm is the "world of concrete personal experiences," where the *pragmatic method* applies, rather than the world of abstract ideas, where speculation is encouraged. ▪ "The pragmatic method is a method of settling metaphysical disputes that otherwise might be interminable." ▪ "There can *be* . . . no difference in abstract truth that doesn't express itself in a difference in concrete fact." ▪ Metaphysical disputes are settled by considering the practical (i.e., observable) difference which it would make *to the individual* if one or the other alternative were true. ▪ "The true is the name of whatever proves itself to be good in the way of belief" (see theories of truth, pp. 7, 8). ▪ "Truth *happens* to an idea; it *becomes* true, is *made* true by events."

Theory of reality—pluralism ▪ Reality consists in many "reals" as experienced in a loosely related ("strung along") rather than rigidly structured ("blocked out") universe; it is a "*pluri*verse." ▪ These reals include a "real God" and relate to each other externally as a part of the "process of becoming." ▪ Reality, including God, is "unfinished," "in the making." ▪ Consciousness is not an entity but a *function in experience.* ▪ "That function is *knowing*" (cf. Husserl and phenomenology, above).

KANT, Immanuel (1724–1804) *Critique of Pure Reason* (an examination of theoretical reason or science). *Critique of Practical Reason* (an examination of practical reason or morality). *Critique of Judgment* (an examination of aesthetic and teleological judgments in art and in nature).

Theory of reality—critical or transcendental idealism ▪ Reality as "thing-in-itself" (*Ding an sich*) or as noumena is unknowable. ▪ Noumena present themselves to minds as phenomena which are knowable (see phenomenalism, p. 11). ▪ Phenomena are the joint product of mind and sense data. ▪ Phenomena are possible only because mind is capable of ordering them in space and time. ▪ Mind knows only what it orders in space and time according to the principle of causality as phenomena or experience. ▪ Mind cannot know what it is as "thing-in-itself." ▪ Mind knows only phenomena because it possesses the requisite faculties that make phenomena possible. ▪ Mind provides the organizing and unifying agency that makes phenomena not only possible and intelligible but also uniform, universal, and communicable. ▪ Reality as noumena—including the self—may be free, as suggested by the demands of practical reason and moral necessity. ▪ The freedom and immortality of man and the existence of God may be affirmed as a moral necessity. ▪ Reality is therefore threefold: (1) noumena, i.e., things-in-themselves; (2) phenomena, i.e., things-as-experienced; and (3) self, i.e., the active, organizing, and transcendental agent or what Kant termed the "transcendental unity of apperception." ▪ Kant's transcendental unity of apperception is analogous to the substance of the rationalists (Descartes, Spinoza, *et al.*); it is the ultimate necessary condition or presupposition of the possibility of experience. ▪ Note: Kant's critical philosophy requires further reading for adequate comprehension.

KIERKEGAARD, Søren A. (1813–1855) *Fear and Trembling. The Concept of Dread. Philosophical Fragments. Concluding Unscientific Postscript.*

Theory of reality and value (as ethics)—Christian existentialism ▪ "The individual is the category through which . . . this age, all history, the human race as a whole must pass." ▪ The particular existing individual is the primary category. ▪ The real is the particular—not the rational or universal, as in Hegel. ▪ Kierkegaard's opposition to Hegel is shown in his theory that the existing particular self is prior to any *concept* of a universal self. ▪ For Hegel, each self is an instance of the universal by virtue of which the particular is a self, i.e., what is *thought* to be a self. ▪ Essence—what is thought and is universal—precedes existence, i.e., what is concretely lived by the particular subject. ▪ Thought is the universal essence of things in Hegel; Kierkegaard reverses the priority of thought and existence. ▪ For him, to think *is* to act. ▪ To think about death meaningfully, e.g., is to experience and to accept the finitude of one's own particular existence—not to refer to the general concept of death. ▪ It is to know that one must die his own death. ▪ Conceptual thinking is abstract, impersonal, and passive; existential thinking is concrete, personal, and passionate, i.e., subjective. ▪ Existential "truth" is subjective because it has to do with ultimate concerns. ▪ The essence of subjectivity is freedom. ▪ Freedom is not merely metaphysical indeterminism; it is implied in choice. ▪ What one is to become must be freely chosen in an unconditional act or "leap" of faith. ▪ This "leap" brings a reciprocal movement of the unconditioned—God—into human existence and is what is meant by living by faith.

KÖHLER, Wolfgang (1887–   ) *Gestalt Psychology.*

Theory of mind—Mind is the organized and dynamic structure of the whole of experience and behavior. ▪ Mind is "the structural correspondence of excitory fields in the brain with the experienced contents of consciousness" (Warren) (isomorphism).

■ Mental phenomena occur and interact in fields (cf. field physics, p. 16). ■ There is "a psychophysiological correspondence between experienced order in space and time and the underlying dynamical context of physiological processes" (Patrick). ■ Mind is therefore the form or function of body.

LEIBNI(T)Z, Gottfried Wilhelm (1646–1716) *Monadologie.*

Theory of reality—spiritualistic atomism or panpsychism ■ Reality is a harmonious whole governed by the laws of mathematics and logic. ■ This harmonious whole is a manifestation of an infinite number of forces as dynamic entities. ■ Force is the "fountain of the mechanical world." ■ Space is the result of the harmonious coexistence of forces. ■ The primary unit of force is the monad. ■ Leibniz developed Bruno's idea of the monad as a spiritual atom (panpsychism). ■ Monads are "worlds-in-themselves," i.e., entities that "mirror the world" in themselves. ■ Monads are not in space but produce spaces that pattern or structure their particular worlds. ■ Space is therefore relative (cf. relativity theory, pp. 14, 16, 17). ■ The monads vary through a whole spectrum of consciousness from the minimal awareness of inanimate objects to the full self-consciousness of man. ■ No two monads are exactly alike, for if they were, they would be identical monads (the law of the identity of indiscernibles). ■ Yet there are no breaks in the spectrum from the stone to God (the law of continuity). ■ God is the original and highest monad—the monad of monads, i.e., pure force or activity *(actus purus).* ■ Each individual monad develops with an inner necessity; it is "charged with the past" and "big with the future." ■ There is a preestablished harmony of the mental and the physical in all phenomena. ■ Man functions as a harmoniously operating "divine machine" in a "best of all possible worlds" according to the all-encompassing and divine purpose of God.

LOCKE, John (1632–1704) *An Essay Concerning Human Understanding.*

Theory of knowledge—representative realism, British empiricism ■ The mind at birth is a *tabula rasa* (blank tablet) on which are impressed experiences (impressions) which produce simple ideas. ■ Simple ideas are joined by reflection to form complex ideas. ■ Even abstract ideas such as cause, substance, or logical implication reduce to simple ideas. ■ There are no universal, necessary, or *a priori* innate ideas independent of experience (see pp. 3, 4, 9, 10). ■ Certain qualities—such as extension, shape, etc.—are presented to all knowers as the objective primary qualities. ■ These give rise to the subjective (or secondary qualities), such as taste, color, etc.

MARX, Karl (1818–1883) *Theses on Feuerbach. Dühring's Revolution,* with Friedrich Engels (1820–1895).

Theory of reality—dialectical materialism ■ Reality is the manifestation of a fundamental strife in all matter, expressed as motion. ■ This strife is a dialectical opposition, which yields a process and self-transmutation. ■ Human society also reflects this process (cf. Hegel above). ■ This process involves three fundamental laws (Engels): (1) the law of strife—all reality is an unstable unity and interpenetration of opposites; (2) the law of transformation—qualitative change is the concomitant of quantitative change; (3) the law of negation of negation—change constitutes a synthesis of earlier contradictions or oppositions, i.e., theses and antitheses, which in turn issue in new contradictions and new syntheses.

MERLEAU-PONTY, Maurice (1908–1961) *Phenomenology of Perception. The Structure of Behavior.*

Theory of reality—existential phenomenology, existentialism, humanism ■ Philosophy is phenomenology. ■ "True philosophy is a re-learning to see the world," i.e., becoming fully conscious of the "inalienable presence" of the world in concrete situations. ■ "I am present to myself [only] by being present to the world." ■ *Being-in-the-world,* as a concrete set of relations, is prior to Being (as opposed to Heidegger) or to pure consciousness (as opposed to Sartre). ■ The meaning of the world is not created by man (as in Sartre) nor disclosed by Being itself (as in Heidegger) but *ambiguously* involved in the concrete given world. ■ One can no more say that everything has meaning than that everything is nonsense. ■ Meaning must be clarified in each concrete but ambiguous situation (see Chart 24).

MILL, John Stuart (1806–1873) *Examination of Sir William Hamilton's Philosophy.*

Theory of knowledge—phenomenalism ■ Ideas such as matter and causality are admitted if interpreted phenomenalistically, as, e.g., "possibilities of sensation." ■ Knowledge of God is possible as an inference from knowledge of the world (from sense data). ■ The uniformity of nature makes possible knowledge of a world as cause of sense data.

Theory of reality—"Matter is the permanent possibility of sensation." ■ Reality is not an independent mental or material substance but a complex of actual and possible sensations. ■ Material and mental entities are constructed from sense data. ■ Sense data belong to a subjective mind (as in idealism) *and* the objective world (as in realism). ■ Realism is ordered by an invariable principle of causality (determinism).

MOORE, George Edward (1873–1958) *Principia Ethica. Philosophical Studies.*

Theory of knowledge and reality—new realism ■ As sensibles (i.e., complexes of sense data), reality exists independent of perception, though perception renders the complexes as physical objects. ■ Locke's objective primary qualities and subjective secondary qualities are reversed, in the sense that it is now the sense data that are objective and the objects that are subjective. ■ Moore's realism approaches Mill's phenomenalism, wherein matter is the "permanent possibility of perception" (see above).

Theory of value (as axiology and ethics)—doctrine of the indefinable good and doctrine of the naturalistic fallacy ■ The meaning of "good" cannot be defined with pleasure or anything else without loss of meaning, as, e.g., "yellow" cannot be reduced to a wavelength without losing the indefinable quality of the experience of "yellow." ■ All attempts to reduce ethical to nonethical terms result in the naturalistic fallacy. ■ Good "is one of those innumerable objects of thought which are themselves incapable of definition because they are the ultimate terms by reference to which whatever is capable of definition must be defined." ■ Goodness is a unique, irreducible property. ■ Values involve indefinable qualities of experience unique to the human situation (see pp. 22, 27, 28).

NIETZSCHE, Friedrich (1844–1900) *The Birth of Tragedy. Beyond Good and Evil. The Genealogy of Morals. Thus Spake Zarathustra. The Will to Power.*

Theory of value (as ethics)—naturalism, nihilism, atheistic existentialism ■ Western man has been corrupted by two major evils: intellectualistic philosophy on the one hand, and the apotheosis of weakness by Christianity on the other; both deny the natural human spirit. ■ A *transvaluation* or reversal of values is needed: instead of sympathy and pity—contempt and aloofness; instead of neighbor love—egoism and ruthlessness. ■ Why? "Life is precisely Will to Power . . . the *fundamental fact* of all history." ■ But the transvaluation is for "free spirits" only, for the Superman. ■ The everyday man is a "bridge," a something to be "surpassed." ▪ The new morality is "beyond good and evil," beyond the values of the "common herd," who sublimate their resentment of the naturally superior in the form of a conventional morality that makes the virtue of superiority "evil" and their own weakness "good." ▪ Altruism is a typical "slave" ideal. ▪ The new morality embodies the realization of the *natural* virtues of strength and power. ▪ "The noble type of man . . . regards *himself* as a determiner of values" (cf. Sartre below).

PEIRCE, Charles Sanders (1839–1914) *Collected Papers.*

Theory of knowledge—realism, pragmaticism ▪ The pragmatic method is interpreted more nearly as the scientific method (see pp. 5, 6, 7, 8). ▪ Knowledge is more social in nature, and verification more public in emphasis, than in James (above). ▪ Theory of knowledge turns on semiotic or theory of signs and is realistic (see p. 14). ▪ Knowledge can never attain complete verification or absolute certainty; this is the principle of fallibilism.

Theory of reality—pluralism, process philosophy ▪ Reality is a many-sided pluralistic process realizing limited actualities but possessing unlimited possibilities. ▪ Matter is directly apprehended through sensation as a "brutal fact." ▪ The only legitimate metaphysics is empirical or phenomenological and seeks to identify three universal and pervasive aspects of all phenomena: quality, fact, and law. ▪ These Peirce labels the categories of firstness, secondness, and thirdness.

PERRY, Ralph Barton (1876–1957) *Present Philosophical Tendencies. General Theory of Value.*

Theory of mind—Mind consists in three elements: biological interests, adaptive behavior, and mental contents. ▪ The meaning of mind depends on whether it is viewed from within or from without. ▪ "Mind as observed introspectively differs . . . from mind as observed in nature and society."

Theory of reality—new realism ▪ Reality is a neutral datum "given independently of whatever ideas may be formed about it . . . indifferent . . . to thought, which may reveal, but does not constitute or create its object." ▪ Reality consists in a plurality of entities, relations, etc., presented directly to consciousness as logical or material.

PLATO (Aristocles) (427–347 B.C.) Partial list of dialogues: 1st (Socratic) period: *Apology, Meno, Protagoras, Euthyphro, Gorgias.* 2nd period: *Symposium, Phaedo, Republic, Phaedrus, Parmenides, Theaetetus.* 3rd and 4th periods: *Sophistes, Timaeus, Laws.*

Theory of knowledge and reality—rationalism, intuitionism, doctrine of ideas, dualism, Platonism, Platonic idealism, Platonic realism, classical idealism ▪ With Democritus, Plato starts from Protagoras's perception theory of knowledge. ▪ Reason and insight discover in perceptual phenomena the universals, i.e., the Ideas, or intelligible forms of reality (rationalism and intuitionism). ▪ Knowledge develops through three stages, corresponding to the relative development of the three levels of the soul: (1) *doxa*—opinion or mere belief deriving directly from senses; (2) *dianoia*—rational or discursive understanding; (3) *noesis*—direct intuition of the Ideas. ▪ Knowledge has as its object (1) what really is, i.e., being, essence (*ousia*), the Ideas or the Forms; and (2) virtue. "Virtue is to be gained only through right knowledge [and] knowledge is cognition of true Being" (Windelband). ▪ Plato's theory of knowledge is best summarized by his figure of the divided line from Book VI of the *Republic*. ▪ The moral universals or ideals of Socrates acquire ontological status, i.e., become the basis of reality (see Socrates below). ▪ The Ideas are (1) eternal and perfect; (2) real—"the 'forms' of true reality, knowledge of which constitutes virtue, are the spe-

cies of class concepts" (Windelband); (3) suggested, approximated, or imitated by the things of the world of phenomena; (4) grasped by reason and intuition; (5) objective—independent of minds or knowers, as compared to modern idealism (see objectivism as Platonic realism, p. 10); (6) ordered in a hierarchy under the higher and more universal ideas of being, virtue, beauty, and truth, which in turn participate in the absolutely universal Idea of the Good; (7) ordered toward the idea of the good as the ultimate limitation, purpose (teleology); (8) the intelligible ideals that structure the endless flux or becoming of phenomena; (9) revealed to the soul (mind) by a process of recollection or memory of a past existence. ▪ The two fundamental kinds of reality are (1) the Ideas, which are independently real; and (2) phenomena, which are dependently real. To these could be added the agent or creator—God—who forms the world according to the Ideas. ▪ Phenomena comprise the spatial-temporal world that approximates the eternal and real world of the Ideas.

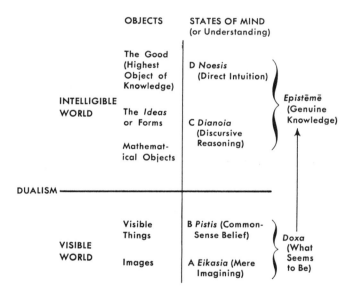

PLATO'S FIGURE OF THE DIVIDED LINE

Theory of mind (soul) and value (as ethics)—spiritualism, self-realization, doctrine of immortality ▪ The soul (mind) is preexistent and immortal (doctrine of immortality—*Phaedo*). ▪ The soul (mind) links the body as phenomena (becoming) to the Ideas (being). ▪ The soul (mind) brings life and knowledge to the body. ▪ The soul (mind) establishes this link through three functions: (1) appetite—impulses or sensuous desires (*epithymia*) originating in the belly; (2) will—ambitions or spiritual energies (*thymos*) originating in the breast; (3) reason—insight or understanding (*noesis*) originating in the mind and corresponding to, as well as yearning for, the immortal world of the Ideas—which is its source. ▪ The soul (mind) is likened to a chariot; two horses—appetite and will—move it, under the guidance of reason. ▪ The three functions of the soul are correlated to the (1) three kinds of knowledge (see above); (2) three classes of the ideal state (*Republic*); (3) nature and goals of education (*Republic*). ▪ The harmony of society is analogously related to the harmony of functioning of the soul. ▪ Realization of the ideal harmony of functioning is justice (*Republic*). ▪ The supreme good (*summum bonum*) is justice (see Aristotle above). ▪ Justice is obtained with temperance of appetite and courage of will guided by wisdom of the soul. ▪ Wisdom is desire and search for (*eros*) and finally knowledge (*epistēmē*) of the Good (*Symposium*).

PLOTINUS (205–270) *Enneads.*

Theory of reality—neo-Platonism, mysticism, emanationism ■ Reality is the One from which all existence emanates and to which all strives to return. ■ It is of the nature of the One to emanate. ■ Emanation begins with the ideas that structure existence and link Being (the One) to Nonbeing. ■ Ideas emanate souls, which in turn emanate bodies or matter. ■ Matter exhausts emanation in a plurality of physical beings that have a kind of negative existence but are essentially Nonbeing or absence of Being. ■ Souls are individual and animate bodies. ■ Souls participate in the world mind. ■ Souls find their ultimate destiny in escape from matter (Nonbeing) and return to the One (Being).

NEOPLATONIC EMANATIONISM

One (Being)

World Mind (Ideas)

World Soul (Souls)

Matter (Nonbeing)

PROTAGORAS of Abdera (c. 480–410 B.C.)

Theory of knowledge—sensualism, relativism, skepticism, phenomenalism ■ All mental activity consists in, or is reducible to, perceptions, which are the product of the motion of the knower and the motion of the things known. ■ What is known is sense data, not independent objects. ■ What is known is relative to the knower and to the instant of perception. ■ Hence "man is the measure of all things, of things that are that they are and of things that are not that they are not." ■ Secondary qualities (as e.g., color, taste) are subjective (cf. Democritus, Galileo, and Locke).

RUSSELL, Bertrand (1872–1970) *Our Knowledge of the External World. Analysis of Matter.*

Theory of reality—logical atomism ■ Reality consists in a plurality of events in space-time and the abstract logical relations that structure these events. ■ Mental events are not distinguished from material events. ■ Sense data relate both to objects they constitute as physical facts and to the minds that perceive them as mental facts. ■ Sense data are subjective; i.e., they do not exist unperceived. ■ Yet "there really are objects other than ourselves and our sense data which have an existence not dependent on our perceiving them." ■ These objects are "perceptual objects" or "logical constructions" rather than physical being as such (see pp. 9, 10, 11, 12, 13).

RYLE, Gilbert (1900–   ) *The Concept of Mind. Dilemmas.*

Theory of language—Oxford School of analysis, ordinary language philosophy, behaviorism ■ "Philosophical arguments . . . are intended not to increase what we know about minds, but to rectify the logical geography of the knowledge which we already possess." ■ The "logical geography" of one concept needing rectification is the "official doctrine" of the "dogma of the Ghost in the Machine," i.e., historically, Descartes's beliefs concerning mind and body (see Descartes above). ■ This "dogma" arises from a mistaken analysis of ordinary expressions about, e.g., what the "mind" or "body" does, etc. ■ The specific error is the *category mistake,* which consists in "the presentation of facts belonging to one category in the idioms appropriate to another" or in the allocation of "concepts to logical types to which they do not belong" (see Russell's theory of types, p. 13). ■ Concerning the mind-body problem, Ryle holds that all statements that refer to minds are really statements about current bodily behavior or hypothetical statements about predicted bodily behavior.

SANTAYANA, George (1863–1952) *Scepticism and Animal Faith. Realms of Being.*

Theory of reality—critical realism ■ Reality consists in a plurality of material existences known through the essences (cf. Plato above). ■ Essences are the ideally possible modes or forms of matter. ■ Material existences including minds embody essences. ■ Minds intuit essences—not material existences. ■ Material existences must be accepted on "animal faith."

SARTRE, Jean-Paul (1905–   ) *The Transcendence of the Ego. Nausea. Theory of the Emotions. Being and Nothingness. Critique of Dialectical Reason. Existentialism Is Humanism.*

Theory of reality—existential phenomenology, existentialism, atheism ■ Develops a "phenomenological ontology" (*Being and Nothingness*) centering on a reflexive analysis of consciousness, wherein "consciousness of something" is distinguished from the self-consciousness that is reflexively implicit or "mirrored" in "consciousness of something." ■ As *being-in-itself,* the world is everything that is given meaning or structured by *being-for-itself* in the *act* of consciousness. ■ As free and *transcending* self-consciousness, *being-for-itself* is nothingness. ■ When one becomes self-conscious, one reflects on the *prereflective* consciousness of something else. ■ The self of which I become conscious is not the *subject* performing the reflection, but its intentional object which has emerged in retrospect. ■ In-itself it is nothingness. ■ Though the world is objective, what it is in-itself—its structure—must be conferred by the knower as the creator of all meaning in the act of knowing. ■ There is no antecedent human nature as a substantial self, as in Descartes, or transcendental self, as in Kant or Husserl (see Chart 3). ■ Also there is no God, whose essence is existence. ■ There is only man, whose consciousness is existence without essence, i.e., nothingness. ■ Existence is not the *fact* of existing in the usual sense. ■ Existence is consciousness, and consciousness is nothingness. ■ "Existence [of consciousness] precedes essence." ■ Essence, i.e., *meaning,* or what something is, etc., must be chosen. ■ Consciousness *for-itself* must choose itself by its acts or choices; this implies freedom. ■ But freedom exists only as consciousness *acts* in relation to the world. ■ Man *is* only as he "defines himself by his goals," i.e., only as he chooses his future.

SCHLICK, Moritz (1882–1936) *Problems of Ethics. Allgemeine Erkenntnisslehre.*

Theory of knowledge—scientific empiricism ■ Founder of the Vienna Circle. ■ Rejected synthetic *a priori* knowledge (see Chart 23 and p. 4). ■ Viewed philosophy as primarily logical analysis. ■ Emphasized the analytical and *a priori* character of logic and mathematics (see p. 4). ■ Distinguished empirical or factual from relational or logical knowledge. ■ Limits knowledge to the empirical and the logical. ■ Advocated a revised correspondence theory of truth (empirical realism).

SCHOPENHAUER, Arthur (1788–1860) *The World as Will and Idea* (or *Representation*).

Theory of reality—voluntaristic idealism ■ Reality is a blind, irrational will, objectifying itself as man and the phenomena of his world. ■ This will is Kant's "thing-in-itself" but can be introspectively and intuitively known (see p. 11). ■ In man, the will becomes self-conscious and presents to itself by construction a phenomenal world of ideas or representations. ■ This world is ordered in terms of the principle of causality, which is necessary to the conception of phenomena. ■ Mind is a manifestation of will which is self-conscious and capable of understanding the forms of existence, i.e., the forms by which will objectifies itself. ■ Phenomena appear to be plural, but in reality manifest the one universal will. ■ Phenomena appear to be orderly and good, but in reality hide an irrational and evil will.

Theory of aesthetics—The world as will representing itself to itself develops through several stages: (1) the ideas that limit objectification to particular things; (2) and a final objectification as human consciousness and its world of phenomena as representations. ▪ Ordinary knowledge is the activity of the will. ▪ Knowledge of the ideas bypasses this activity and turns the will on itself and its ideas or limitations; hence knowledge of the ideas no longer further objectifies will. ▪ Art penetrates the representations to the ideas, thus revealing reality. ▪ Tragedy, e.g., reveals the blindness and necessity of will. ▪ Music is the most revealing and liberating art, for it reveals the will itself.

SOCRATES (c. 470–399 B.C.)

Theory of knowledge—rationalism ▪ Agreed with the Sophists (see Protagoras above) that knowledge of reality is uncertain. ▪ But moral knowledge is possible: "Virtue is knowledge," and there is virtue. ▪ Moral knowledge is universal (moral absolutism). ▪ Universal principles open to reason are those moral concepts in which all particular ideas agree (see pp. 9, 45). ▪ The Socratic method is dialectical and inductive: universals are derived from particulars by noting differences in identities and identities in differences (see p. 45).

THE INFLUENCE OF SOCRATES IN ANCIENT PHILOSOPHY

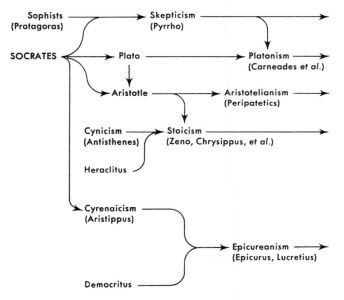

SPENCER, Herbert (1820–1903) *First Principles.*

Theory of reality—evolutionism ▪ The world is a vast evolutionary process of matter, motion, and force. ▪ "Matter, Motion, and Force . . . are not themselves ultimate realities, but represent . . . the *limits* of knowledge" as modes of the unknowable. ▪ The redistribution of matter, motion, and force proceeds from the relatively indefinite state of homogeneity to the relatively heterogeneous integration and differentiation of matter. ▪ The principle of evolution applies to all aspects of existence from cosmology to culture. ▪ Knowledge of the source of evolution—the Unknowable—is not forthcoming (agnosticism).

SPINOZA, Baruch (Benedict) (1632–1677) *Ethics Based on Geometry. Theologico-Political Treatise.*

Theory of reality—monism, pantheism ▪ Reality is Infinite Substance or God. ▪ "By God, I mean a being absolutely infinite— a substance consisting in infinite attributes." ▪ From the human standpoint, two attributes are intelligible: consciousness (mind) and extension (matter) (cf. Cartesianism, p. 41). ▪ Mind and body, thought and motion, are parallel; the causal succession of physical events is paralleled by the logical succession of ideas (parallelism) (see p. 18). ▪ God and the universe are one (pantheism). ▪ God is immanent cause—not creator. ▪ All events are interdependent and necessary (determinism). ▪ "The whole endless series of bodies with their divisions, forms, and motions, are the modes of extension (matter), just as the endless series of minds with their ideas and volitions are the modes of consciousness (mind)" (Windelband). ▪ Spinoza's monism attempts the reconciliation of idealism and materialism.

St. THOMAS AQUINAS (1224–1274) *Summa Theologica. Summa Contra Gentiles.*

Theory of knowledge—Aristotelian realism, classical realism ▪ Unaided reason alone is not enough for knowledge either of the world or of God. ▪ There is a "given" element both in knowledge of the world, i.e., experience, and in knowledge of God, i.e., revelation. ▪ St. Thomas Aquinas follows Aristotle in holding that there is nothing in the intellect that is not first in experience. ▪ But, opposing Aristotle, he holds that man is created for a supernatural end and is therefore incomplete in himself or in this world, just as natural knowledge is incomplete without revelation. ▪ Material objects are real and are in *act* not only to exist but also to produce perceptions for the intellect (mind). ▪ Intellects (minds) are also real and are in *act* not only to exist but also to *abstract* the forms (ideas) of essences, i.e., things or substances. ▪ The intellect acts to use experience as a means of getting to know real independent things; i.e., it uses both sensory images and concepts or universal ideas abstracted from particulars as the means by which it gets to know things. ▪ Concepts such as, e.g., roundness are universally in minds as well as things, making objective knowledge possible.

Theory of reality—absolute theism, Thomism, Aristotelianism, scholasticism, supernaturalism ▪ The task of philosophy is metaphysical in Aristotle's sense, which is to start with the concrete existing world, to inquire into what its being is, how it exists, and what the conditions of its existence are. ▪ The world is created from nothing (from St. Augustine) by a God in whom alone is *essence*, i.e., substance, identical with *existence* (supernaturalism). ▪ God is Pure Act, i.e., necessary; rather than contingent existence, existence itself. ▪ Essence and existence are the two constituent metaphysical principles of all finite beings. ▪ No essence without existence, and no existence without essence. ▪ The world, including man, is a plurality and hierarchy of real things (substances or essences) which, in varying degrees, combine *act* and *potency*, God alone being Pure Act or Act Itself (Aristotelianism). ▪ But God is not merely a philosophical first principle. ▪ God possesses those characteristics and mysteries of the Christian personal God (theism). ▪ "Existence . . . is neither an essence nor part of an essence; it is the act by which the essence [i.e., substance as, e.g., a particular person] has being" (Copleston).

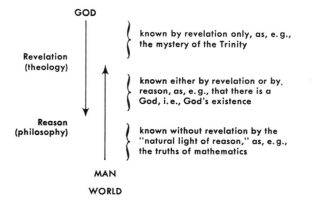

TILLICH, Paul (1886–1965)   *The Courage to Be. The New Being. Systematic Theology* (3 vols.).

Theory of reality—religious existentialism, idealism ▪ Being is that in which all existence is grounded, but from which human existence is estranged. ▪ "Man is estranged from the ground of his being, from other beings, and from himself." ▪ Whereas Sartre sees an existential estrangement of human consciousness from all there is, i.e., being-in-itself, and a realization that in-itself consciousness is nothingness, Tillich sees an existential estrangement from the *ground of being*, i.e., the *ground* of all there is, including, e.g., human relations. ▪ He calls for a *courage to be* in the face of the various threats of *nonbeing* arising from estrangement. ▪ The goal is a *new being*, which occurs in a relationship of openness and acceptance to being. ▪ The new being is found in a *love* which manifests the *power of being* as a power of reconciling the estranged. ▪ Existential estrangement, e.g., arises from ultimate concern about that which is not ultimate. ▪ What *ought* to arouse ultimate concern is the unconditioned *ground of being* itself. ▪ Hence concern, e.g., for a theistic God who is a personal being, but nonetheless a being alongside other beings, is not concern for *being itself*. ▪ The concern perpetuates estrangement because only *being itself* transcends all that exists as its ground, and only the concern for it that is manifested as *love* can bring about the *new being*.

VAIHINGER, Hans (1852–1933)   *The Philosophy of As-If.*

Theory of knowledge—fiction(al)ism, skepticism, pragmatism ▪ All abstract ideas are useful fictions that serve as instruments of the will to live. ▪ Knowledge is a means of orientation, prediction, and control in a world of sensations. ▪ "Because our conceptual world is a product of the real world, it cannot be a reflection of the real world." ▪ Knowledge does not reveal reality but helps us cope with it.

WHITEHEAD, Alfred North (1861–1947)   *Process and Reality. Science and the Modern World. Adventures in Ideas.*

Theory of reality—organism, process philosophy, realism ▪ Whitehead combines elements of Platonism, realism, panpsychism, and relativity physics. ▪ Originally, Whitehead was a realist ("I am in the world; the world is not in me."—1925). He becomes more idealistic ("I am in the world, and the world is in me."—1933). ▪ Reality is pictured as a network or process of interrelated events comprising mutually sensitive fields which "prehend" each other and form "minds." ▪ When actualized, events are structured by the "eternal objects" or forms of existence (cf. Plato above; also see Whitehead on God, p. 33).

WISDOM, John (1904–   )   *Other Minds. Philosophy and Psychoanalysis. Paradox and Discovery.*

Theory of language—Cambridge School of analysis, therapeutic philosophical analysis, linguistic analysis ▪ Philosophy is conceptual therapy, but not just the emancipation of the puzzled philosopher from the "bewitchment" (Wittgenstein) of language. ▪ "A purely linguistic treatment of philosophical conflicts is often inadequate." ▪ Philosophers puzzling over paradoxes *have* noticed something about the world that must be taken seriously. ▪ The issue is *not merely* one of a confusing or misleading use of language, since what is said that may appear to be absurd may also be calling attention to some feature of the world that has escaped attention or is obscured by linguistic habits. ▪ But "philosophical theories such as 'Matter (or Mind) does not exist' are . . . paradoxes; and philosophical questions are not questions (scientific) nor problems (logic)—but . . . riddles." ▪ The philosopher's proposals concerning the nature of the world may be fruitful suggestions for showing us "not new things but old things anew." ▪ "A philosophical answer is really a *verbal recommendation*." ▪ As metaphysical statements, they are not (mere) nonsense (cf. logical positivism, pp. 6, 7, 23, 33) but significant "nonsense." "Wisdom places emphasis on *seeing* what is so, not *saying* what is so" (Newell). ▪ Although metaphysical statements are not factual statements *per se*, they are not, as a consequence, of emotive value only; they help one to see facts in a new way. ▪ Also reasoning is not solely either empirical induction or deduction, i.e., logical *demonstration*, but in actual use is more nearly a referring to or *comparing* of particular cases. ▪ "Reasoning will not be effective until it leads to or comes from a new apprehension of the familiar."

WITTGENSTEIN, Ludwig (1889–1951)   *Tractatus Logico-Philosophicus. Philosophical Investigations. The Blue and Brown Books.*

Theory of language—(early Wittgenstein of the *Tractatus*)— logical atomism (later Wittgenstein of the *Investigations*)— linguistic analysis, ordinary language philosophy ▪ For a statement of Wittgenstein's philosophy and his approach to philosophy, see pp. 6, 12, 13, concerning the logical atomism of the *Tractatus*. ▪ For his rejection of logical atomism and the development of ordinary language philosophy, see Chart 23.

Part VI

Chronology with References

The "v" indicates inclusion in Part V.
Chart numbers are shown in **boldface** type.

THALES (c. 600 B.C.), 15, 19; **8, 16**

ANAXIMANDER (c. 611–547 B.C.), 15, 17; **8**

PYTHAGORAS (c. 600 B.C.), 8, 15; **1, 2, 4, 5, 16, 22**

ANAXIMENES (c. 550 B.C.), 15, 19; **8, 16**

HERACLITUS (c. 500 B.C.), 15, 47; **1, 2, 8, 14, 16, 19, 20**

PARMENIDES (c. 500 B.C.), 15, 19; **1, 2, 8**

ANAXAGORAS (c. 500–428 B.C.), 15, 17; **1, 2, 12, 16**

ZENO OF ELEA (c. 475 B.C.), 9, 14; **1, 2**

LEUCIPPUS (c. 475 B.C.), **3, 12**

EMPEDOCLES (c. 490–435 B.C.), 15, 17, 18; **12, 16**

v PROTAGORAS (c. 480–410 B.C.), 14, 26, 36, 41, 45, 46, 47; **1, 2, 3, 13, 16, 17, 19**

v SOCRATES (c. 470–399 B.C.), 1, 14, 26, 36, 45, 47; **1, 2, 4, 8, 11, 15, 16, 17, 19, 20, 21, 22**

v DEMOCRITUS (c. 460–360 B.C.), 8, 10, 15, 19, 39, 41, 45, 47; **1, 2, 3, 12, 17, 19**

ANTISTHENES (c. 444–360 B.C.), 47; **8, 20, 22**

v PLATO (427–347 B.C.), 2, 9, 10, 14, 15, 19, 21, 22, 24, 26, 28, 31, 35, 36, 38, 39, 42, 43, 45, 47; **1, 2, 4, 5, 7, 8, 9, 11, 14, 15, 16, 17, 19, 20, 21, 22**

v ARISTOTLE (384–322 B.C.), 1, 4, 5, 7, 8, 9, 13, 14, 15, 17, 21, 22, 24, 25, 26, 29, 31, 35, 36, 38, 39, 40, 45, 47; **2, 3, 8, 9, 11, 14, 15, 17, 19, 20, 22, 23**

PYRRHO (c. 360–270 B.C.), 47; **1, 13, 19**

ZENO OF CITIUM (c. 350–258 B.C.), 47; **8, 20, 22**

EPICURUS (342–270 B.C.), 15, 24, 26, 35, 47; **1, 2, 3, 12, 17**

ARCESILAUS (316–241 B.C.), **1, 4, 5, 13, 19**

v CHRYSIPPUS (282–209 B.C.), 29, 40, 47; **2, 8, 15, 20**

CARNEADES (214–129 B.C.), 47; **1, 4, 5, 13, 18, 19**

PANAETIUS (c. 180–111 B.C.), **8, 20, 22**

CICERO (106–32 B.C.), **8, 20**

LUCRETIUS (95–52 B.C.), 17, 32, 47; **3, 12, 17**

PHILO (born c. 20 B.C.), **4, 11, 22**

SENECA (4 B.C.–A.D. 65), **8, 20, 22**

AENESIDEMUS (c. A.D. 50), **13, 19**

EPICTETUS (c. A.D. 60), 25; **8, 20, 22**

MARCUS AURELIUS (121–180), **8, 18, 20**

CLEMENT OF ALEXANDRIA (Christian) (c. 150), **4, 22**

TERTULLIAN (Christian) (c. 155–222), **22, 24**

ORIGEN (Christian) (c. 185–254), **4, 5, 22**

v PLOTINUS (205–270), 46; **2, 4, 5, 9, 14, 16, 20, 22**

SEXTUS EMPIRICUS (c. 300), **1, 13, 19**

v ST. AUGUSTINE (354–430), 9, 15, 21, 26, 30, 31, 32, 35, 36, 38, 40, 47; **2, 4, 5, 8, 9, 11, 15, 16, 20, 21, 22, 24**

BOETHIUS (Christian?) (480–524), **20**

SCOTUS ERIGENA (Christian) (c. 800–877), **2, 4, 9**

AVICENNA (980–1036), **9, 11, 15**

ST. ANSELM (1033–1109), 35; **4, 5, 11**

ROSCELLINUS (c. 1050–1122), **12, 13**

ABÉLARD (1079–1142), 42; **12, 13, 22**

JOHN OF SALISBURY (c. 1115–1180), **4, 5**

AVERROËS (1126–1198), **11**

MAIMONIDES (1135–1204), **11**

ALBERTUS MAGNUS (1206–1280), **2, 11, 22**

ROGER BACON (c. 1214–1294), **12**

ST. BONAVENTURE (1231–1274), 9; **4, 5, 9**

v ST. THOMAS AQUINAS (1224–1274), 9, 15, 21, 22, 30, 32, 34, 35, 36, 38, 47; **2, 5, 11, 14, 15, 22**

MEISTER ECKHART (c. 1250–1329), **2, 4, 9, 24**

DUNS SCOTUS (c. 1274–1308), 26, 35; **2, 5, 11, 21, 22**

WILLIAM OF OCKHAM (Occam) (c. 1349), 14, 26; **1, 2, 5, 11, 12, 13, 21, 22**

BURIDAN (c. 1297–1358), **12, 13**

LEONARDO DA VINCI (Italian) (1452–1519), 31; **12**

MACHIAVELLI (Italian) (1469–1527), **18**

LUTHER (German) (1483–1546), **4, 5, 22**

MONTAIGNE (French) (1533–1592), **1, 13, 17, 19**

BRUNO (Italian) (1548–1600), **14**

FRANCIS BACON (English) (1561–1626), 8, 36; **1, 2, 12, 13, 14, 18**

GALILEO (Italian) (1564–1641), 2, 8, 9, 10, 15, 16, 42; **1, 12**

v HOBBES (English) (1588–1679), 17, 26, 36, 42; **1, 2, 3, 12, 15, 17, 18, 19**

v DESCARTES (French) (1596–1650), 4, 8, 9, 10, 14, 15, 19, 21, 25, 30, 35, 36, 41, 42, 43, 46; **1, 2, 3, 6, 10, 15, 16, 20, 21, 24**

PASCAL (French) (1623–1662), **22 24**

v SPINOZA (Dutch Jewish) (1632–1677), 5, 11, 13, 21, 22, 24, 26, 29, 31, 32, 35, 36, 38, 43, 47; **5, 6, 10, 11, 15, 20**

CHRONOLOGICAL
AND
THEMATIC
CHARTS

SUBJECTIVISTIC THEORIES OF KNOWLEDGE
(Things in themselves are not known.)

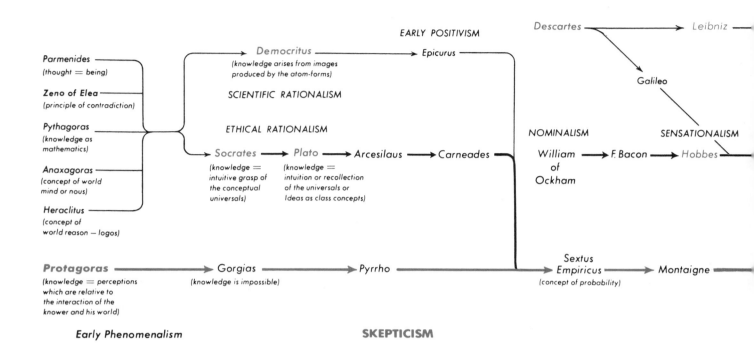

EARLY POSITIVISM

Parmenides ——
(thought = being)

Zeno of Elea ——
(principle of contradiction)

Pythagoras ——
(knowledge as mathematics)

Anaxagoras ——
(concept of world mind or nous)

Heraclitus ——
(concept of world reason — logos)

Democritus ——
(knowledge arises from images produced by the atom-forms)
→ Epicurus

SCIENTIFIC RATIONALISM

ETHICAL RATIONALISM

Socrates → Plato → Arcesilaus → Carneades
(knowledge = intuitive grasp of the conceptual universals)
(knowledge = intuition or recollection of the universals or Ideas as class concepts)

Descartes ———→ *Leibniz* ——

Galileo

NOMINALISM   SENSATIONALISM

William of Ockham → F. Bacon → *Hobbes*

Protagoras ———→ Gorgias ———→ *Pyrrho* ———
(knowledge = perceptions which are relative to the interaction of the knower and his world)
(knowledge is impossible)

Sextus Empiricus ——→ *Montaigne* ——
(concept of probability)

Early Phenomenalism   **SKEPTICISM**

Although the problem of knowledge is of perennial concern, demanding the attention of philosophers during all ages, it became particularly technical and urgent with the emergence of post-Renaissance modern philosophy and has tended to occupy the center of attention since Descartes. This preoccupation with the problem of knowledge has been encouraged by the advance of the various sciences. As the world of *common sense* became less intelligible to common sense, and science sought comprehension and control, questions arose as to the nature of the knowledge sought and the *methods* of acquiring it. Development of the *experimental method* and the rise of various forms of *empiricism* greatly influenced theories of the *nature of truth* and the source of knowledge.

Traditionally, intuitionist and idealist theories of knowledge have been strong in Western philosophy, but the twentieth century witnessed their general decline and, in various degrees, the rise of various forms of *realism, pragmatism, phenomenalism, positivism,* and **analytical philosophy** (see pp. 9–13). Of these, the most recent and perhaps most influential are the various analytical theories of knowledge. **Positivism** combined developments in *logic, science,* and the *analysis of language* with the tradition of empiricism. It is best known as **logical positivism.** From the standpoint of historical development, logical positivism is chiefly the outcome of Hume's **phenomenalism** and **skepticism** (see Chart 23).

Skepticism denies the possibility both of knowledge as a whole and of the immediate apprehension of things as such. Instead, skepticism stresses the importance of particular perceptions. Skepticism is found in many forms, all of which *doubt* knowledge in some respect or limit knowledge to what Hume called the "stream of perceptions" (see pp. 9, 42, 43). Western skepticism has its first great spokesman in the Sophist **Protagoras.** In recent times it is associated with **logical positivism** and other forms of **analytical philosophy** (see Chart 23).

Contrary to the intuitive emphasis of *Continental rationalism,* a tradition of English philosophers developed strictly *empirical* theories of knowledge which may be traced to the *nominalism* of William of Ockham and to the philosophy of Francis Bacon. Together with Kant, this tradition provides the major source of inspiration for contemporary theories of knowledge. After Hume, **British empiricism** became the contemporary empirical schools of **pragmatism, positivism, phenomenalism,** and **analytical philosophy** (see Chart 23).

All theories of knowledge of this kind hold that the objects of knowledge are *made up* out of perceptions, sense data, or whatever is given in experience. Things are as they *appear* to us (**Kant,** see p. 43). Things are *logical constructs* (**Russell, Ayer,** see pp. 11–13 and 43). Entity words are useful *ideas* (**James,** see p. 11).

CHART 1

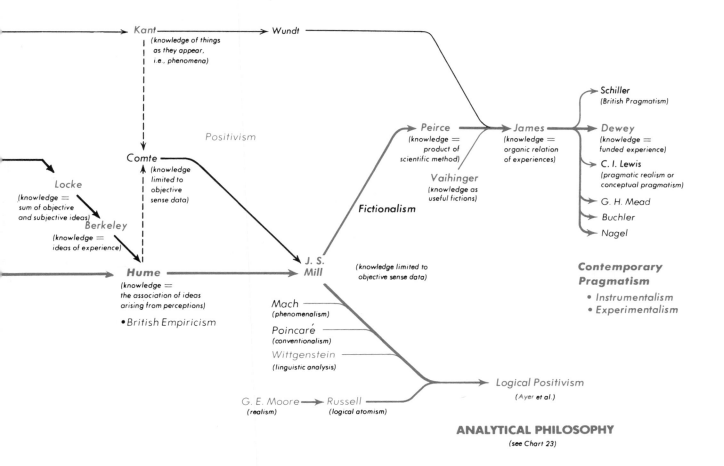

Kant
(knowledge of things as they appear, i.e., phenomena)

Wundt

Positivism

Locke
(knowledge = sum of objective and subjective ideas)

Berkeley
(knowledge = ideas of experience)

Comte
(knowledge limited to objective sense data)

Peirce
(knowledge = product of scientific method)

James
(knowledge = organic relation of experiences)

Schiller
(British Pragmatism)

Dewey
(knowledge = funded experience)

C. I. Lewis
(pragmatic realism or conceptual pragmatism)

G. H. Mead

Buchler

Nagel

Vaihinger
(knowledge as useful fictions)

Fictionalism

Hume
(knowledge = the association of ideas arising from perceptions)

• *British Empiricism*

J. S. Mill

(knowledge limited to objective sense data)

Contemporary Pragmatism

• *Instrumentalism*
• *Experimentalism*

Mach
(phenomenalism)

Poincaré
(conventionalism)

Wittgenstein
(linguistic analysis)

G. E. Moore
(realism)

Russell
(logical atomism)

Logical Positivism

(Ayer et al.)

ANALYTICAL PHILOSOPHY
(see Chart 23)

OBJECTIVISTIC THEORIES OF KNOWLEDGE
(Knowledge refers to a reality apart from the knower.)

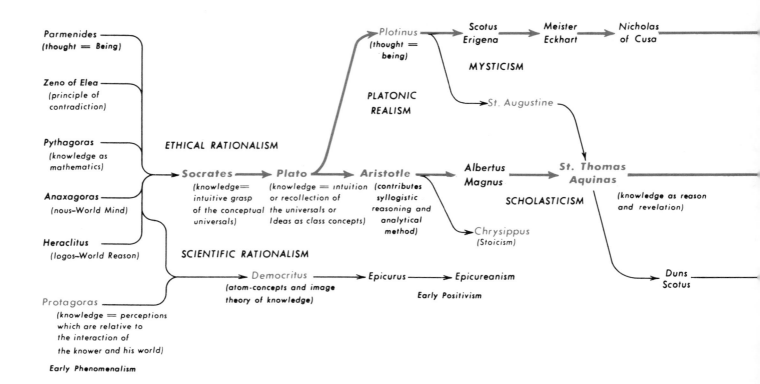

INTUITIONISM
(knowledge = immediate apprehension of the real)

Parmenides
(thought = Being)

Zeno of Elea
(principle of contradiction)

Pythagoras
(knowledge as mathematics)

Anaxagoras
(nous–World Mind)

Heraclitus
(logos–World Reason)

Protagoras
(knowledge = perceptions which are relative to the interaction of the knower and his world)

Early Phenomenalism

ETHICAL RATIONALISM

Socrates
(knowledge= intuitive grasp of the conceptual universals)

Plato
(knowledge = intuition or recollection of the universals or Ideas as class concepts)

Aristotle
(contributes syllogistic reasoning and analytical method)

SCIENTIFIC RATIONALISM

Democritus
(atom-concepts and image theory of knowledge)

Epicurus

Epicureanism

Early Positivism

Plotinus
(thought = being)

PLATONIC REALISM

St. Augustine

Albertus Magnus

Chrysippus
(Stoicism)

Scotus Erigena

Meister Eckhart

Nicholas of Cusa

MYSTICISM

St. Thomas Aquinas
(knowledge as reason and revelation)

SCHOLASTICISM

Duns Scotus

Historical expressions of the various objectivistic theories of knowledge are not identical, but are sufficiently similar to suggest that most contemporary forms of objectivism are modifications and refinements of older and recurring responses to questions having to do with knowledge. Four objectivistic streams may be identified in the history of theories of knowledge: intuitionism, Aristotelianism-Thomism, objective idealism, and contemporary realism (see pp. 9, 10). All four are metaphysical theories of knowledge.

Intuitionism is the view that reality is immediately apprehended as sensible or intelligible. It is invoked by both *rationalism* and *mysticism*. As immediate apprehension of reality, *intuition* may be an end product of a progressive advance in insight (as it was for Plato) or it may simply be a way in which the knower functions psychologically in his role as knower (as it is for the psychologist Jung). As the theory of knowledge of mysticism, intuitionism links the knower directly to reality. To know reality is to be united with it; the knower and his

world are one (see theories of reality in Part II). Western intuitionism has its origins in Parmenides and Plato and terminates in thinkers like Bergson (see pp. 40, 45). It also forms the basis of the theory of knowledge of *Continental rationalism.*

Objective idealism has its origin in Continental rationalism. Descartes and his successors through Kant stressed the role of the mind and the processes of thought in gaining knowledge of the world investigated by science. They believed, e.g., that some knowledge is self-evident or *innate* to minds. In other words, it is *a priori*, i.e., known independently of experience. This knowledge could be relied upon to form the basis of all knowledge. Also, since the world is rational, human reason has access to it.

Aristotelianism-Thomism has its origin in Aristotle's theory of knowledge and in his metaphysics. It flourished during the latter part of the Middle Ages as the theory of knowledge of most *scholasticism* and, as developed by St. Thomas Aquinas, has been revived and reasserted in the contemporary Thomistic

CHART 2

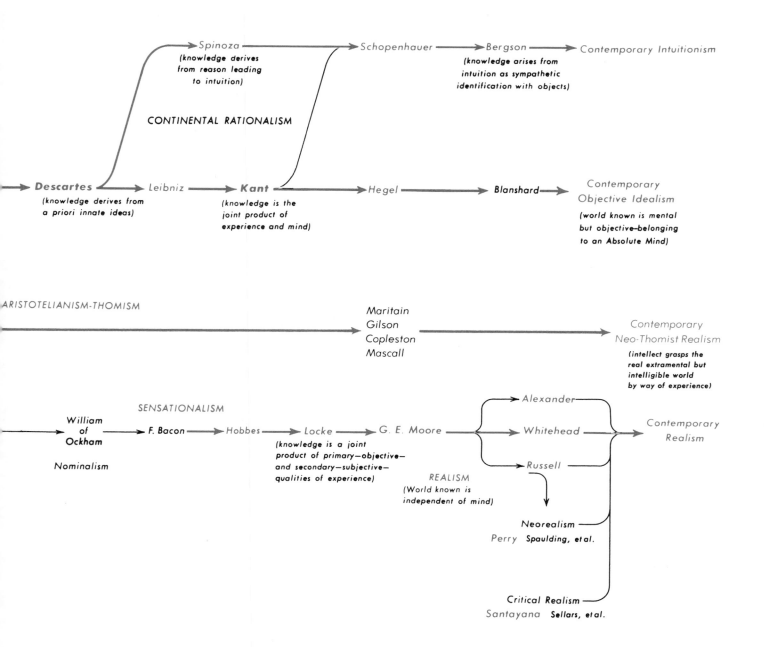

philosophy. Thomism believes that experience is the medium through which the intellect is able to grasp an intelligible reality. Things as they really are, are really known (see p. 47).

As a contemporary theory of knowledge, *epistemological realism* arose from the revolt of G. E. Moore in England and William James in the United States against the prevailing influence of *idealism*, specifically *Hegelianism*. **Contemporary realism** is not to be confused with *Platonic realism*, for it teaches the independent reality of material objects and relations, not the Ideas of Plato. There is a wide variety of realistic theories of knowledge. These range from a *maximum of realism*, as in *common-sense* or *naïve realism*, to a *minimum of realism*, as in *critical realism*, wherein mind plays a greater role in knowledge. In general, epistemological realism may be identified by the belief that an objective material or neutral world of substance, process, or events exists independent of knowers.

NATURALISTIC THEORIES OF MIND
(Mind is not substantive or spiritual.)

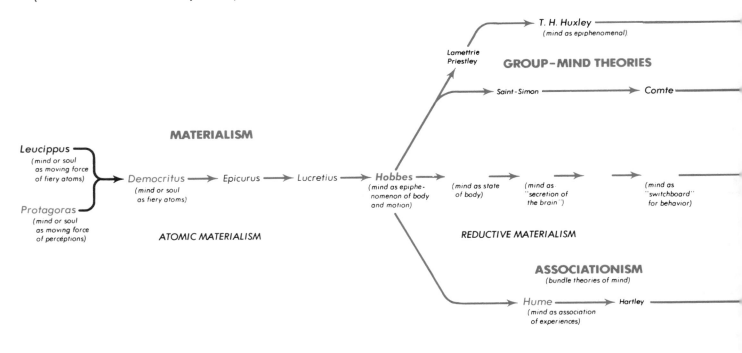

MATERIALISM

Leucippus
(mind or soul as moving force of fiery atoms)

Protagoras
(mind or soul as moving force of perceptions)

Democritus → Epicurus → Lucretius → **Hobbes** →
(mind or soul as fiery atoms)
(mind as epiphenomenon of body and motion)

ATOMIC MATERIALISM

T. H. Huxley
(mind as epiphenomenal)

Lamettrie
Priestley

GROUP-MIND THEORIES

Saint-Simon → Comte

(mind as state of body) → *(mind as "secretion of the brain")* → *(mind as "switchboard" for behavior)*

REDUCTIVE MATERIALISM

ASSOCIATIONISM
(bundle theories of mind)

Hume → Hartley
(mind as association of experiences)

PSYCHOANALYSIS

Schopenhauer → Nietzsche → Freud

Husserl
(mind as intentionality)

Naturalistic theories of mind agree generally that there is no entity mind, either as a substance, as, e.g., in **Descartes** (see Chart 16), or as an active rational principle, as, e.g., in **Aristotle** (see Chart 15). A characteristic naturalistic theory is **epiphenomenalism,** which interprets mind as a by-product of bodily activity and therefore never causally antecedent to behavior (see pp. 18, 42).

Behaviorism in one form or another characterizes most naturalistic theory today. Mechanistic or metaphysical behaviorism is a form of metaphysical monism which holds **materialism** as a theory of reality. Most contemporary forms of behaviorism are nonmechanistic and nonmetaphysical, however, claiming only that all references to the mental are actually references to observable behavior of some sort or a disposition to behave in certain ways. Most psychology is behavioristic in this methodological and nonmetaphysical sense. A well-known philosophical expression of this view is that of **Ryle,** who is famous for his denial of the "ghost in the machine" and for his attempt to reduce all discourse about the mental to discourse about dispositions to behave in certain observable ways (see p. 46). Recent **analytical** and **behavioristic** theories of this sort are likely to be **identity theories,** according to which references to the mental are held to be the same as references to the physical, even though no metaphysical claim is made that as a matter of fact the mental is nothing but the material.

Most naturalistic theories have their origin in **Hobbes,** who anticipated them in a remarkable way (see p. 42). Important naturalistic rivals of behaviorism and epiphenomenalism are the **group-mind** and **psychoanalytic theories. Group-mind theories** approach the mind problem sociologically. Durkheim and **Marx** believed that since man is a social creature, the individual mind mirrors the beliefs and expectations of the group or class of which it is a part (see pp. 32, 44). **Psychoanalytic theories** are usually associated with **Freud** or his disciples and have their origin in philosophies like those of **Nietzsche** and **Schopenhauer,** which give primacy to will and the unconscious (see pp. 41, 44–

CHART 3

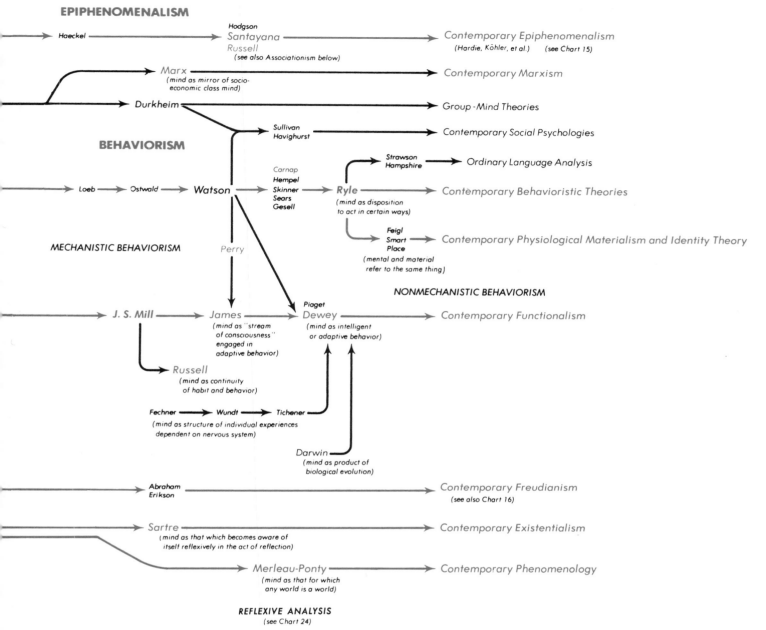

EPIPHENOMENALISM

Haeckel → Hodgson
Santayana
Russell
(see also Associationism below)
→ Contemporary Epiphenomenalism
(Hardie, Köhler, et al.)   (see Chart 15)

Marx → Contemporary Marxism
(mind as mirror of socio-
economic class mind)

Durkheim → Group-Mind Theories

Sullivan
Havighurst → Contemporary Social Psychologies

BEHAVIORISM

Strawson
Hampshire → Ordinary Language Analysis

Loeb → Ostwald → Watson → Carnap
Hempel
Skinner
Sears
Gesell
→ Ryle → Contemporary Behavioristic Theories
(mind as disposition
to act in certain ways)

MECHANISTIC BEHAVIORISM

Perry

Feigl
Smart
Place → Contemporary Physiological Materialism and Identity Theory
(mental and material
refer to the same thing)

NONMECHANISTIC BEHAVIORISM

Piaget
J. S. Mill → James → Dewey → Contemporary Functionalism
(mind as "stream   (mind as intelligent
of consciousness"   or adaptive behavior)
engaged in
adaptive behavior)

Russell
(mind as continuity
of habit and behavior)

Fechner → Wundt → Tichener
(mind as structure of individual experiences
dependent on nervous system)

Darwin
(mind as product of
biological evolution)

Abraham
Erikson → Contemporary Freudianism
(see also Chart 16)

Sartre → Contemporary Existentialism
(mind as that which becomes aware of
itself reflexively in the act of reflection)

Merleau-Ponty → Contemporary Phenomenology
(mind as that for which
any world is a world)

REFLEXIVE ANALYSIS
(see Chart 24)

47). Like Hobbes, they find that man is not primarily a rational being for whom knowledge of an independent rational world is available.

A unique approach to the problem of mind in contemporary philosophy is the reflexive analysis of existentialism and phenomenology. Both derive their theory mainly from Husserl, for whom mind is that which arises in consciousness and acts to give meaning to experience (see p. 43). An act of consciousness "intends" what it is conscious of by endowing it with meaning and identifying it as "something." Sartre pictures the mind in the analogy of a mirror, i.e., as a "self" of which we are conscious in the act of being "conscious of something" (see p. 46). Mind doesn't underlie experience as something antecedent to it, but arises in it as the meaningful component intended by us. We can only find our "selves" as we are "mirrored" in our acts and experiences. We may be "objects" for others, but not directly for ourselves (see Chart 24).

PLATONIC DUALISM
(Reality is spiritual.)

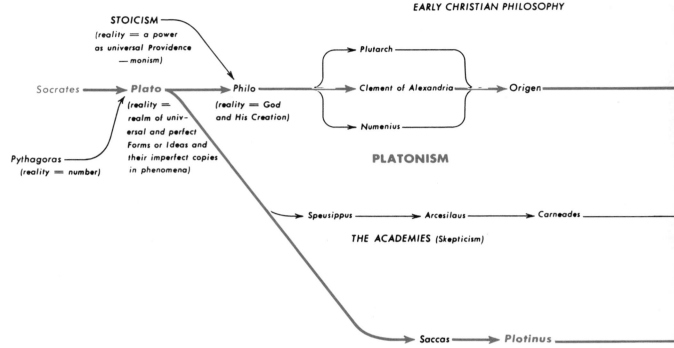

STOICISM
(reality = a power
as universal Providence
— monism)

EARLY CHRISTIAN PHILOSOPHY

Socrates ⟶ **Plato** ⟶ Philo

Plato
(reality =
realm of univ-
ersal and perfect
Forms or Ideas and
their imperfect copies
in phenomena)

Pythagoras ⟶
(reality = number)

Philo
(reality = God
and His Creation)

Plutarch ⟶
Clement of Alexandria ⟶ ⟶ Origen ⟶
Numenius ⟶

PLATONISM

Speusippus ⟶ Arcesilaus ⟶ Carneades

THE ACADEMIES (Skepticism)

Saccas ⟶ **Plotinus**
(reality = the ineffable One)

NEO-PLATONISM
(monism)

Thought and experience tend to structure the world in terms of the opposites characteristic of *dualism,* such as mind and matter, good and evil, reality and appearance. This prevalent tendency is opposed by another tendency of reflective thought, to seek unity in the apparent diversity of the world. Hence when a cosmic dualism is advanced, it is often subordinated to some overarching and absolute reality such as God or the *Idea of the Good,* as in **Plato** (see p. 45). Popular thought, however, finds the dualistic distinctions of mental and material, this world and the next, easier to comprehend.

In Western philosophy, **Platonism** established the character of most dualism until it was modified by **St. Augustine** into its Christian form as **Augustinianism.** Until challenged and largely replaced by *Aristotelianism* in the thirteenth century, Platonism (or, as it was later called, Augustinianism) was the predominant philosophy of the West. The Renaissance, the Protestant Reformation, and the scientific revolt of early modern Europe tended to revive its influence. It has exhibited a perennial vitality either as a dualistic form of *idealism* or as *mysticism.*

Platonism is characterized by a spiritualistic view of life and a high regard for the capacity of the human mind to discover absolute truth. It is the ancient origin of both *dualism* and *idealism* in the West, and it has permanently influenced the character and concerns of Christian theology and philosophy.

CHART 4

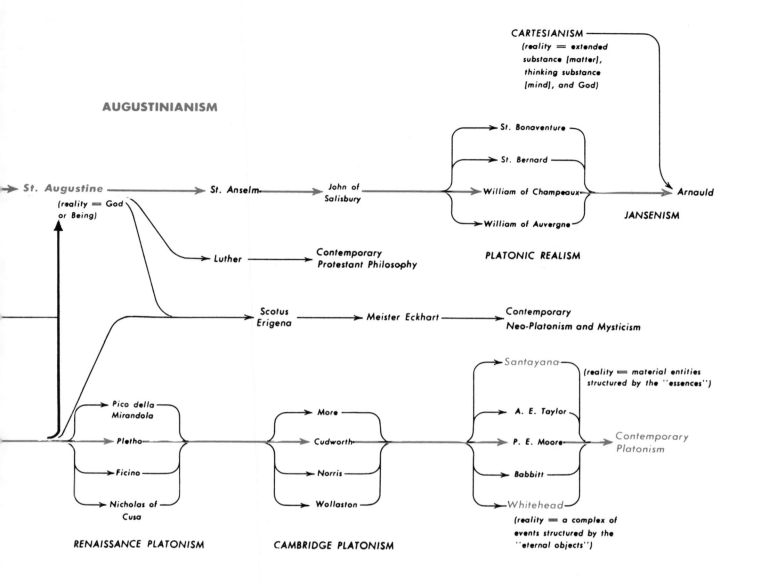

CARTESIANISM
(reality = extended
substance [matter],
thinking substance
[mind], and God)

AUGUSTINIANISM

St. Bonaventure

St. Bernard

St. Augustine ──────→ St. Anselm ──────→ John of ─────→ William of Champeaux ─────→ Arnauld
(reality = God   Salisbury   JANSENISM
or Being)   William of Auvergne

Luther ──────→ Contemporary   PLATONIC REALISM
               Protestant Philosophy

Scotus ──────→ Meister Eckhart ──────→ Contemporary
Erigena   Neo-Platonism and Mysticism

Santayana   (reality = material entities
                   structured by the "essences")

A. E. Taylor

Pico della   More   P. E. Moore ──────→ Contemporary
Mirandola   Platonism

Pletho ──────→   Cudworth ──────→   Babbitt

Ficino   Norris   Whitehead

Nicholas of   Wollaston   (reality = a complex of
Cusa   events structured by the
                                                      "eternal objects")

RENAISSANCE PLATONISM   CAMBRIDGE PLATONISM

RELIGIOUS DUALISM (AUGUSTINIANISM)
(Reality is God and a created world.)

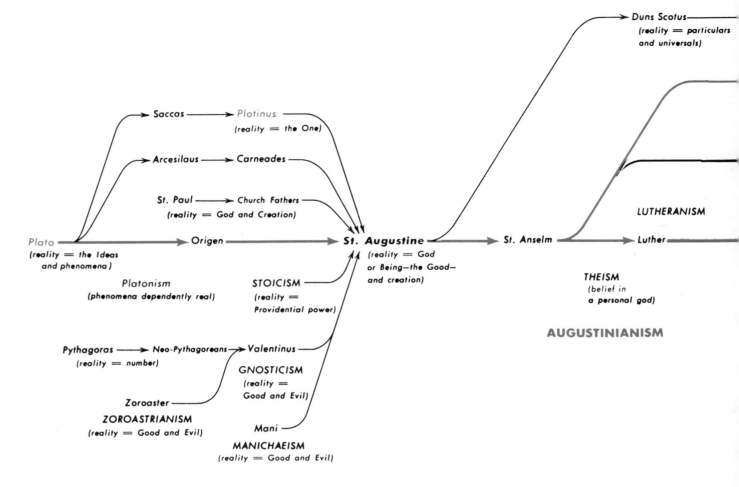

SCOTISM

→ Duns Scotus————
*(reality = particulars
and universals)*

→ Saccas———→ Plotinus———
(reality = the One)

→ Arcesilaus———→ Carneades———

St. Paul———→ Church Fathers———
(reality = God and Creation)

Plato———————————→ Origen————————————→ St. Augustine ———————→ St. Anselm ——————→ Luther————
*(reality = the Ideas
and phenomena)*

*(reality = God
or Being—the Good—
and creation)*

LUTHERANISM

Platonism
(phenomena dependently real)

STOICISM———
*(reality =
Providential power)*

THEISM
*(belief in
a personal god)*

AUGUSTINIANISM

Pythagoras———→ Neo-Pythagoreans—→ Valentinus———
(reality = number)

GNOSTICISM
*(reality =
Good and Evil)*

Zoroaster————

ZOROASTRIANISM
(reality = Good and Evil)

Mani————

MANICHAEISM
(reality = Good and Evil)

St. Augustine integrated several philosophies with Platonism, yielding a distinctly religious form of dualism that persists to the present. To Plato he fused the *neo-Platonism* of Plotinus and *Pauline Christianity*. He was also influenced by the *skepticism* of the Academies and by *Manichaeism*. The latter taught a struggle between the forces of light and goodness and the forces of darkness and evil (see p. 40).

Though always important in Western thought, Augustinianism yielded ground to *Thomism* during the thirteenth century. The Protestant Reformation revived it, and it continues today as Christian evangelicalism and other forms of Christian philosophy. As a theory of reality, Augustinianism may be identified by its distinctly dualistic and religious character. For Augustinianism, God is the central fact of reality; although in some forms of Christian existentialism and contemporary radical theology, some theory of the *death of God* holds.

CHART 5

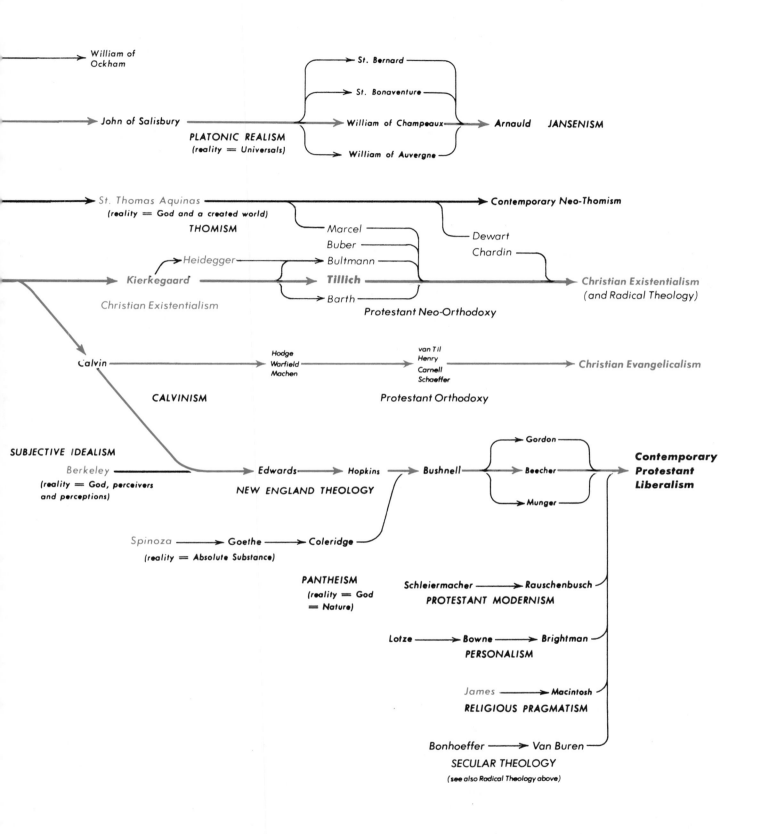

William of Ockham

John of Salisbury

PLATONIC REALISM
(reality = Universals)

St. Bernard

St. Bonaventure

William of Champeaux

William of Auvergne

Arnauld   JANSENISM

St. Thomas Aquinas ————————————————→ Contemporary Neo-Thomism
(reality = God and a created world)
THOMISM

Marcel

Buber

Dewart

Chardin

Heidegger ———→ Bultmann

Kierkegaard ———→ *Tillich*

Christian Existentialism

Barth

Protestant Neo-Orthodoxy

Christian Existentialism
(and Radical Theology)

Calvin

Hodge
Warfield
Machen

van Til
Henry
Cornell
Schaeffer

Christian Evangelicalism

CALVINISM

Protestant Orthodoxy

SUBJECTIVE IDEALISM

Gordon

Beecher

Munger

**Contemporary
Protestant
Liberalism**

Berkeley
*(reality = God, perceivers
and perceptions)*

Edwards ———→ Hopkins ———→ Bushnell

NEW ENGLAND THEOLOGY

Spinoza ———→ Goethe ———→ Coleridge
(reality = Absolute Substance)

PANTHEISM
*(reality = God
= Nature)*

Schleiermacher ———→ Rauschenbusch
PROTESTANT MODERNISM

Lotze ———→ Bowne ———→ Brightman
PERSONALISM

James ———→ Macintosh
RELIGIOUS PRAGMATISM

Bonhoeffer ———→ Van Buren
SECULAR THEOLOGY
(see also Radical Theology above)

CARTESIAN DUALISM
(Reality is mind and matter.)

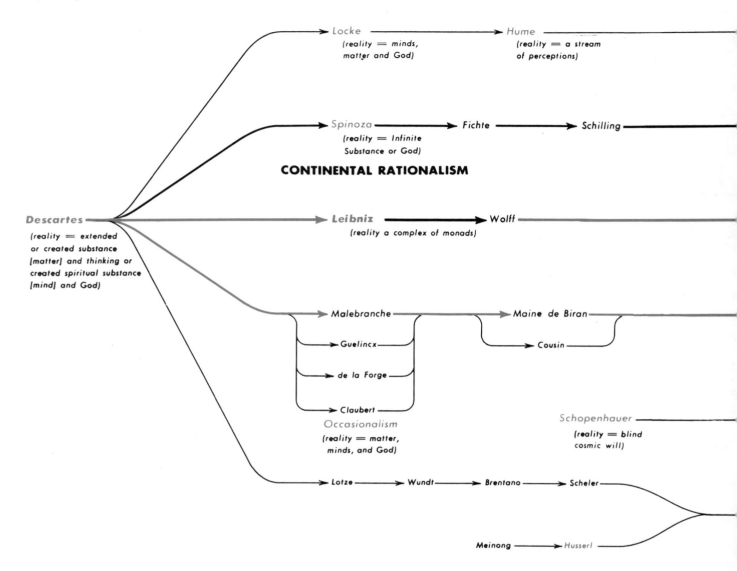

Descartes
(reality = extended
or created substance
[matter] and thinking or
created spiritual substance
[mind] and God)

Locke
(reality = minds,
matter and God)

Hume
(reality = a stream
of perceptions)

Spinoza
(reality = Infinite
Substance or God)

Fichte

Schilling

CONTINENTAL RATIONALISM

Leibniz
(reality a complex of monads)

Wolff

Malebranche

Maine de Biran

Guelincx

Cousin

de la Forge

Claubert

Occasionalism
(reality = matter,
minds, and God)

Schopenhauer
(reality = blind
cosmic will)

Lotze — Wundt — Brentano — Scheler

Meinong — Husserl

In many respects, the Cartesian revolution initiated the spirit of the modern world. Where contemporary dualism is not religious in character, it is likely to be Cartesian. Cartesian dualism is the popular philosophy that separates the mental or spiritual from the material or scientific. It commends itself by the ease with which scientific and religious matters may be kept apart (see p. 41).

The Cartesian revolution owes its importance to the fact that Descartes's philosophy enabled the modern scientific revolution to get under way. This was partly because Descartes pictured the world as a vast mathematical order discoverable by a reason chastened by the method of doubt. By separating the spiritual from the material, Descartes enabled the new science to proceed in its inquiries into the *mechanism* of an *orderly material world* unhampered by the arbitrary intervention of a providential God or the unpredictable irregularities of nature.

God became the cosmic watchmaker who created an orderly world and minds to learn of it. Moreover, by clearing the mind of uncertain knowledge, Descartes believed that one could proceed by deduction from first principles to all there was to know about the world. Buttressed by the similar convictions of other rationalists, Descartes fortuitously contributed a philosophy that sparked the scientific revolt.

Cartesianism influenced a number of philosophies which diverged from its *dualism*. Known also as Continental rationalism, Cartesianism became *monistic* in Spinoza and, through Spinoza and Kant, developed into the monistic idealism of Hegel. Deriving also from Descartes was the occasionalism of Malebranche and later the dualistic metaphysics of Bergson's vitalism. Contemporary phenomenology is also an expression of Cartesianism (see Chart 24).

CHART 6

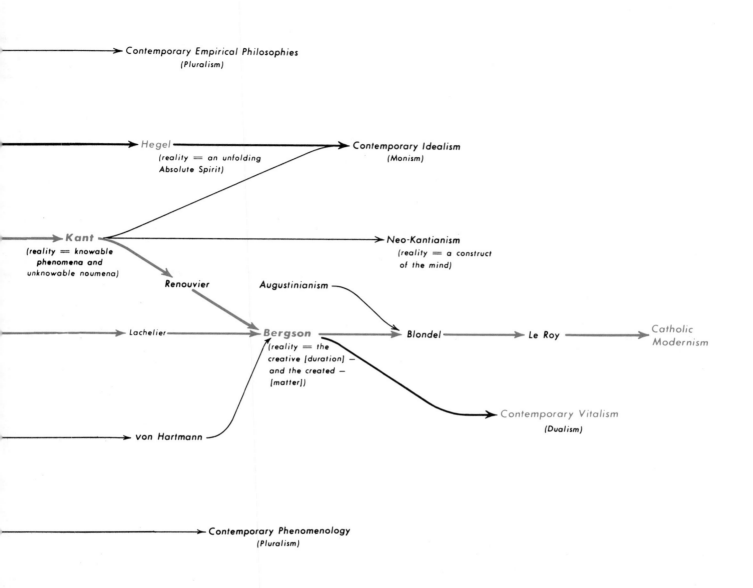

KANTIANISM (DUALISM)
(Reality includes a spiritual realm.)

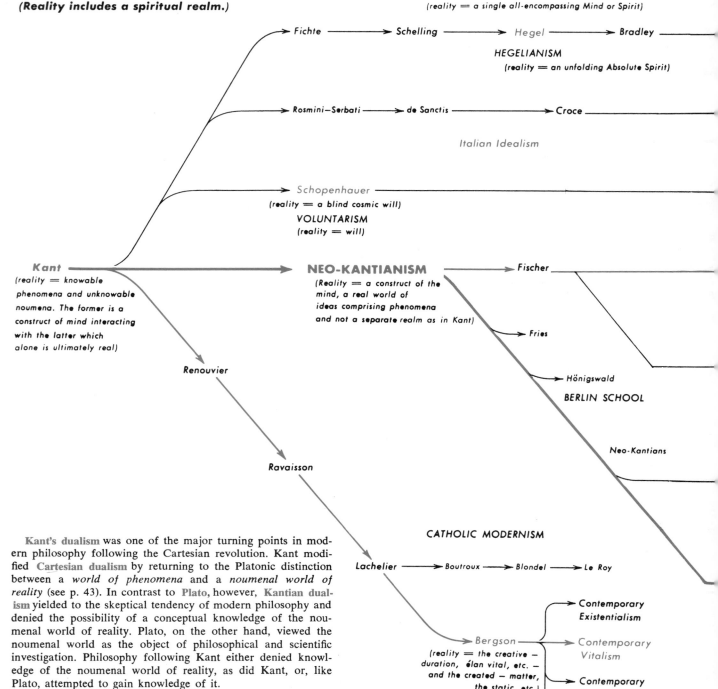

Fichte ——→ Schelling ——→ Hegel ——→ Bradley

HEGELIANISM
(reality = an unfolding Absolute Spirit)

Rosmini–Serbati ——→ de Sanctis ——→ Croce

Italian Idealism

Schopenhauer
(reality = a blind cosmic will)
VOLUNTARISM
(reality = will)

Kant
(reality = knowable
phenomena and unknowable
noumena. The former is a
construct of mind interacting
with the latter which
alone is ultimately real)

NEO-KANTIANISM
(Reality = a construct of the
mind, a real world of
ideas comprising phenomena
and not a separate realm as in Kant)

Fischer

Fries

Hönigswald
BERLIN SCHOOL

Neo-Kantians

Renouvier

Ravaisson

CATHOLIC MODERNISM

Lachelier ——→ Boutroux ——→ Blondel ——→ Le Roy

Bergson
(reality = the creative —
duration, élan vital, etc. —
and the created — matter,
the static, etc.)

→ *Contemporary
Existentialism*

→ *Contemporary
Vitalism*

→ *Contemporary
Process Philosophy*

→ *Contemporary
Latin American Philosophy*

Kant's dualism was one of the major turning points in modern philosophy following the Cartesian revolution. Kant modified **Cartesian dualism** by returning to the Platonic distinction between a *world of phenomena* and a *noumenal world of reality* (see p. 43). In contrast to **Plato**, however, **Kantian dualism** yielded to the skeptical tendency of modern philosophy and denied the possibility of a conceptual knowledge of the noumenal world of reality. Plato, on the other hand, viewed the noumenal world as the object of philosophical and scientific investigation. Philosophy following Kant either denied knowledge of the noumenal world of reality, as did Kant, or, like Plato, attempted to gain knowledge of it.

Kant's influence was considerable and encouraged not only dualistic theories of reality but monistic and pluralistic forms of **idealism** as well. Through Kant, **Cartesianism** exerted a continuing influence—particularly in **Bergson**, who became one of the major metaphysical dualists of the twentieth century (see p. 40).

Kant's influence on **Protestant liberalism** is also considerable (see Chart 22). When Kant denied freedom to the phenomenal world of science, he suggested the possibility that freedom and moral and spiritual values might belong to the noumenal world. Moreover, he further suggested that although knowledge in the usual sense cannot apply to reality, nevertheless moral requirements suggest that reality is a moral order and that there is a purpose operative in nature. Kant's attempt to establish the legitimate realms of both science and religion met with favor among certain religiously inclined thinkers and provided a major influence on the ethical emphasis of liberal Protestant philosophy.

Certain of Kant's followers, known as neo-Kantians, regarded the noumenal world of Kant as a limiting concept rather than as an actual realm of reality. The **idealism** of **neo-Kantianism** avoided Kant's **dualism** by viewing reality as a construct of the mind embracing all contents of thought—phenomenal or noumenal—and consisting in an ideational or symbolic world. A major expression of contemporary neo-Kantian thought is the philosophy of Ernst Cassirer.

CHART 7

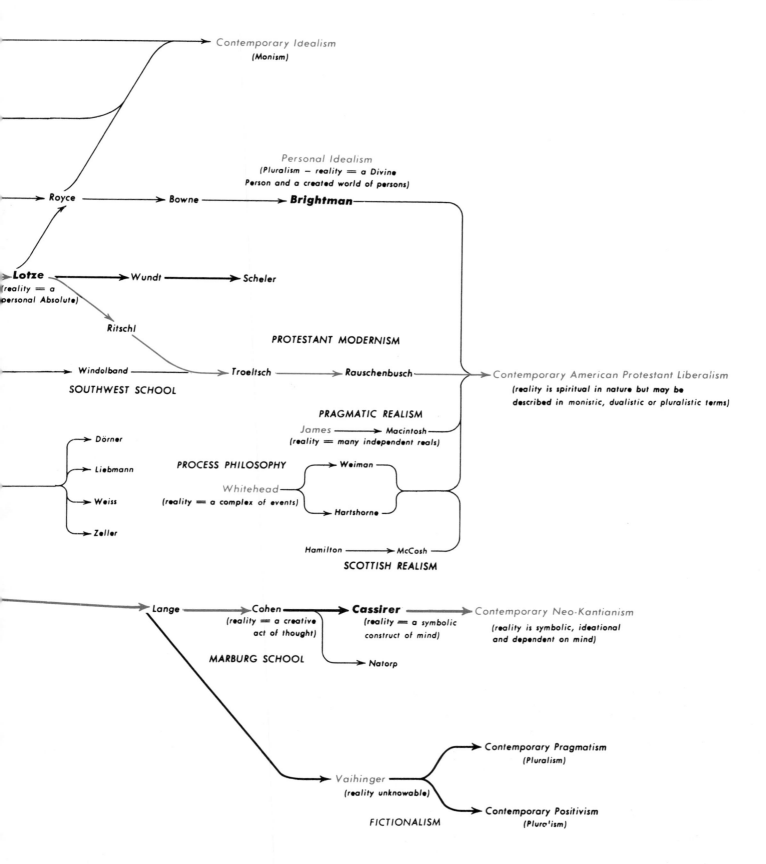

Contemporary Idealism
(Monism)

Personal Idealism
(Pluralism — reality = a Divine
Person and a created world of persons)

Royce ——————→ Bowne ——————→ **Brightman**

Lotze ——————→ Wundt ——————→ Scheler
(reality = a
personal Absolute)

Ritschl

PROTESTANT MODERNISM

Windolband ——————→ Troeltsch ——————→ Rauschenbusch ——————→ Contemporary American Protestant Liberalism
SOUTHWEST SCHOOL   (reality is spiritual in nature but may be
                                                                    described in monistic, dualistic or pluralistic terms)

PRAGMATIC REALISM
James ——————→ Macintosh
(reality = many independent reals)

Dörner

Liebmann   PROCESS PHILOSOPHY ——————→ Weiman

Weiss   Whitehead ——————→
                  (reality = a complex of events)
Zeller   ——————→ Hartshorne

                  Hamilton ——————→ McCosh
                  SCOTTISH REALISM

Lange ——————→ Cohen ——————→ **Cassirer** ——————→ Contemporary Neo-Kantianism
              (reality = a creative   (reality = a symbolic   (reality is symbolic, ideational
              act of thought)   construct of mind)   and dependent on mind)

              MARBURG SCHOOL ——————→ Natorp

                                                    Contemporary Pragmatism
                                                    (Pluralism)

              Vaihinger ——————→
              (reality unknowable)
                                                    Contemporary Positivism
              FICTIONALISM   (Pluraism)

MONISM: STOICISM
(Reality is a purposive power.)

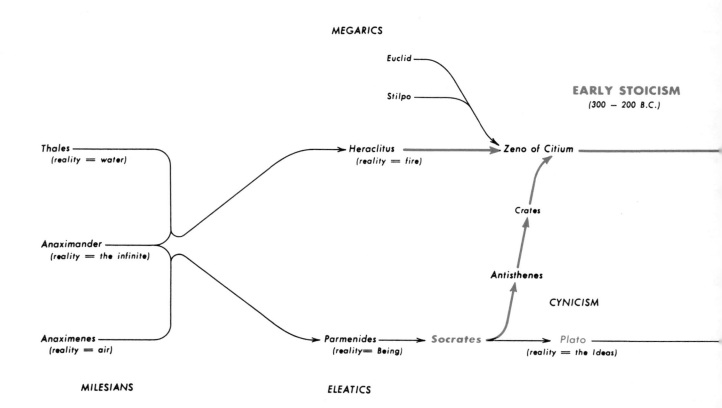

MEGARICS

Euclid ——

Stilpo ——

EARLY STOICISM
(300 – 200 B.C.)

Thales ——
(reality = water)

Heraclitus ——→ Zeno of Citium ——
(reality = fire)

Crates

Anaximander ——
(reality = the infinite)

Antisthenes

CYNICISM

Anaximenes ——
(reality = air)

Parmenides ——→ Socrates ——→ Plato ——
(reality = Being)   (reality = the Ideas)

MILESIANS

ELEATICS

"The tendency to seek for unity in plurality, to find the One in the Many, as Plato said, is persistent in the human mind, so that there has always been a strong hope among philosophers of finding some one elementary form of being . . . the various manifestations of which will make up our world of experience" (Patrick). As the metaphysical doctrine that reality is one, monism meets the demand for economy of explanation, for a satisfying unity which reason demands even though experience may contest.

In ancient philosophy, Parmenides spoke of an all-encompassing *Being* which occupies all space and thought and is changeless. Heraclitus, on the other hand, taught that reality is change, a kind of process ordered by a vital principle, or *logos*. His monism interpreted oneness in terms of structure or law whose rule is *necessary* and *universal*. These ideas form the basis of Stoicism, which flourished for hundreds of years in the Greco-Roman world and greatly influenced early Christianity and Western philosophy. As one of the major streams

of thought in the ancient world, Stoicism combined a variety of theories of reality. It derived its major ideas from Heraclitus and from the Cynics. Its founder is generally considered to be Zeno of Citium (Cyprus, 340–265 B.C.).

Early Stoicism was developed by Zeno, Cleanthes, and Chrysippus, who gave it a systematic formulation (see p. 41). Middle Stoicism arose when Panaetius (180–110 B.C.) introduced Stoicism to Rome. Roman Stoicism culminated the school. Unlike earlier Stoicism, the Stoicism of Panaetius directed attention to ethical issues instead of to the problem of reality. Stoic theories of reality became highly eclectic. In the Roman period, they became more religious in character.

Although more *eclectic* than Stoic, Cicero espoused many Stoic ideas and, through his writings, influenced St. Augustine. In many ways, Stoicism paralleled Christianity. When it finally yielded to Christianity, Stoicism left an enduring influence on Christian thought.

CHART 8

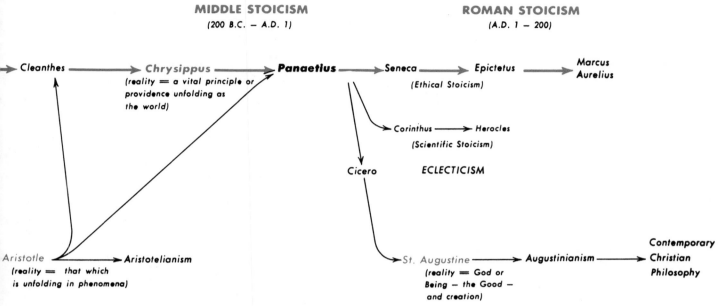

MIDDLE STOICISM
(200 B.C. — A.D. 1)

ROMAN STOICISM
(A.D. 1 — 200)

Cleanthes

Chrysippus
(reality = a vital principle or
providence unfolding as
the world)

Panaetius

Seneca
(Ethical Stoicism)

Epictetus

Marcus
Aurelius

Corinthus ──→ Herocles
(Scientific Stoicism)

Cicero

ECLECTICISM

Aristotle
(reality = that which
is unfolding in phenomena)

Aristotelianism

St. Augustine
(reality = God or
Being — the Good —
and creation)

Augustinianism

Contemporary
Christian
Philosophy

MONISM: MYSTICISM
(Reality is a Divine Ground.)

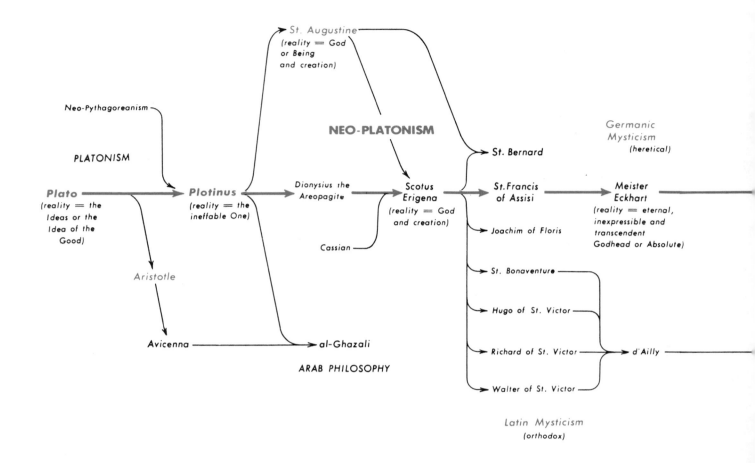

Neo-Pythagoreanism

PLATONISM

St. Augustine
(reality = God
or Being
and creation)

NEO-PLATONISM

*Germanic
Mysticism*
(heretical)

Plato
(reality = the
Ideas or the
Idea of the
Good)

Plotinus
(reality = the
ineffable One)

*Dionysius the
Areopagite*

*Scotus
Erigena*
(reality = God
and creation)

St. Bernard

St. Francis
of Assisi

*Meister
Eckhart*
(reality = eternal,
inexpressible and
transcendent
Godhead or Absolute)

Aristotle

Cassian

Joachim of Floris

St. Bonaventure

Hugo of St. Victor

Richard of St. Victor

d'Ailly

Avicenna ⟶ al-Ghazali

Walter of St. Victor

ARAB PHILOSOPHY

Latin Mysticism
(orthodox)

Mysticism is the supremely monistic philosophy which attempts to transcend the category **monism** itself as well as all categories of *metaphysics* (see p. 33). While other monisms may view reality as various forms of one substance or one mind, the mystic may avoid such categories of description as oneness, changelessness, or Being and speak only in *negative terms*. It is not proper to ascribe to the ineffable *One* or *Godhead* or *Ground* the property of this or that, for *It* is all of these or none of these and yet something else.

Mysticism teaches four general doctrines:

(1) All aspects of the *phenomenal* world are "the manifestation of a Divine Ground within which all partial reality have their being, and apart from which they would be nonexistent" (A. Huxley).

(2) This Divine Ground may be known by *inference* and *intuition*. Knowledge of it unites knower and thing known.

(3) Man has a *spiritual self* as well as a phenomenal ego. This is the true self and it may be united with the *Cosmic Self*.

(4) The goal of life is this *knowledge of reality* and *unification with it*.

The mystic stream in Western philosophy has its origin in **Plato** and particularly in **Plotinus**, whose **neo-Platonism** constitutes the major fountainhead of *Western mysticism* (see p. 46). Eastern influence is considerable. During the Middle Ages, "mysticism accompanied scholasticism as a shadow" (Wood). During the fourteenth century, it diverged into two forms—one supporting orthodoxy and the Church, and the other, as, e.g., in Meister Eckhart, tending toward neo-Platonism and heresy. The major offense was *pantheism,* as opposed to the *theism* of orthodoxy. The influence of mysticism was considerable in philosophical and scientific thought as well as in religion. Shortly prior to the modern period, it diverged again into Protestant and Catholic streams, and during the nineteenth and twentieth centuries, *Eastern mysticism* again asserted its influence. Today mysticism may be found in a wide variety of philosophies.

CHART 9

CATHOLIC MYSTICISM

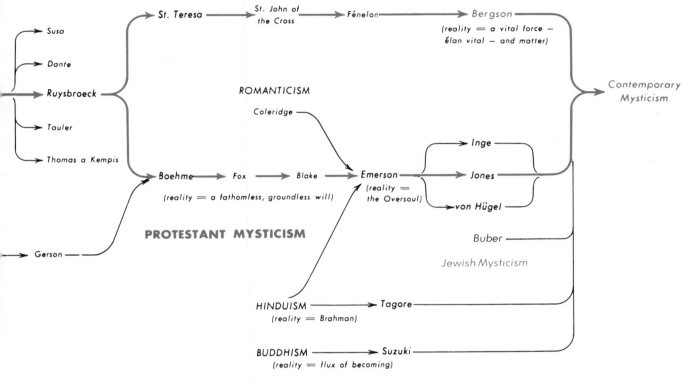

Susa

Dante

Ruysbroeck

Tauler

Thomas a Kempis

St. Teresa → St. John of the Cross → Fénelon → Bergson
(reality = a vital force — élan vital — and matter)

ROMANTICISM

Coleridge

Boehme → Fox → Blake → Emerson
(reality = a fathomless, groundless will)

Emerson
(reality = the Oversoul)

Inge

Jones

von Hügel

PROTESTANT MYSTICISM

Gerson

Buber

Jewish Mysticism

Contemporary Mysticism

HINDUISM → Tagore
(reality = Brahman)

BUDDHISM → Suzuki
(reality = flux of becoming)

Eastern Mysticism

MONISM: IDEALISM
(Reality is Mind.)

During the seventeenth century, *Cartesianism* separated reality into the mental and the material. This *dualism* prompted a *monistic reaction,* wherein it was argued that reality is either mental or material, but not both. Spinoza, however, transcended Cartesian dualism to develop a monistic theory of reality which remains as one of the most thoroughgoing monistic metaphysics ever developed. For him, all is *Substance* or *God. Mind* and *matter* are but *Attributes* of Substance (see p. 47). Spinoza's in-

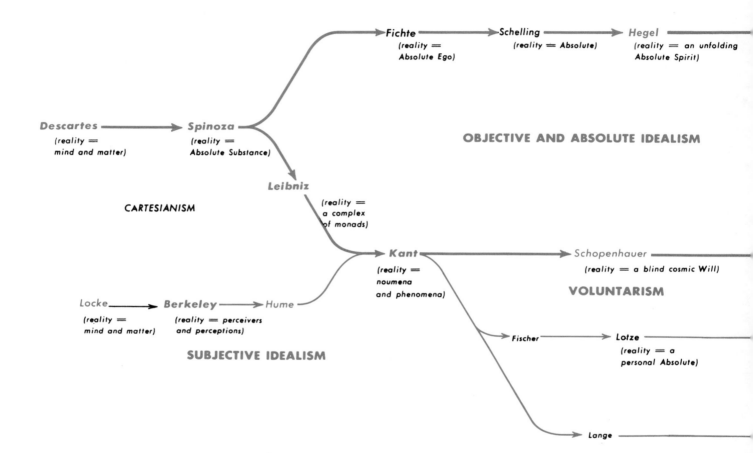

Fichte
(reality =
Absolute Ego)

Schelling
(reality = Absolute)

Hegel
(reality = an unfolding
Absolute Spirit)

OBJECTIVE AND ABSOLUTE IDEALISM

Descartes
(reality =
mind and matter)

Spinoza
(reality =
Absolute Substance)

Leibniz
(reality =
a complex
of monads)

CARTESIANISM

Kant
(reality =
noumena
and phenomena)

Schopenhauer
(reality = a blind cosmic Will)

VOLUNTARISM

Locke
(reality =
mind and matter)

Berkeley
(reality = perceivers
and perceptions)

Hume

SUBJECTIVE IDEALISM

Fischer

Lotze
(reality = a
personal Absolute)

Lange

NEO-KANTIANISM

fluence on the development of modern monistic idealism is important. His relationship to Hegel, e.g., is clear, and the romantic and idealistic philosophies of nineteenth-century Germany are greatly indebted to him.

Modern idealism takes many forms, which may be monistic, dualistic, or pluralistic theories of reality. Its most widely influential form in Eastern as well as Western philosophy is monism and, like many highly developed dualistic or pluralistic theories of reality, tends to transcend these categories to become a form of *mysticism.*

Idealism holds that reality is of the order of mind. Idealism approaches reality from the standpoint of the self—from "the inside out"—as compared with *realism,* which approaches reality from "the outside in." Reality is understood in terms of self-knowledge. Man is, in a small way, what reality is as a whole. Hence idealism interprets reality in terms of *consciousness,* ideas, and the *process of thought* or *personality.* Whatever may confront man as reality, it is *his* reality; he is part of it; and his ideas are involved in his thought about it.

Historically, six types of idealism may be identified as *theories of reality:*

(1) Platonic or Classical idealism, which is dualistic and axiological—value-centered (see p. 45).

(2) Berkeleyan or subjective idealism, which is a pluralistic theory of reality (see p. 40).

(3) Kantian or critical idealism, which is also dualistic and axiological, like Platonic idealism, but skeptical (see p. 43).

(4) Voluntaristic idealism, as in Schopenhauer, which is monistic and interprets reality as a will (see pp. 46, 47).

(5) Lotzean or personal idealism, which is pluralistic and interprets reality in terms of the character of personality (see Chart 16).

CHART 10

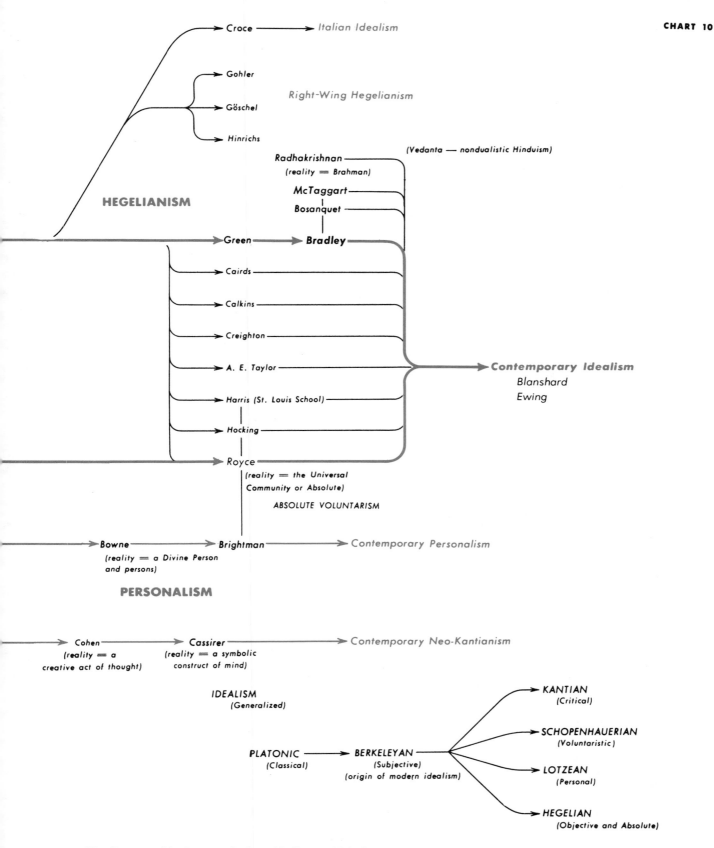

(6) **Hegelian** or **objective** or **absolute idealism,** which is monistic, logical, and historical in emphasis (see pp. 41, 42).

These types are found in Indian and Chinese as well as Western philosophy. They are not mutually exclusive, but stress different aspects of the problem of reality. Most idealistic theories of reality involve elements of all six theories as, e.g., the idealism of Josiah Royce.

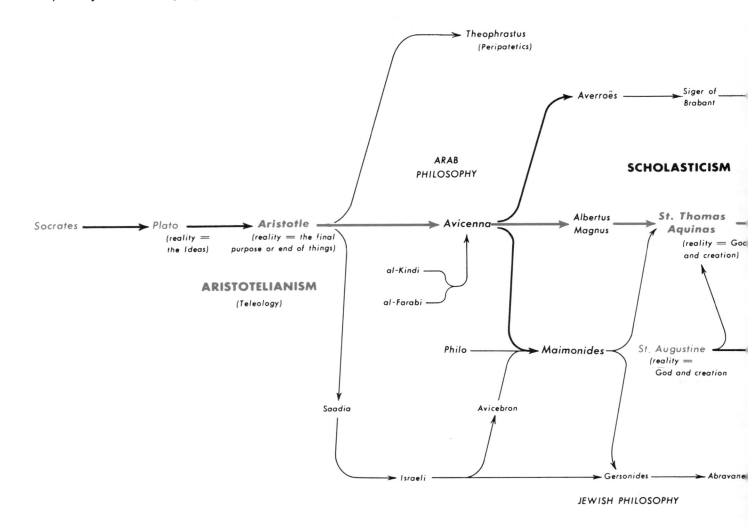

The tradition of **Aristotelianism** is a long and highly developed one, persisting into the present. Though not clearly monistic, *monism* is implied. Aristotle's doctrine that reality is in particulars constitutes a *pluralistic realism,* but his view that the fundamental reality in particulars is their purpose and that this purpose contributes to and compromises a final and transcendent purpose or end is monistic (see pp. 39–40).

As revised by **St. Thomas Aquinas,** Aristotelianism acquired a distinctly theistic and dualistic character. This was because of the inherent *dualism* of **St. Augustine's** Christian philosophy and theology which St. Thomas reinterpreted in Aristotelian terms. Aristotelianism became the basis of **scholasticism** during its peak of influence in the thirteenth century. Until the pronouncement of Pope Leo XIII in 1879 urging the study of St. Thomas, Aristotelianism declined—particularly in the face of the scientific revolution and the rise of empirical and nominalistic philosophies.

Neo-Aristotelianism (also **neo-Thomism** or **neoscholasticism**) is an influential contemporary philosophy, particularly in Roman Catholic circles. It revives the Aristotelian confidence in reason as an instrument of metaphysical knowledge. Its theory of reality is realistic and pluralistic. There is an independently real world of many beings created by an independently real Being—God (*theism*). The starting point of scholasticism (and neoscholasticism) is theory of reality (*metaphysics* or *ontology*). Reality can be known through reason and revelation (see p. 47). The problem of knowledge is not central, as it became later for *nominalism, empiricism,* and *skepticism.*

Three stages of medieval scholasticism may be identified:

(1) Formative (ninth to twelfth centuries). *Platonism, neo-Platonism,* and *Augustinianism* predominate. Emphasis is *dualistic.* Plato's Ideas (universals) are *essences* of and prior to things (*ante res*), as in St. Anselm's medieval *realism* (see p. 9).

(2) Peak (thirteenth century). **Aristotelianism** predominates. Emphasis is more *monistic* and *pluralistic.* Ideas (universals) are real, but in things (*in rebus*), not prior to things, as in Albertus Magnus and **St. Thomas Aquinas** (see p. 9). This stage forms the basis for **contemporary neoscholasticism.**

(3) Decline (fourteenth century). *Nominalism* and *pluralism* rise in influence together with *mysticism.* Ideas (universals) are not real, but names of things; only things are real; universals are after things (*post res*), as in William of Ockham (see p. 9).

CHART 11

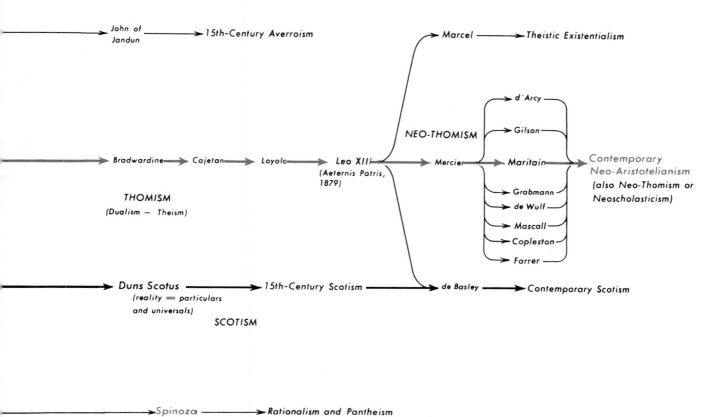

John of Jandun ────────► 15th-Century Averroism

Marcel ────────► Theistic Existentialism

Bradwardine ──► Cajetan ──► Loyola ──► Leo XIII ──► Mercier ──► Maritain ──► *Contemporary Neo-Aristotelianism (also Neo-Thomism or Neoscholasticism)*
(Aeternis Patris, 1879)

NEO-THOMISM

d'Arcy
Gilson
Maritain
Grabmann
de Wulf
Mascall
Copleston
Farrer

THOMISM
(Dualism — Theism)

Duns Scotus ────────► 15th-Century Scotism ────────► de Basley ────────► Contemporary Scotism
(reality = particulars and universals)

SCOTISM

Spinoza ────────► *Rationalism and Pantheism*
(reality = Absolute Substance)

PLURALISM: MATERIALISTIC ATOMISM
(Reality is made up of material atoms.)

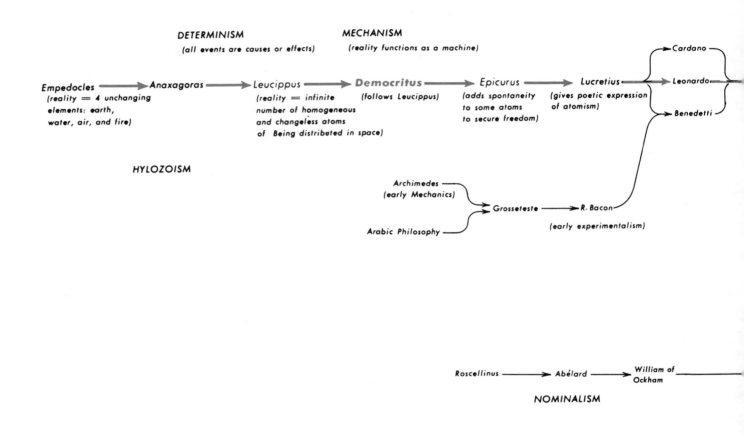

DETERMINISM

(all events are causes or effects)

MECHANISM

(reality functions as a machine)

Empedocles ⟶ Anaxagoras ⟶ Leucippus ⟶ Democritus ⟶ Epicurus ⟶ Lucretius ⟶ Cardano ⟶ Leonardo ⟶ Benedetti

(reality = 4 unchanging elements: earth, water, air, and fire)

(reality = infinite number of homogeneous and changeless atoms of Being distributed in space)

(follows Leucippus)

(adds spontaneity to some atoms to secure freedom)

(gives poetic expression of atomism)

HYLOZOISM

Archimedes
(early Mechanics)

Arabic Philosophy ⟶ Grosseteste ⟶ R. Bacon

(early experimentalism)

Roscellinus ⟶ Abélard ⟶ William of Ockham

NOMINALISM

Pluralism is the metaphysical doctrine that reality consists in many reals. The most obvious form of pluralism is atomic materialism, wherein the basic view of the ancient Greek philosophers Leucippus and Democritus holds: reality consists in discrete, indestructible atoms rearranging themselves in space in the many objects that present themselves to the senses (see p. 41).

There are, however, no clear distinctions among monistic, dualistic, and pluralistic interpretations of reality. A pluralist like Leibniz may be interpreted as a monist when his *spiritual atoms* (*monads*) are considered as organized into the unified spiritual whole suggestive of monistic *idealism* (see p. 44). Also, most materialism tends to view matter as the sole reality and is therefore monistic in this sense. Haeckel, e.g., specifically refers to his materialism as *monism*. But in each instance, these philosophies are also pluralistic in the sense that they emphasize the reality of independent particular things.

Pluralism may interpret the many reals as spiritual, mental,

material, perceptual, or simply neutral. Perhaps one of the best examples of a pluralistic theory of reality is the *pragmatism* of William James, who described reality as many reals "strung-along" (see p. 43 and Chart 14).

For materialistic atomism, reality consists in some space-occupying *substance* distributed throughout space as discrete entities, or *atoms*. Empedocles first suggested the existence of elements as unchanging substances varying in motion and combination. Anaxagoras animated his elements with a kind of "thought stuff," or *nous*. The classical materialism of early modern science unaltered by recent scientific developments was first suggested by Leucippus and developed by Democritus. Leucippus viewed reality as an infinite number of homogeneous atoms distributed throughout empty space in an infinite variety of forms.

Materialistic atomism was generally ignored during the Middle Ages, but was revived by Galileo and other early modern scientific thinkers of the sixteenth and seventeenth centuries.

CHART 12

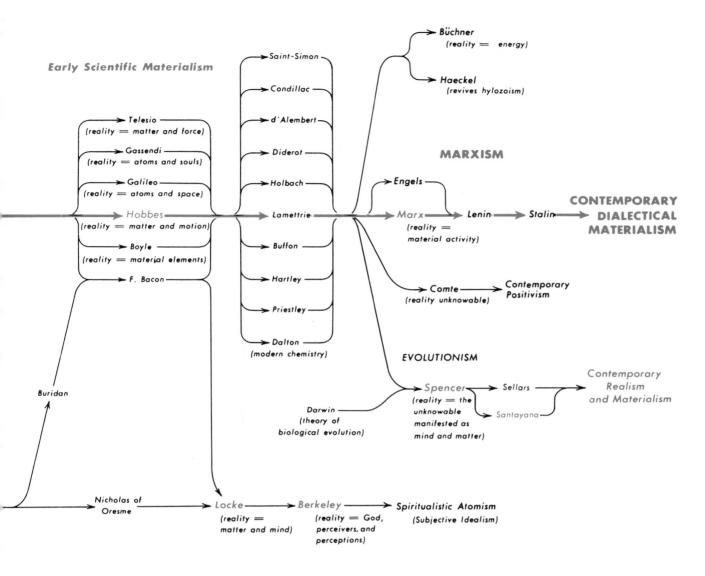

MATERIALISM

Early Scientific Materialism

Büchner
(reality = energy)

Haeckel
(revives hylozoism)

Saint-Simon

Condillac

d'Alembert

Diderot

Holbach

Lamettrie

Buffon

Hartley

Priestley

Dalton
(modern chemistry)

Telesio
(reality = matter and force)

Gassendi
(reality = atoms and souls)

Galileo
(reality = atoms and space)

Hobbes
(reality = matter and motion)

Boyle
(reality = material elements)

F. Bacon

MARXISM

Engels

Marx
(reality =
material activity)

Lenin

Stalin

**CONTEMPORARY
DIALECTICAL
MATERIALISM**

Comte
(reality unknowable)

Contemporary
Positivism

EVOLUTIONISM

Spencer
(reality = the
unknowable
manifested as
mind and matter)

Sellars

Santayana

Contemporary
Realism
and Materialism

Darwin
(theory of
biological evolution)

Buridan

Nicholas of
Oresme

Locke
(reality =
matter and mind)

Berkeley
(reality = God,
perceivers, and
perceptions)

Spiritualistic Atomism
(Subjective Idealism)

Most of these thinkers retained the independent status of the soul, mind, or spirit. Hobbes and Lamettrie, however, developed a mechanistic interpretation of man pointing to some of the theories of the contemporary behavioral sciences (see p. 42). Dalton developed the key ideas of early modern chemistry based on atomic materialism.

Impressed by Hegel's *dialectic,* Marx adapted it to materialistic atomism and gave the latter a social interpretation stressing the role of strife at the root of reality. The result was a **dialectical materialism,** which constitutes the basis of contemporary Marxist philosophy (see p. 44).

Contemporary forms of materialism tend to be highly sophisticated, in that *energy* or *activity* is stressed rather than *substance* as such. In other words, matter is what it does. Materialism has also come to be associated with *realism, positivism,* and *evolutionism.*

PLURALISM: PHENOMENALISM AND SKEPTICISM
(Reality outside experience is unknowable.)

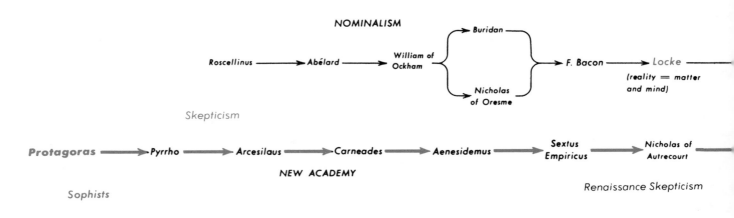

NOMINALISM

Roscellinus ⟶ Abélard ⟶ William of Ockham ⟶ Buridan / Nicholas of Oresme ⟶ F. Bacon ⟶ *Locke*

(reality = matter and mind)

Skepticism

Protagoras ⟶ Pyrrho ⟶ Arcesilaus ⟶ Carneades ⟶ Aenesidemus ⟶ Sextus Empiricus ⟶ Nicholas of Autrecourt

NEW ACADEMY

Sophists

Renaissance Skepticism

Phenomenalism holds that we only know things as they appear. Skepticism holds that we can't know things at all. In its weaker form, called agnosticism, skepticism holds that we don't know whether we can know things. Phenomenalism, skepticism, and agnosticism refer reality to *perceptions*. Things are perceptions or constructs of them (see p. 11).

Although these theories are *antimetaphysical* in temper, their view of reality is *pluralistic*. No claim is made that the world is one or more substances or that it emerges from anything. The world is what it appears to be—a vast variety of phenomena.

The skeptical emphasis of contemporary philosophy has been encouraged by developments in scientific method and by the study of the nature of language and logic. Denial of the possibility of a knowledge of reality outside experience or, for that matter, any certain or universal knowledge whatever also finds an early advocate in the great Sophist Protagoras (see p. 46). Though generally discouraged during the Middle Ages, skepticism nevertheless found expression in the *nominalism* of William of Ockham (see p. 14).

Hume is the key figure in modern skepticism and phenomenalism (see pp. 42, 43). Deriving his skepticism from a logical development of Locke's and Berkeley's *empiricism*, Hume paved the way for most of contemporary empirical philosophy and the antimetaphysical tendencies that may be found in all forms of *positivism, pragmatism,* and *phenomenalism* (see pp. 9, 44, and Charts 14, 23). The emergence of these philosophies during the nineteenth century and more recently of *analytical philosophy* has established skepticism as a dominant emphasis and has minimized interest in metaphysical issues like the problem of the nature of reality (see Chart 1).

CHART 13

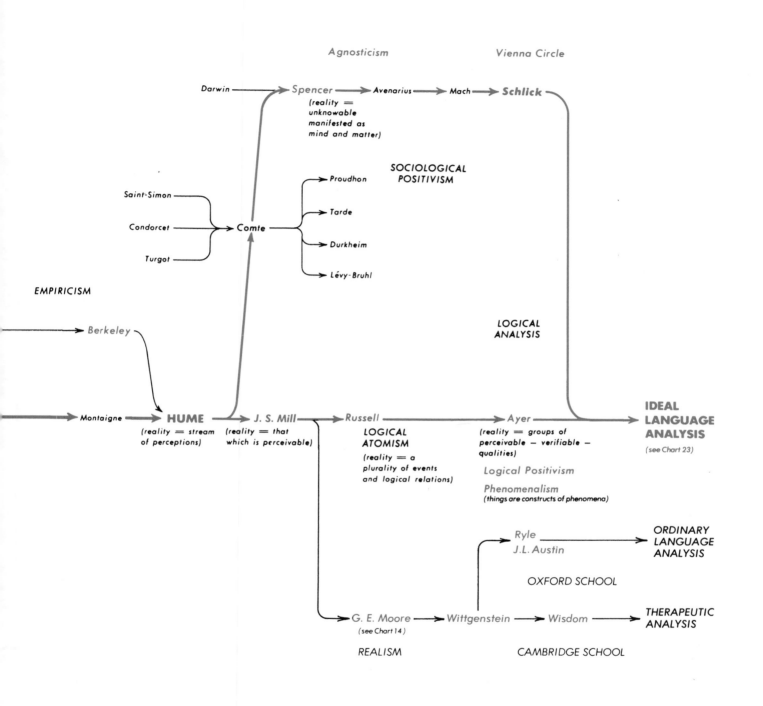

Agnosticism   Vienna Circle

Darwin ——— Spencer ——→ Avenarius ——→ Mach —→ **Schlick**
(reality =
unknowable
manifested as
mind and matter)

SOCIOLOGICAL
POSITIVISM

Saint-Simon ——————→ Proudhon

Condorcet ———→ Comte ——→ Tarde

Turgot ——————————→ Durkheim

——→ Lévy-Bruhl

EMPIRICISM

LOGICAL
ANALYSIS

Berkeley

IDEAL
LANGUAGE
ANALYSIS

Montaigne ——→ **HUME** ——→ *J. S. Mill* ——→ *Russell* ——————————→ *Ayer* ————————→
(reality = stream   *(reality = that*   LOGICAL   *(reality = groups of*   *(see Chart 23)*
of perceptions)   *which is perceivable)*   ATOMISM   *perceivable — verifiable —*
                                  (reality = a   *qualities)*
                                    plurality of events
                                    and logical relations)   *Logical Positivism*

                                                   Phenomenalism
                                                   (things are constructs of phenomena)

Ryle ——————————→ ORDINARY
J.L. Austin   LANGUAGE
                  ANALYSIS

OXFORD SCHOOL

THERAPEUTIC
G. E. Moore ——→ *Wittgenstein* ——→ *Wisdom* ————→ ANALYSIS
(see Chart 14)

REALISM   *CAMBRIDGE SCHOOL*

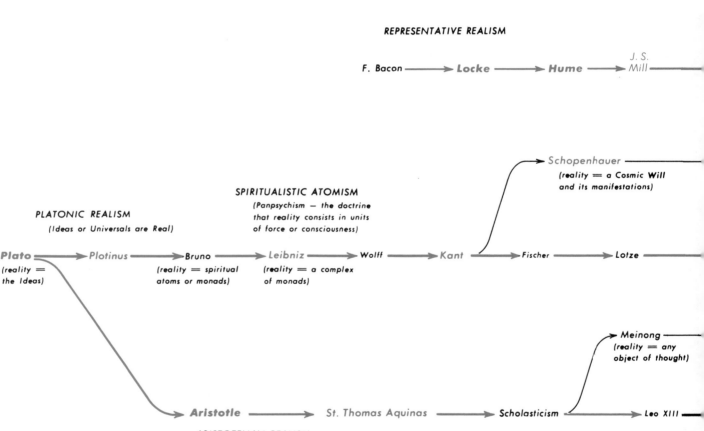

REPRESENTATIVE REALISM

F. Bacon ⟶ **Locke** ⟶ **Hume** ⟶ *J. S. Mill* ⟶

SPIRITUALISTIC ATOMISM

(Panpsychism — the doctrine
that reality consists in units
of force or consciousness)

PLATONIC REALISM

(Ideas or Universals are Real)

⟶ Schopenhauer ⟶

(reality = a Cosmic **Will**
and its manifestations)

Plato ⟹ *Plotinus* ⟶ *Bruno* ⟶ *Leibniz* ⟶ **Wolff** ⟶ **Kant** ⟶ *Fischer* ⟶ *Lotze* ⟶

(reality =
the Ideas)

(reality = spiritual
atoms or monads)

(reality = a complex
of monads)

⟶ Meinong ⟶

(reality = any
object of thought)

Aristotle ⟶ St. Thomas Aquinas ⟶ Scholasticism ⟶ Leo XIII ⟶

ARISTOTELIAN REALISM

The picture of contemporary philosophy—particularly with regard to theory of reality—is complex (see pp. 2, 19, 20). Several distinguishing features may be identified, however:

(1) Its **antimetaphysical tendency,** which becomes an outright **skepticism** for many and a general lack of interest in the problem of reality as such (see skepticism as a theory of knowledge, p. 9 and Charts 23, 24).

(2) Its **pluralism.** Whether the "real" is identified with the flux of experience, with its objects, or with its intended or ideal objects or relations, it is plural in nature. There is not a speculative quest for the "one" of reality or a religious tendency to

a *dualism* of this world and the next or of the actual and the ideal. As *described,* the world exhibits variety and plurality. Contemporary philosophy is pluralistic.

(3) Its **dynamism.** Contemporary philosophy takes its cue from Heraclitus. *Process, activity,* and *emergence* are the key ideas. Whatever may be real, it is relative and changing. *Substance* and *being* are analyzed away. Whatever is, is so by virtue of its power to produce observable results.

(4) Its **realism.** With the possible exception of *personalism,* most contemporary schools, other than those that are pure *skepticism* or *phenomenalism,* exhibit realistic origins or tendencies. However conceived, reality is independent of being

CHART 14

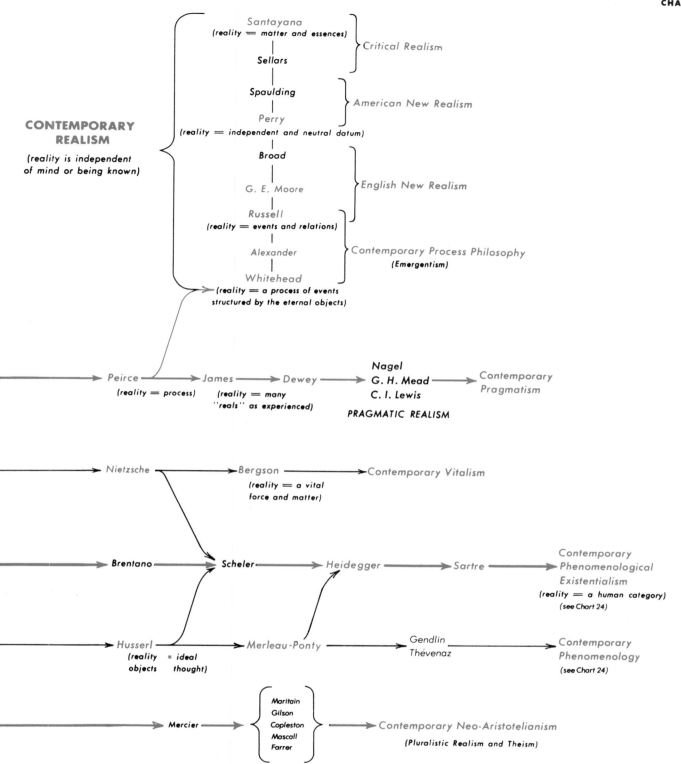

CONTEMPORARY REALISM

(reality is independent of mind or being known)

Santayana
(reality = matter and essences)

Sellars

} Critical Realism

Spaulding

Perry
(reality = independent and neutral datum)

} American New Realism

Broad

G. E. Moore

Russell
(reality = events and relations)

} English New Realism

Alexander

Whitehead
(reality = a process of events structured by the eternal objects)

} Contemporary Process Philosophy
(Emergentism)

Peirce ⟶ James ⟶ Dewey ⟶ Nagel / G. H. Mead / C. I. Lewis ⟶ Contemporary Pragmatism

(reality = process) 　*(reality = many "reals" as experienced)*

PRAGMATIC REALISM

Nietzsche ⟶ Bergson ⟶ Contemporary Vitalism
(reality = a vital force and matter)

Brentano ⟶ Scheler ⟶ Heidegger ⟶ Sartre ⟶ Contemporary Phenomenological Existentialism
(reality = a human category)
(see Chart 24)

Husserl
(reality = ideal objects = ideal thought) ⟶ Merleau-Ponty ⟶ Gendlin / Thévenaz ⟶ Contemporary Phenomenology
(see Chart 24)

Mercier ⟶ { Maritain / Gilson / Copleston / Mascall / Farrer } ⟶ Contemporary Neo-Aristotelianism
(Pluralistic Realism and Theism)

known by some mind, although its meaning may be intentional (see pp. 43, 46). It is an objective process, an organization of relations, or a world of objects. Even contemporary *existentialism* derives from the realism of *phenomenology, vitalism,* and other sources (see Chart 24). In short, reality is not the organized and ideal order of some purposive mind discovered and shared by man, but an independent and neutral—if not unfriendly—complex of objects and events to which man himself gives order and value. This is particularly true of *existentialism* and *pragmatism* (see Charts 23 and 24 for detailed information concerning the major contemporary forms of analytical and existential philosophy).

FUNCTIONALISTIC THEORIES OF MIND
(The mental is a function of the material.)

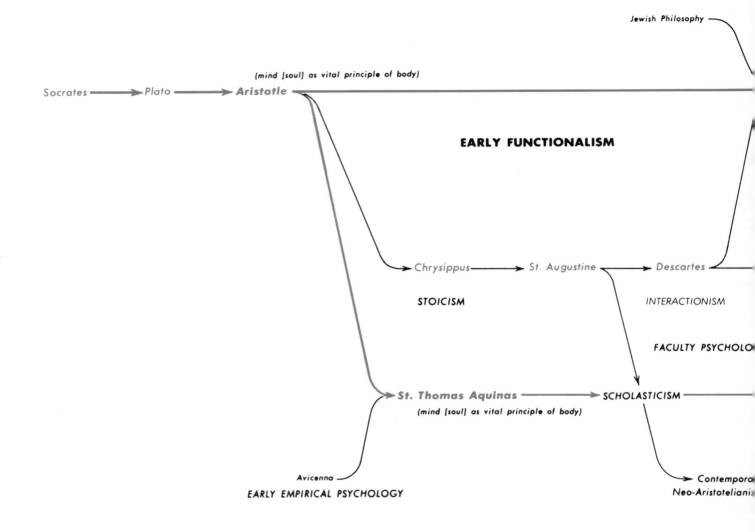

Jewish Philosophy

(mind [soul] as vital principle of body)

Socrates ⟶ Plato ⟶ *Aristotle*

EARLY FUNCTIONALISM

⟶ Chrysippus ⟶ St. Augustine ⟵ Descartes

STOICISM

INTERACTIONISM

FACULTY PSYCHOLO

⟶ *St. Thomas Aquinas* ⟶ SCHOLASTICISM ⟶
(mind [soul] as vital principle of body)

Avicenna

⟶ Contempora
Neo-Aristotelianis

EARLY EMPIRICAL PSYCHOLOGY

Functionalistic theories of mind have their origin in Aristotle, who believed the mental and the material to be inseparable (see pp. 39, 40). For Aristotle, the mental is the organizing and directive tendency of the material. In functional theories, mind is the *form* or *structure* of bodily activity, not a separate soul or substance. Indeed, most contemporary psychologies believe that the term "mind" is no longer necessary, for it points only to *behavior* or the *structure of behavior,* not to an independent entity. Contemporary *experimental psychology* has given great impetus to the study of behavior. As a contemporary school of psychology, functionalism was reformulated by Dewey and Angell under the impact of James and *behaviorism* (see p. 41). From the experimental psychology of Wundt, there arose a kind of pyschology known as structuralism, the most important of which reacted to Wundt's *atomistic* structuralism to produce a *holistic* structuralism, or Gestalt psychology (see pp. 43, 44). In Gestalt

psychology, Aristotelian functionalism reasserts itself. Closely related to Gestalt psychology is the theory that mind is an *emergent*—a unique product of the processes of *evolution* which constitutes a higher *structure* of reality (see pp. 18, 39, 48). All forms of functionalism as identified here were profoundly influenced by Darwin. Contemporary *neo-Thomist* or *neo-Aristotelian* theories of mind are also modified expressions of Aristotelian functionalism.

The *analytical theories* of Wittgenstein and Ryle are also interpreted by some as *functional theories* of mind, insofar as they hold that to refer to mind or the mental is to refer to behavior or to dispositions to behave in certain ways, and not to any mental entity as such. This functionalism, and Dewey's and Gestalt theory generally, are all forms of or related to behaviorism (see Chart 3).

CHART 15

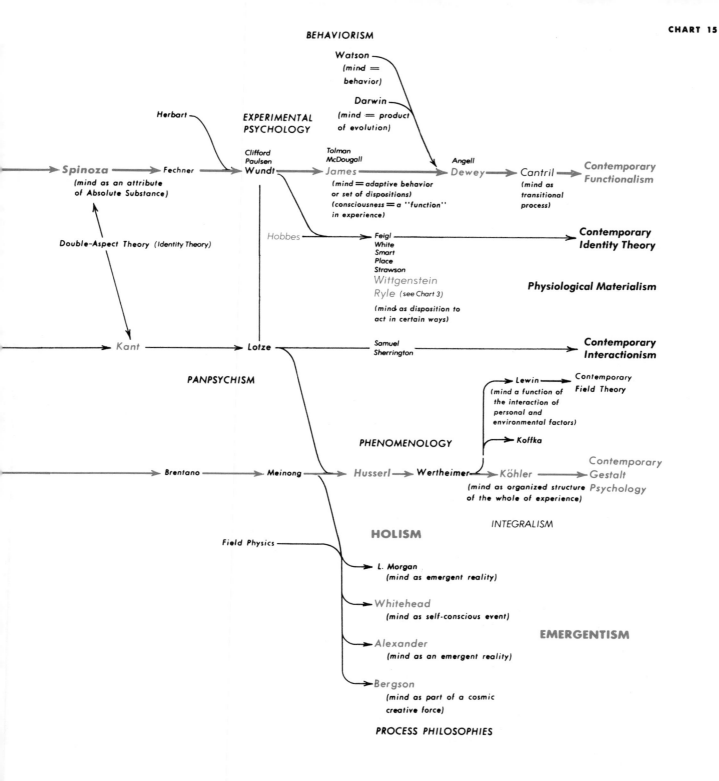

BEHAVIORISM

Watson
(mind =
behavior)

Darwin
(mind = product
of evolution)

Herbart

EXPERIMENTAL
PSYCHOLOGY

Clifford
Paulsen
Wundt

Tolman
McDougall
James
(mind = adaptive behavior
or set of dispositions)
(consciousness = a "function"
in experience)

Angell
Dewey
(mind as
transitional
process)

Cantril

Contemporary
Functionalism

Spinoza
(mind as an attribute
of Absolute Substance)

Fechner

Double-Aspect Theory (Identity Theory)

Hobbes

Feigl
White
Smart
Place
Strawson
Wittgenstein
Ryle (see Chart 3)

(mind as disposition to
act in certain ways)

Contemporary
Identity Theory

Physiological Materialism

Kant

Lotze

Samuel
Sherrington

Contemporary
Interactionism

PANPSYCHISM

Lewin
(mind a function of
the interaction of
personal and
environmental factors)

Contemporary
Field Theory

Koffka

PHENOMENOLOGY

Brentano

Meinong

Husserl

Wertheimer

Köhler

Contemporary
Gestalt
Psychology

(mind as organized structure
of the whole of experience)

INTEGRALISM

HOLISM

Field Physics

L. Morgan
(mind as emergent reality)

Whitehead
(mind as self-conscious event)

EMERGENTISM

Alexander
(mind as an emergent reality)

Bergson
(mind as part of a cosmic
creative force)

PROCESS PHILOSOPHIES

SPIRITUALISTIC THEORIES OF MIND
(Mind or soul has a unique and irreducible existence of its own.)

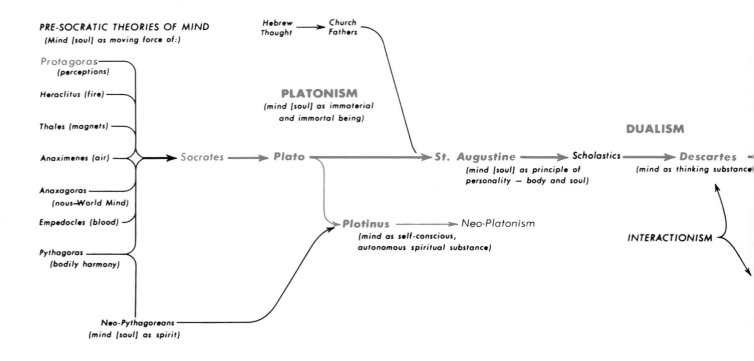

PRE-SOCRATIC THEORIES OF MIND
(Mind [soul] as moving force of:)

Protagoras
(perceptions)

Heraclitus (fire)

Thales (magnets)

Anaximenes (air)

Anaxagoras
(nous—World Mind)

Empedocles (blood)

Pythagoras
(bodily harmony)

Socrates → Plato

Neo-Pythagoreans
(mind [soul] as spirit)

Hebrew Thought → Church Fathers

PLATONISM
(mind [soul] as immaterial
and immortal being)

St. Augustine
(mind [soul] as principle of
personality — body and soul)

Plotinus
(mind as self-conscious,
autonomous spiritual substance)

Neo-Platonism

DUALISM

Scholastics → Descartes
(mind as thinking substance)

INTERACTIONISM

Spiritualistic theories of mind have their origin in Platonic idealism. Spiritualistic or idealistic theories of mind teach that, by whatever name, mind possesses a degree of independence or reality not accounted for in other theories of mind. In Platonism, a dualism separates matter from mind, attributing to the latter *spirituality* and *immortality* (see p. 19). Dualism was the dominant expression of the spiritual view of mind through Kant (see theories of reality in Part III). Following Kant, spiritualism became monism in objective and absolute idealism, which gave to mind a metaphysical status that subordinated all material activity to it as manifestation of *absolute mind* (see pp. 10, 41, 42). On the other hand, the highly *personalistic* tradition of St. Augustine and Descartes was revived in Lotze, who became an inspiration for various forms of personal idealism, or personalism, and personalistic psychologies. All forms of personalism stress the central reality of self or personality. From Kant there also arose philosophies of voluntarism, which interpreted the world and mind as manifestations of *will* or irrational forces, as, e.g., in Schopenhauer. Coupled with this development was the introduction of the idea of the *unconscious mind*. Freud's *psychoanalytic* theory of mind utilized these ideas on a *biological* and *materialistic* foundation (see p. 41). The function of *group mind* was also introduced through the role of the *super-ego* (see Freud's theory of mind). More personalistic, however, were the theories of Adler and Jung. The latter repudiated Freud's *materialism* and stressed instead the reality of *psyche* in personalistic and social terms (see Chart 3).

CHART 16

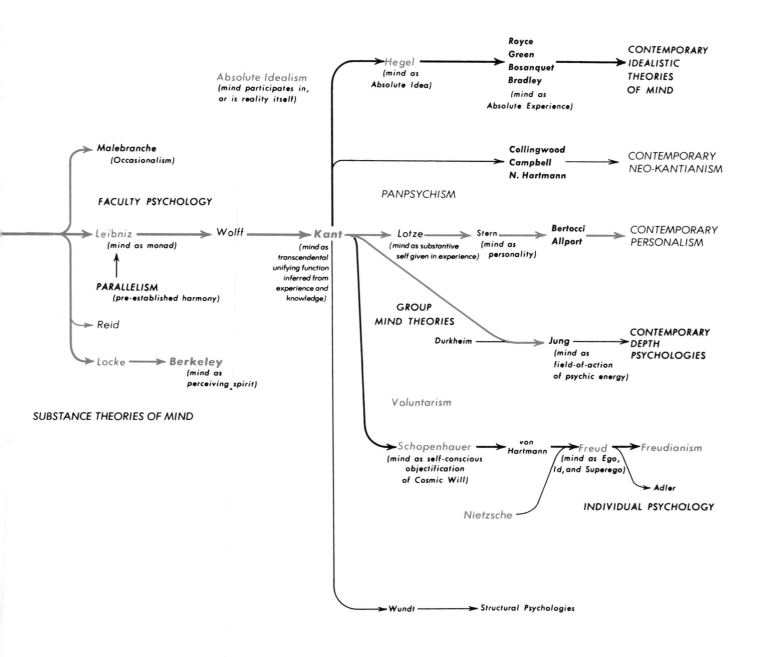

Absolute Idealism
*(mind participates in,
or is reality itself)*

Malebranche
(Occasionalism)

FACULTY PSYCHOLOGY

Hegel
*(mind as
Absolute Idea)*

**Royce
Green
Bosanquet
Bradley**
*(mind as
Absolute Experience)*

CONTEMPORARY
*IDEALISTIC
THEORIES
OF MIND*

**Collingwood
Campbell
N. Hartmann**

CONTEMPORARY
NEO-KANTIANISM

PANPSYCHISM

Leibniz
(mind as monad)

Wolff

Kant
*(mind as
transcendental
unifying function
inferred from
experience and
knowledge)*

Lotze
*(mind as substantive
self given in experience)*

Stern
*(mind as
personality)*

**Bertocci
Allport**

CONTEMPORARY
PERSONALISM

PARALLELISM
(pre-established harmony)

**GROUP
MIND THEORIES**

Reid

Durkheim

Jung
*(mind as
field-of-action
of psychic energy)*

CONTEMPORARY
*DEPTH
PSYCHOLOGIES*

Locke → **Berkeley**
*(mind as
perceiving spirit)*

Voluntarism

SUBSTANCE THEORIES OF MIND

Schopenhauer
*(mind as self-conscious
objectification
of Cosmic Will)*

von
Hartmann

Freud
*(mind as Ego,
Id, and Superego)*

Freudianism

→ Adler

INDIVIDUAL PSYCHOLOGY

Nietzsche

Wundt → Structural Psychologies

HEDONISM
(Good = pleasure in some form, or seeking pleasure and avoiding pain.)

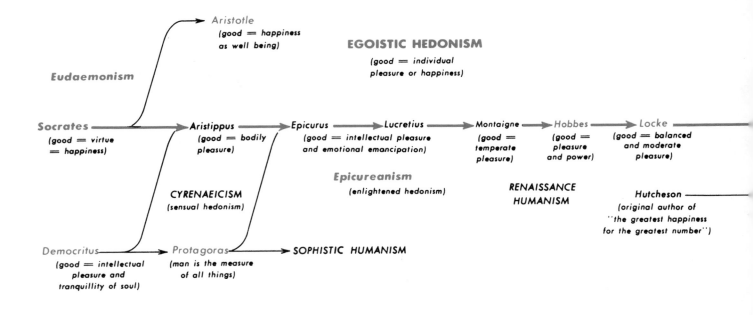

EGOISTIC HEDONISM
(good = individual pleasure or happiness)

Eudaemonism

Aristotle
(good = happiness as well being)

Socrates
(good = virtue = happiness)

Aristippus
(good = bodily pleasure)

Epicurus
(good = intellectual pleasure and emotional emancipation)

Lucretius

Montaigne
(good = temperate pleasure)

Hobbes
(good = pleasure and power)

Locke
(good = balanced and moderate pleasure)

Epicureanism
(enlightened hedonism)

RENAISSANCE HUMANISM

CYRENAEICISM
(sensual hedonism)

Democritus
(good = intellectual pleasure and tranquillity of soul)

Protagoras
(man is the measure of all things)

SOPHISTIC HUMANISM

Hutcheson
(original author of "the greatest happiness for the greatest number")

The Enlightenment

Hedonistic theories of the good constitute one of the major bodies of ethical theory in Western philosophy. Initially, the *naturalistic* theory of hedonism takes one of two general forms: (1) the simple pursuit of *pleasure*, in Democritus and Aristippus, and (2) the pursuit of *eudaemonia*, or *personal well-being* (happiness), in Socrates (see pp. 39, 40, 47). Eudaemonism characterizes most of *Greek ethics* and involves an achievement far surpassing the simple goal of finding pleasure and avoiding pain. All in all, however, Greek ethics were primarily *teleological*, i.e., concerned with the goal of good living or the nature of the good as the goal of life.

As it developed in Plato, eudaemonism became distinctly *nonnaturalistic* in the sense that the good is not reducible to pleasant feelings or any other natural phenomena but instead enjoys metaphysical status as the essence of ultimate reality itself. For Plato, the Idea of the Good informs all particular examples of the good (see p. 45). The ethics of Socrates, Plato, and Aristotle are best characterized as nonnaturalistic, rather than naturalistic, notwithstanding the elements of hedonism present in each.

Early hedonism was egoistic (individual). During the early modern period, Cumberland and Bentham converted it into its characteristic contemporary form—utilitarian hedonism (see p. 24). Bentham developed a *quantitative* form of utilitarian hedonism based on the *principle of utility*, wherein "the greatest happiness of the greatest number" constitutes the *universal moral standard.*

Recognizing certain inherent inadequacies in Bentham's utilitarianism, J. S. Mill modified it in the direction of a more *qualitative* interpretation (see p. 24). From the socially oriented ethical theory of Mill, there developed the *instrumental* or *pragmatic* ethics of Dewey (see p. 24). Also deriving from Mill is an ethical theory identifying the good with all *intrinsic values*, rather than with the usual hedonistic goals of pursuing pleasure and avoiding pain. As *ideal utilitarianism*, in G. E. Moore, e.g., utilitarianism becomes linked to *ethical intuitionism* (see p. 24). Taken in its most general sense, utilitarianism is the ethical doctrine that an act or class of acts *ought* to be judged by the *goodness* of its *consequences.*

Act utilitarianism specifically asks: "What effect will *my* doing *this* act in *this* situation have on the consequences?" Rule utilitarianism asks: "What would be the consequences if *everyone* were to do *this* act in *this* situation?" Thus, act utilitarianism holds that one ought to do that particular *act* which will produce the most intrinsic good, and rule utilitarianism holds that one ought to act according to the *rule* whose adoption will produce the most intrinsic good. Rule utilitarianism differs with both act utilitarianism on the one hand and deontological ethics on the other (see p. 24 and Chart 21).

CHART 17

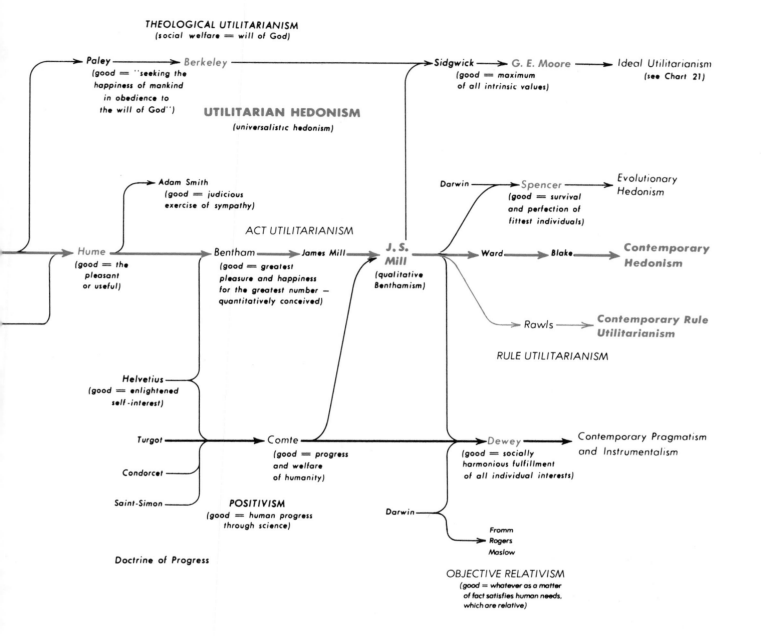

THEOLOGICAL UTILITARIANISM
(social welfare = will of God)

Paley ──────────► Berkeley ──────────────────────────► Sidgwick ──► G. E. Moore ──────► Ideal Utilitarianism
(good = "seeking the   (good = maximum   (see Chart 21)
happiness of mankind   of all intrinsic values)
in obedience to
the will of God")

UTILITARIAN HEDONISM
(universalistic hedonism)

Adam Smith
(good = judicious
exercise of sympathy)

ACT UTILITARIANISM

Darwin ──────► Spencer ──────► Evolutionary
                (good = survival   Hedonism
                and perfection of
                fittest individuals)

Hume ──────────► Bentham ──► James Mill ──► J. S.   Ward ──► Blake ──► Contemporary
(good = the   (good = greatest   Mill   Hedonism
pleasant   pleasure and happiness   (qualitative
or useful)   for the greatest number —   Benthamism)
                 quantitatively conceived)
                                                            Rawls ──► Contemporary Rule
                                                                      Utilitarianism

                                                            RULE UTILITARIANISM

Helvetius
(good = enlightened
self-interest)

Turgot ──────────► Comte ────────────────────────► Dewey ──────► Contemporary Pragmatism
                    (good = progress   (good = socially   and Instrumentalism
Condorcet   and welfare   harmonious fulfillment
                    of humanity)   of all individual interests)
Saint-Simon ──────
                    POSITIVISM
                    (good = human progress   Darwin ──────►
                    through science)
                                                            Fromm
                                                            Rogers
Doctrine of Progress   Maslow

                                                    OBJECTIVE RELATIVISM
                                                    (good = whatever as a matter
                                                    of fact satisfies human needs,
                                                    which are relative)

NATURALISM: ETHICS OF POWER
(Good = power.)

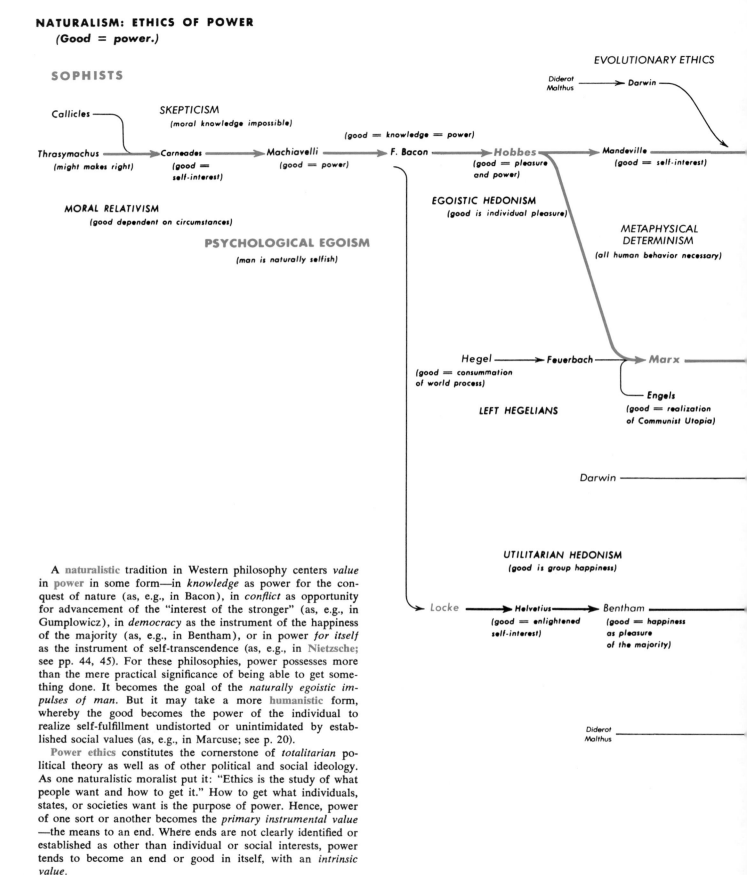

SOPHISTS

EVOLUTIONARY ETHICS

Diderot
Malthus → Darwin

Callicles

SKEPTICISM
(moral knowledge impossible)

(good = knowledge = power)

Thrasymachus → Carneades → Machiavelli → F. Bacon → Hobbes → Mandeville
(might makes right) | (good = self-interest) | (good = power) | | (good = pleasure and power) | (good = self-interest)

MORAL RELATIVISM
(good dependent on circumstances)

EGOISTIC HEDONISM
(good is individual pleasure)

METAPHYSICAL DETERMINISM
(all human behavior necessary)

PSYCHOLOGICAL EGOISM
(man is naturally selfish)

Hegel → Feuerbach → Marx
(good = consummation of world process)

LEFT HEGELIANS

Engels
(good = realization of Communist Utopia)

Darwin

UTILITARIAN HEDONISM
(good is group happiness)

Locke → Helvetius → Bentham
(good = enlightened self-interest) | (good = happiness as pleasure of the majority)

Diderot
Malthus

A naturalistic tradition in Western philosophy centers *value* in power in some form—in *knowledge* as power for the conquest of nature (as, e.g., in Bacon), in *conflict* as opportunity for advancement of the "interest of the stronger" (as, e.g., in Gumplowicz), in *democracy* as the instrument of the happiness of the majority (as, e.g., in Bentham), or in power *for itself* as the instrument of self-transcendence (as, e.g., in Nietzsche; see pp. 44, 45). For these philosophies, power possesses more than the mere practical significance of being able to get something done. It becomes the goal of the *naturally egoistic impulses of man*. But it may take a more humanistic form, whereby the good becomes the power of the individual to realize self-fulfillment undistorted or unintimidated by established social values (as, e.g., in Marcuse; see p. 20).

Power ethics constitutes the cornerstone of *totalitarian* political theory as well as of other political and social ideology. As one naturalistic moralist put it: "Ethics is the study of what people want and how to get it." How to get what individuals, states, or societies want is the purpose of power. Hence, power of one sort or another becomes the *primary instrumental value* —the means to an end. Where ends are not clearly identified or established as other than individual or social interests, power tends to become an end or good in itself, with an *intrinsic value*.

Because of their crucial role as links in the chain of theory, certain philosophers, like Locke and Mill, are included, whose ethics are *not* the ethics of power. Also, the *democratic* expressions of the search for power and self-expression are to be clearly distinguished from totalitarian power theories.

CHART 18

SOCIAL DARWINISM

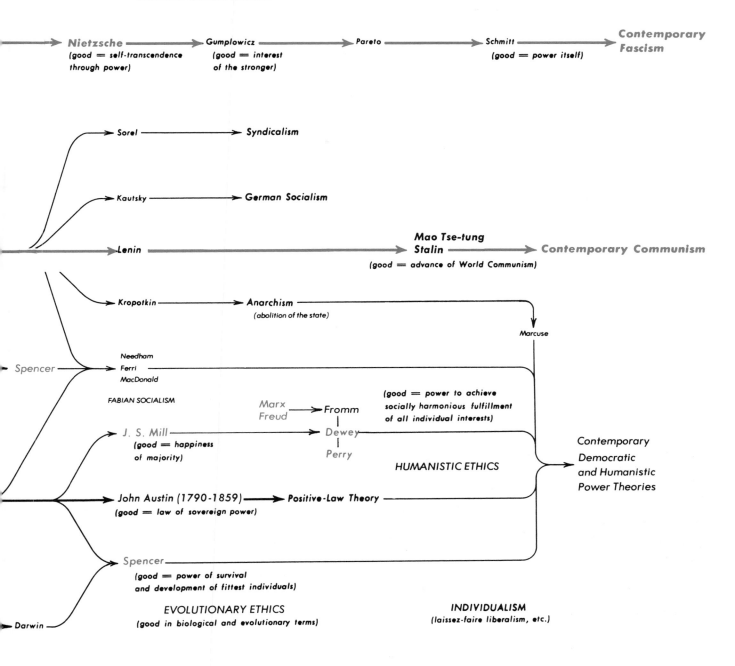

Nietzsche
(good = self-transcendence
through power)

Gumplowicz
(good = interest
of the stronger)

Pareto

Schmitt
(good = power itself)

Contemporary
Fascism

Sorel ⟶ Syndicalism

Kautsky ⟶ German Socialism

Lenin

Mao Tse-tung
Stalin ⟶ Contemporary Communism
(good = advance of World Communism)

Kropotkin ⟶ Anarchism
(abolition of the state)

Marcuse

Spencer

Needham
Ferri
MacDonald

FABIAN SOCIALISM

Marx
Freud ⟶ Fromm

(good = power to achieve
socially harmonious fulfillment
of all individual interests)

J. S. Mill
(good = happiness
of majority)

Dewey

Perry

HUMANISTIC ETHICS

Contemporary
Democratic
and Humanistic
Power Theories

John Austin (1790-1859) ⟶ Positive-Law Theory
(good = law of sovereign power)

Spencer
(good = power of survival
and development of fittest individuals)

EVOLUTIONARY ETHICS
(good in biological and evolutionary terms)

INDIVIDUALISM
(laissez-faire liberalism, etc.)

Darwin

NATURALISM: ETHICAL SKEPTICISM, SUBJECTIVISM, AND RELATIVISM
(Moral knowledge as objective moral truth is denied.)

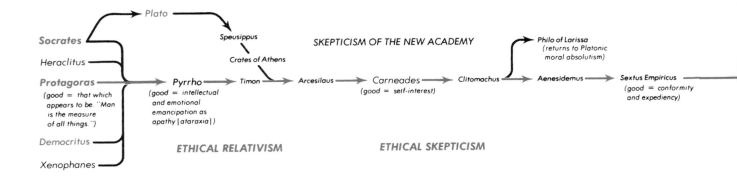

Ethical skepticism is the denial of the possibility of moral knowledge as such. According to the moral skeptic, moral statements *may* inform us concerning certain psychological, sociological, or even theological facts; e.g., "I approve *x*," "Society approves *x*," or "God approves *x*"—i.e., facts about someone's *attitudes* (subjectivism), but not objective moral facts as in ethical objectivism (see p. 27 and Chart 21). Moreover, since attitudes concerning right and wrong, good and bad, or values generally appear to vary widely, the ethical skeptic is likely to be an ethical relativist, whereby he will say not only that morals and values *are* relative but also that they *ought to be* relative. Hence, if one culture, e.g., believes that *x* is right, it cannot be mistaken, because there are no universal or absolute standards or because there would be no way in which one could attain objective moral knowledge that didn't turn out to be objective empirical knowledge, as, e.g., facts about attitudes, mores, personal convictions, etc. (see p. 28). Thus, most ethical skepticism is *naturalistic,* either in the sense that (1) ethics has to do with the natural, empirical world and not a moral or spiritual realm, or in the sense that (2) ethical statements translate into statements about what *is,* i.e., the empirical (see discussion of the naturalistic fallacy, p. 28).

The first form of naturalism is *metaphysical* because it is a theory about the nature of reality, e.g., that there is a moral order (natural law theory). The second form of naturalism is *metaethical* because it is a theory about the nature of moral statements, e.g., that they are really statements about what people approve (Hume; see p. 23).

Emotivism is an even stronger statement of skepticism (see pp. 23, 27). According to emotivism, moral statements are not statements at all, but *expressions* of approval, disapproval, etc. (Ayer). Emotivism denies moral knowledge on the grounds that there is no *nonempirical* knowledge of any kind. Subjectivism denies peculiarly moral knowledge on the grounds that it is really a kind of *empirical* knowledge, i.e., knowledge of approval, etc.

More recent forms of analytical philosophy (see Chart 23) reject the emotivist view that moral statements are mere expressions of feeling or attitude, mere commands, or arbitrary decisions or commitments. Rather they interpret moral statements as evaluations, recommendations, prescriptions, etc., and stress the fact that when we say of something that it is good, we imply that there are *good reasons* for our judgment (e.g., Toulmin)—that we are not merely evincing a feeling or reporting that we have such a feeling, etc. (see p. 27). Recent analytical theories may even hold that moral judgments can be said to be true or false, although not in the same sense as empirical judgments. Thus emotivism is ameliorated by noting the wide variety of things performed by moral language and allowing that reasoning and factual information are relevant to moral judgment.

The emotivist belief that ethics has to do primarily with behavior and the analysis of moral language (metaethics), and not with metaphysical knowledge, is retained but altered to allow for the fact that any ordinary use of moral language involves more than giving vent to feelings.

The existentialist's denial of objective moral knowledge as, e.g., in Sartre, is another important kind of contemporary ethical skepticism. However, the existentialist's denial of moral knowledge is not based on logical or metaethical grounds, but on certain metaphysical grounds that have to do with the human situation and the nature of reality as such. Like Aristotle, the existentialist rejects Plato's universal moral absolutes for personal moral absolutes. Unlike Aristotle, however, he denies that moral absolutes are relative to the individual as part of his *essence*. Rather, personal moral absolutes must be freely chosen and human essence established by these choices (see Sartre's "Existence precedes essence," p. 46 and Chart 24).

CHART 19

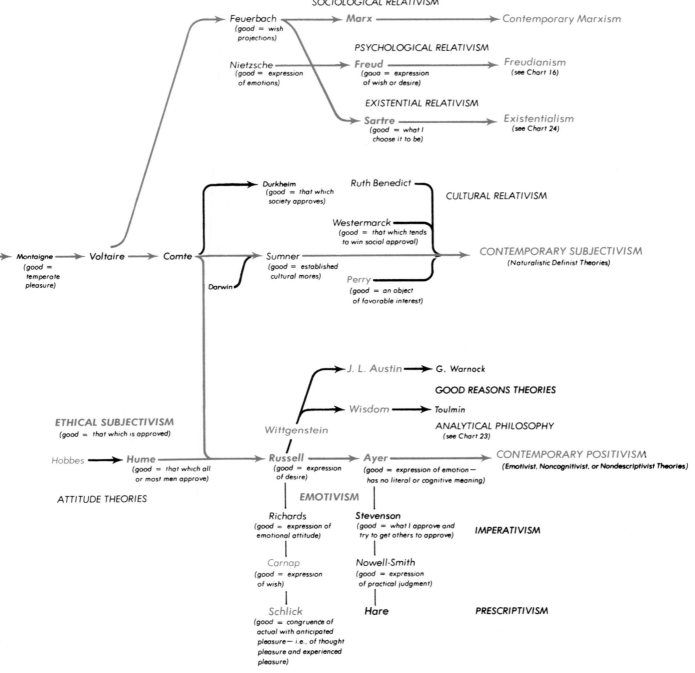

SOCIOLOGICAL RELATIVISM

Feuerbach
(good = wish
projections)

Marx

Contemporary Marxism

PSYCHOLOGICAL RELATIVISM

Nietzsche
(good = expression
of emotions)

Freud
(good = expression
of wish or desire)

Freudianism
(see Chart 16)

EXISTENTIAL RELATIVISM

Sartre
(good = what I
choose it to be)

Existentialism
(see Chart 24)

Durkheim
(good = that which
society approves)

Ruth Benedict

CULTURAL RELATIVISM

Westermarck
(good = that which tends
to win social approval)

Montaigne
(good =
temperate
pleasure)

Voltaire

Comte

Darwin

Sumner
(good = established
cultural mores)

Perry
(good = an object
of favorable interest)

CONTEMPORARY SUBJECTIVISM
(Naturalistic Definist Theories)

J. L. Austin

G. Warnock

GOOD REASONS THEORIES

Wisdom

Toulmin

ANALYTICAL PHILOSOPHY
(see Chart 23)

ETHICAL SUBJECTIVISM
(good = that which is approved)

Wittgenstein

Hobbes

Hume
(good = that which all
or most men approve)

Russell
(good = expression
of desire)

Ayer
(good = expression of emotion—
has no literal or cognitive meaning)

CONTEMPORARY POSITIVISM
(Emotivist, Noncognitivist, or Nondescriptivist Theories)

ATTITUDE THEORIES

EMOTIVISM

Richards
(good = expression of
emotional attitude)

Stevenson
(good = what I approve and
try to get others to approve)

IMPERATIVISM

Carnap
(good = expression
of wish)

Nowell-Smith
(good = expression
of practical judgment)

Schlick
(good = congruence of
actual with anticipated
pleasure— i.e., of thought
pleasure and experienced
pleasure)

Hare

PRESCRIPTIVISM

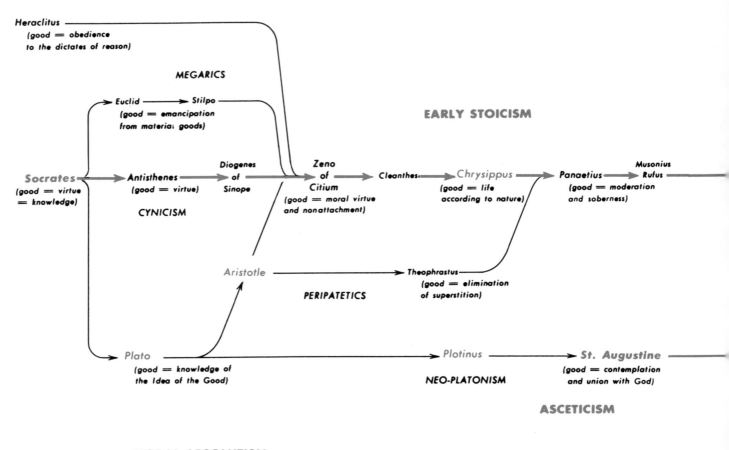

Heraclitus
(good = obedience
to the dictates of reason)

MEGARICS

Euclid → Stilpo
(good = emancipation
from material goods)

EARLY STOICISM

Socrates
(good = virtue
= knowledge)

Antisthenes
(good = virtue)

CYNICISM

Diogenes
of
Sinope

Zeno
of
Citium
(good = moral virtue
and nonattachment)

Cleanthes

Chrysippus
(good = life
according to nature)

Panaetius
(good = moderation
and soberness)

Musonius
Rufus

Aristotle

PERIPATETICS

Theophrastus
(good = elimination
of superstition)

Plato
(good = knowledge of
the Idea of the Good)

Plotinus

NEO-PLATONISM

St. Augustine
(good = contemplation
and union with God)

ASCETICISM

MORAL ABSOLUTISM

Socrates, Plato, and **Aristotle** believed that man is a *rational* being whose unique function is the exercise of *reason* and whose supreme goal is the life of reason (see pp. 39, 40, 45, 47). The metaphysical systems of Plato and Aristotle attest to the rational character of the *reality* which rational men try to understand. Heraclitus spoke of an underlying cosmic principle, which he characterized as the *logos* (reason). Under the leadership of Zeno, early Stoicism appropriated the *logos* idea to develop a *rational cosmology* and *teleology*. The universe is a vast purposive order in which all men share a common reason. Beginning with Panaetius and under the Roman Stoics, Stoicism developed an ethic of *humanitarianism* and *self-control* rivaling the ethics of early Christian teachers. Central to Stoic ethics were (1) the life of reason taught by Socrates, Plato, and Aristotle, (2) the principle of nonattachment to things over which control is not possible, and (3) obedience to the sense of duty. Contrary to the Epicureans (*hedonists*), the Stoics developed an indifference or outright antipathy to pleasure (see Chart 8).

Kantian formalism constitutes a distinctly different variety of **ethical rationalism**—one that does not depend on cosmological theory. For Kant, man's own rational nature is the basis of a *moral obligation* which is *unconditional*. Only a rational will is *intrinsically good*. Only a good will is *unconditionally good*. Kant spoke of moral obligation as a **categorical imperative**. Hence there is an emphasis on *motive* (deontological ethics) and on a rational *method* that binds all rational men (see p. 25).

Kant's philosophy provided the basis for many subsequent philosophies. In particular, his emphasis on the role of reason and the importance of mind led to the development of various forms of **idealism**. Ethical idealists, as, e.g., Bradley, taught an ethic of **self-realization** approximating the ethics of *Platonic* and *Christian idealism*. A variant, **personal idealism** or **personalism**, linked modern *idealist ethics* to specifically *religious ethics* and the *ethics of self-realization*.

CHART 20

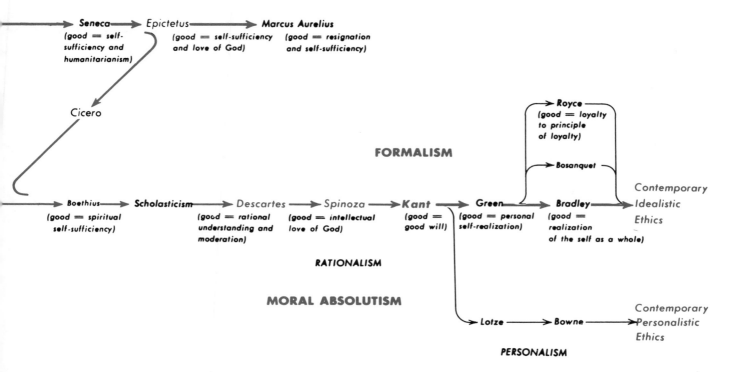

ROMAN STOICISM
*(good as rational understanding
and obedience of the Law of Nature)*

Seneca ⟶ *Epictetus* ⟶ **Marcus Aurelius**
(good = self-   *(good = self-sufficiency*   *(good = resignation*
sufficiency and   *and love of God)*   *and self-sufficiency)*
humanitarianism)

Cicero

FORMALISM

⟶ Royce
*(good = loyalty
to principle
of loyalty)*

⟶ Bosanquet

Contemporary
Idealistic
Ethics

Boethius ⟶ Scholasticism ⟶ *Descartes* ⟶ *Spinoza* ⟶ *Kant* ⟶ Green ⟶ Bradley
(good = spiritual   *(good = rational*   *(good = intellectual*   *(good =*   *(good = personal*   *(good =*
self-sufficiency)   *understanding and*   *love of God)*   *good will)* *self-realization)* *realization*
                        moderation)   *of the self as a whole)*

RATIONALISM

MORAL ABSOLUTISM

⟶ Lotze ⟶ Bowne ⟶ *Contemporary*
Personalistic
Ethics

PERSONALISM

ETHICAL INTUITIONISM: OBJECTIVISM
(Normal human beings have an immediate awareness of moral right or good.)

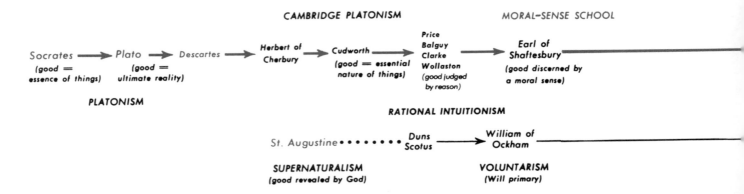

The term intuitionism is derived from the Latin *intueor*, "to look at" or "to have direct acquaintance with." In ethics, it denotes those theories which hold that the good or right can be directly known, as the eye perceives the redness of an apple. But whatever else may accompany "redness," "goodness," or "rightness," they remain independent, unique, and real properties of things or realities themselves. Morally sensitive or rationally responsible persons have an immediate awareness of the *good, right,* or *value* either as the property of some things (Moore) or as the reality of the things themselves (Plato; see pp. 10, 11, 25, 27).

In ancient thought, Plato's *noetic* vision of the Good, the True, and the Beautiful is an example of an appeal to **intuition** as the source of knowledge of the good. For Christianity, a kind of moral sense or conscience discerns one's *duty* in any given situation (see p. 26). This sense of duty is joined with the rational insight of *Platonism* in J. Butler (1692–1752) to suggest a conscience as a *rational* faculty of moral insight. Perhaps the best statement ever written of the case for reason as the source of moral awareness is that of Richard Price (1723–1791). On the contrary, Shaftesbury and Hutcheson found moral awareness in the exercise of an *empirical* moral sense. The British Moral-Sense School and the Scottish Common-Sense School are examples of the continuing tradition of ethical intuitionism in the eighteenth century.

Unable to cope with the influence of modern *naturalistic* ethics, ethical intuitionism lost its influence during the latter half of the nineteenth century, but has returned as an important form of contemporary ethical theory. Four major developments revived ethical intuitionism:

(1) G. E. Moore's doctrine of the indefinable good and his rapprochement with utilitarianism, which resulted in ideal utilitarianism and a doctrine of axiological intuitionism (see p. 28).

(2) H. A. Prichard's revival of the deontological emphasis of Kant with regard to the concern for *duty* and his combining it with elements from ideal utilitarianism to develop a deontological intuitionism (see p. 25).

(3) The influential school of German *phenomenology* under Hartmann and Scheler, as another form of axiological intuitionism.

(4) Bergson's last great work, *The Two Sources of Morality and Religion,* which established a renewed interest in the role of mysticism and in creative behavior.

All forms of intuitionism favor axiological objectivism, in the sense that *values are intuited;* i.e., they are found or discovered as independently real qualities or natures of things (see p. 22). Today the term "intuitionism" is used interchangeably with nonnaturalism and objectivism, since all three take moral judgments to be statements of moral fact.

CHART 21

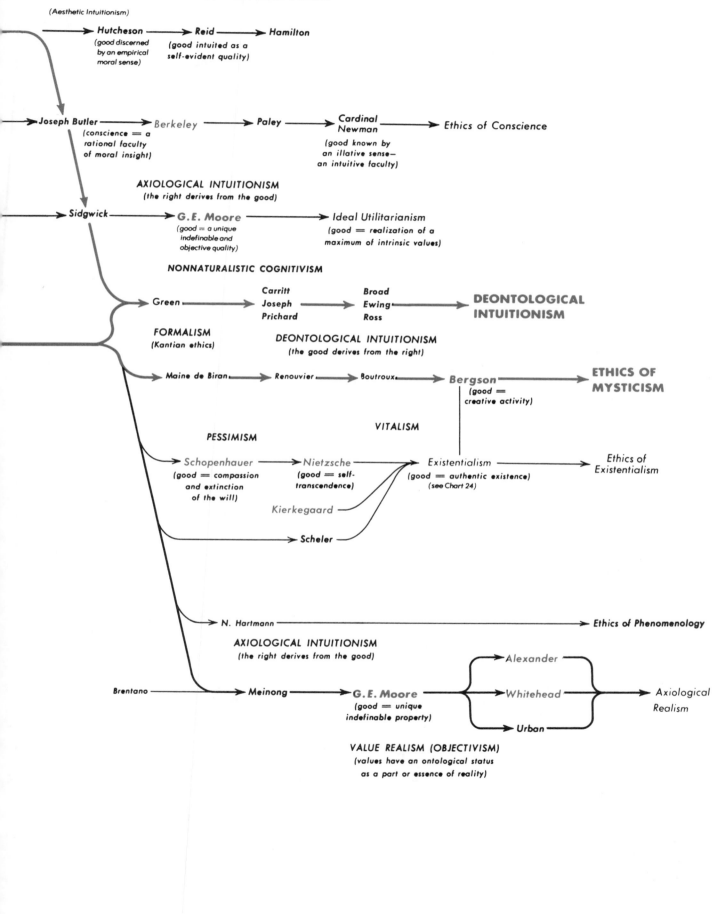

COMMON–SENSE SCHOOL

(Aesthetic Intuitionism)

Hutcheson ⟶ Reid ⟶ Hamilton
(good discerned
by an empirical
moral sense)
(good intuited as a
self-evident quality)

Joseph Butler ⟶ Berkeley ⟶ Paley ⟶ Cardinal Newman ⟶ Ethics of Conscience
(conscience = a
rational faculty
of moral insight)
(good known by
an illative sense—
an intuitive faculty)

AXIOLOGICAL INTUITIONISM
(the right derives from the good)

Sidgwick ⟶ G. E. Moore ⟶ Ideal Utilitarianism
(good = a unique
indefinable and
objective quality)
(good = realization of a
maximum of intrinsic values)

NONNATURALISTIC COGNITIVISM

Green ⟶ Carritt / Joseph / Prichard ⟶ Broad / Ewing / Ross ⟶ DEONTOLOGICAL INTUITIONISM

FORMALISM
(Kantian ethics)

DEONTOLOGICAL INTUITIONISM
(the good derives from the right)

Maine de Biran ⟶ Renouvier ⟶ Boutroux ⟶ Bergson ⟶ ETHICS OF MYSTICISM
(good =
creative activity)

VITALISM

PESSIMISM

Schopenhauer ⟶ Nietzsche ⟶ Existentialism ⟶ Ethics of Existentialism
(good = compassion
and extinction
of the will)
(good = self-
transcendence)
(good = authentic existence)
(see Chart 24)

Kierkegaard

Scheler

N. Hartmann ⟶ Ethics of Phenomenology

AXIOLOGICAL INTUITIONISM
(the right derives from the good)

Brentano ⟶ Meinong ⟶ G. E. Moore ⟶ Alexander / Whitehead / Urban ⟶ Axiological Realism
(good = unique
indefinable property)

VALUE REALISM (OBJECTIVISM)
(values have an ontological status
as a part or essence of reality)

RELIGIOUS ETHICS
(Good is love of God and neighbor in obedience to God's will. God is the source of value.)

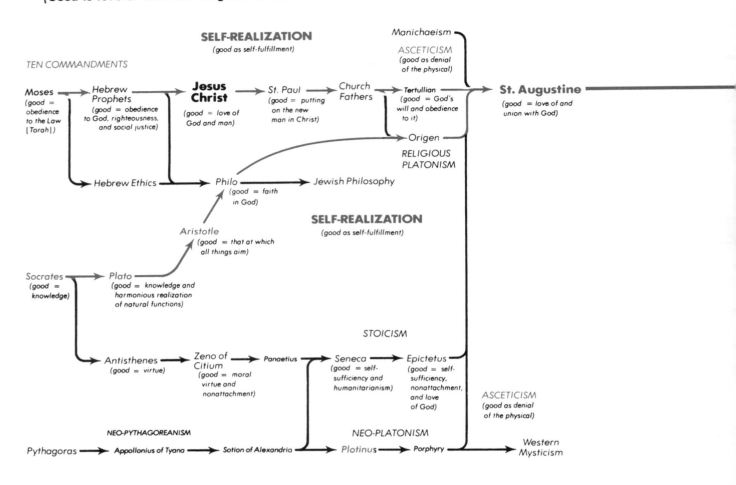

Traditional religious ethics are grounded in the belief in a God and a moral universe. Some forms of contemporary religious existentialism reject traditional theism. Most reject any form of supernaturalism or authoritarianism. Instead, *non-theistic* grounds are given for ethics (Tillich; see p. 48); or radical theology may identify the religious with the secular because of the "death of God," so that ethics becomes primarily humanistic and universalistic as well as existential. The development of existentialist ethics, or the New Morality as it is often called, is shown on Chart 24, since it is more closely bound to contemporary existentialism than to either traditional forms of philosophy or traditional forms of religious thought.

For traditional religious ethics, *God* is identified with the *Good* (St. Augustine) or limited by the *Good* (Plato), and is the source and sustainer of all values. As a moral universe, the world is governed by moral laws which establish the physical order of things (St. Thomas Aquinas) or reveal themselves in the unknowable reality of inner selves (Kant). In most expressions of traditional religious ethics, God is the governor of all things. What He wills as a personal God (*theism*) may be good simply because He wills it (William of Ockham). On the other hand, the good may not be *any* possible pronouncement of God, but specifically "the happiness of mankind" (Paley). In all cases, obedience to God is central for traditional religious ethics.

Although most traditional religious ethics are theistic, a mystical strain (originating primarily in Plotinus) may ground all values in a *pantheistic* conception of God, wherein the goal of life is union with God. In the instance of Plotinus, the world is an *emanation* from God and hence *lower* or *lesser* than Ultimate Goodness itself (see p. 46). By contrast, in strongly *dualistic* philosophies, the world may be associated with an evil or "fallen" state (Manichaeism); hence the good constitutes escape by one means or another from the world "of the flesh and the devil" (*asceticism*). In these philosophies, there arises an intimate association of the idea of *salvation* with the idea of the good. On the other hand, where God is pictured as having created His world in the past or is now engaged in the continuing act of creation, or both, participation or cooperation in the fulfillment of His creative goals is interpreted as the good. This is particularly true of self-realization theories of ethics, wherein realization of the potential self is the goal of life (Jesus Christ). In all traditional religious ethics, however, the authority of God prevails as the ultimate sanction of all goodness (authoritarianism). But this may call for a supernatural "putting on" of Christ (evangelicalism).

Traditional religious ethics are primarily deontological, i.e., based on the centrality of the problem of duty, obligation, or right conceived as act (see pp. 25, 26). As it is sometimes put, "So act that you will be in the center of God's will." The questions are basically: "What ought I to do?" or "What is right?" in obedience to God's will or to the demands of moral reason. "What is my duty to myself, to man, or to God?" One answer widely acclaimed is the *Golden Rule*. Though Jesus elaborated no ethical theory as such, his ideas are central to Christian religious ethics. The most systematic statement of his teachings

CHART 22

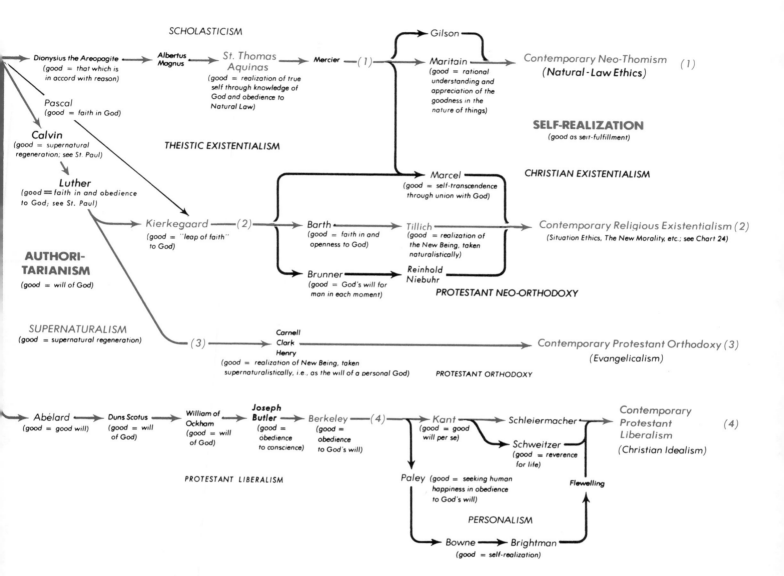

may be found in the *Sermon on the Mount* in the *Gospel according to St. Matthew*. His ethics are *agapistic*, i.e., based on love of God and man, although both *deontological* and *areteic* (see p. 26) elements can be found as well as elements of authoritarianism and supernaturalism.

After St. Augustine, five major streams of religious ethical theory may be identified. One is the tradition of *mysticism* deriving from Plotinus (not shown on the chart). The other four are:

(1) **Thomism,** which continues the tradition of *Aristotelian* and *scholastic* ethics (see p. 32).

(2) **Religious existentialism,** which derives mainly from Kierkegaard, although other influences are apparent (see pp. 32, 33, 43).

(3) **Protestant orthodoxy** and **evangelicalism,** which stress Biblical authoritarianism and supernaturalism along mainly Pauline and Calvinist lines (see p. 32).

(4) **Protestant liberalism,** which has its origins not only in religious thought but also in the moral philosophy of Kant, the various forms of recent **idealism,** and the growing tradition of *humanism* in Western thought (see p. 33).

Analytical philosophy as it is practiced today (mainly in English-speaking countries) has its origin in the ideas of Russell and Moore, both of whom rejected Bradley's belief that metaphysics can "comprehend the universe . . . as a whole." The major influence on the recent course of analytical philosophy, however, is Wittgenstein, who influenced both Russell and Moore and was, in turn, influenced by them (see pp. 12, 13).

The development of Wittgenstein's own analytical philosophy reflects the general development of analytical philosophy as a whole. His first major work, the *Tractatus Logico-Philosophicus* (1921), expressed ideas similar to Russell's and gave impetus to the idea that a logically perfect language, free of the misleading tendencies of ordinary language, might be made the goal and interest of philosophy (see p. 12). "Russell's merit," he writes, "is to have shown that the apparent logical form of a proposition need not be its real form."

The *Tractatus*, together with Russell's logical atomism, paved the way for interest in various attempts to reduce ordinary language, i.e., language in use, to categories that precisely distinguish between literally meaningful language and that which is not. The logical positivists made it their task to work out this distinction by invoking the verifiability-falsifiability criterion of meaning (see pp. 6, 7, 14). They defined as literally meaningful the necessarily true statements of logic and mathematics (i.e., tautologies) and empirical statements that were, in principle, verifiable or falsifiable (see pp. 6, 7).

Logical positivism—or logical empiricism, with which it is closely related—eventually developed into a form of analytical philosophy which stresses symbolic logic as the basis for a more perfect language in which to express or reason about empirical truths. Logical positivism and its later derivatives are one major form of analytical philosophy that has most of its adherents among native and naturalized American philosophers, such as, e.g., Quine and Carnap. For our purposes, it will be identified as ideal language analysis. Its main ideas are as follows:

(1) "Philosophy is the logical analysis of the concepts and sentences of the sciences" (Carnap; see pp. 40, 41).

(2) To understand thought, one must examine language, since it is in language that thought finds its expression, and only a universal and logically perfect language is the language of the sciences or the language of any knowledge.

(3) Natural or ordinary language, i.e., language as used, "misleads us both by its vocabulary and by its syntax" (Russell). Hence it must be reduced to or translated into an artificial or ideal language that is purely formal.

(4) The main task of philosophy is to reform language by making its grammatical and syntactical forms conform to their actual logical function (see pp. 6, 7).

(5) Any metaphysics based upon the existence of nonempirical entities or the belief in internal relations (as, e.g., idealism; see p. 10) is rejected. Relations are external. The world is a plurality of externally related sensible or logical entities.

(6) Definitions must be operational. "Our fundamental dictum is that things which cannot be measured have no meaning" (Bridgman; see p. 14).

Wittgenstein's second major work, the *Philosophical Investigations* (1953), developed an approach to analysis suggestive of Moore rather than Russell, because in it Wittgenstein explicitly rejects the idea that ordinary language or language in use contains a hidden structure or meaning that can be properly identified as its true logical form or function. In the *Investigations*, Wittgenstein admonishes his reader to look and see what language does, i.e., to observe each "language game" and to note how each language game does the many things that are similar or bear what he calls a "family resemblance," yet do not hide any ideal form or "essence." He substitutes the "family resemblance" model for the "property in common" model. The philosopher, he argues, must analyze what he sees *as it is* from several illuminating perspectives, but leave things *as they are* rather than attempt to reduce or translate them into some universal or logically perfect language. Wittgenstein rejected his original position and any form of logical atomism (Russell) or logical positivism (Ayer). He rejected any attempt to reform language as both impossible and presumptuous. Thus, in taking language pretty much as it is and in seeking only to clarify and illuminate what was before him, he sought—like Moore—to bring language back from its philosophical and often problematical use to its natural and ordinary use. We are puzzled by language, he argues, when we fail to examine it as part of an activity. We are puzzled when we ask questions like, e.g.,

"What is time?" on the mistaken assumption that "time" is the name of an entity. He urges us instead to look at language in use, to see what it is doing in order to understand what it is. We may, e.g., as philosophers, puzzle over what it is the word "time" names, but we don't puzzle over the everyday use of temporal expressions.

In originating the idea that philosophy is a form of conceptual therapy that relieves us of our metaphysical "cramps," Wittgenstein initiated two major forms of analytical philosophy that are similar in many ways, yet center in different persons and different analytical techniques. Most British analytical philosophy derives from what may be loosely characterized as the Cambridge School or the Oxford School of analysis.

While both the Cambridge and the Oxford School lean heavily on the ideas of both Moore and Wittgenstein, they are each distinct in their approaches to analysis and their goals. Each differs from both Moore and Wittgenstein, and every one of the influential philosophers who may be loosely associated with each school is, in many respects, unique as an analyst and would tend to resist easy categorization. Also, the tendency of some opponents of analytical philosophy to speak of all analytical philosophy as "positivism" is misleading and ignores the important difference between ideal language analysis and ordinary language analysis on the one hand as well as important differences between the Cambridge and the Oxford analysts on the other hand.

The Cambridge School is the earlier center of Wittgensteinian and post-Wittgensteinian analysis. Wittgenstein himself taught at Cambridge, where a school flourished until shortly after World War II. With his death in 1951, the center of philosophical activity shifted to Oxford, where the bulk of English analytical philosophy originates today.

The major philosopher of the Cambridge School is John Wisdom, whose unique approach to analysis sets him apart from both Wittgenstein and the Oxford philosophers (see p. 48). For Wisdom, the task of philosophy is conceptual therapy, or therapeutic analysis. Philosophical problems produce a kind of intellectual anxiety or puzzlement that needs to be relieved, as Wittgenstein had earlier taught. But, unlike Wittgenstein or the positivists, Wisdom saw a special value in metaphysical views—even paradoxical ones. "Philosophical statements are disguised recommendations," he wrote; and though the philosopher might make "outrageous" recommendations, they are nonetheless illuminating proposals concerning how things might be viewed. The philosopher may have good reasons for saying what he does. Hence philosophical or metaphysical "nonsense" is not *mere* or literal nonsense, as positivists like Ayer had claimed, but *important* or *significant* nonsense that serves a useful if not necessary function in one's attempt to understand the world. The object of philosophical (therapeutic) analysis is not to liquidate permanently philosophical or metaphysical puzzles by logical analysis, but rather to make it possible to see things in a new way or to see things again in an already obvious but unnoticed way. Philosophical problems are neither solved, as traditional metaphysicians tried to do, nor are they dissolved, as positivists or ideal language analysts try to do. They are transformed into sources of new insight. Philosophical analysis "leaves us free to begin," Wisdom wrote. Similarly, John Austin of the Oxford School noted that analysis is not the "end-all" but the "begin-all" of philosophy (see p. 40). However, Oxford analysts, as, e.g., Ryle, more readily allow that philosophical problems do have solutions (see p. 46). Oxford analytical philosophy involves a rather large number of influential contemporary philosophers whose work is characterized by a preoccupation with the ordinary use of language. This school has, in particular, made considerable contributions to several major areas of philosophy, as, e.g., in ethical theory in the works of Hare and Toulmin, in the logical and metaphysical studies of Strawson, and in the philosophy of language and mind of Ryle and Austin (see pp. 6, 27), as well as many other areas.

Unlike the logical positivists and ideal language analysts generally, the ordinary language analysts are less pessimistic about the problems and prospects of metaphysics. They are not antimetaphysical, as are the logical positivists, and would agree generally with Wisdom and the Cambridge School that positivist antimetaphysics is itself a metaphysical position. Instead they try, as did the later Wittgenstein, to steer a generally *nonmetaphysical* course in analysis. Recently, however, it has become once again fashionable to see analytical philosophy much more as part of the historically continuing effort in philosophy to come to grips with metaphysical issues such as the nature of mind, knowledge, causality, moral obligation, etc.

Poincaré
|
Mach
|
Boltzmann
|
Brentano

VIENNA CIRCLE

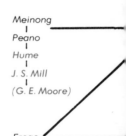

Meinong
|
Peano
|
Hume
|
J. S. Mill
|
(G. E. Moore)

Frege
(mathematics based on logic)

CONCEPTUAL REALISM

Sidgwick

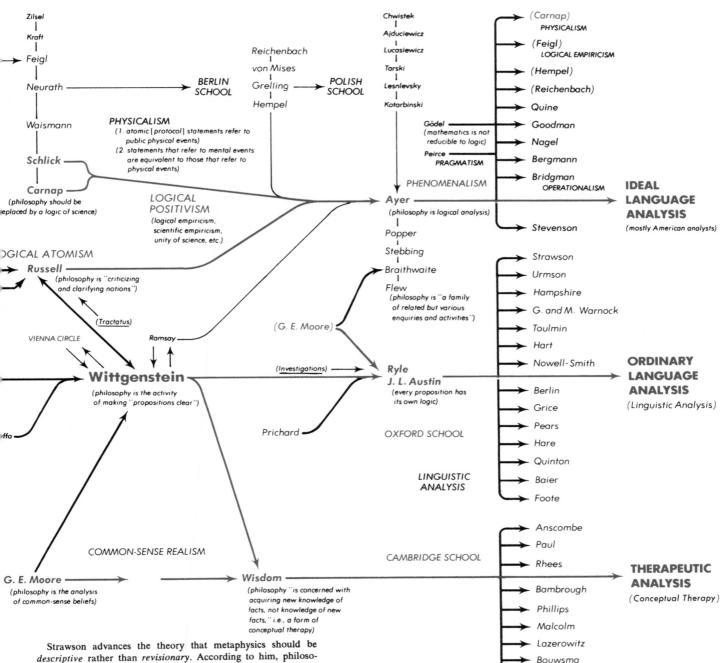

Zilsel
|
Kraft
|
→ Feigl
|
Neurath ——————→ BERLIN SCHOOL
|
Waismann
|
Schlick
|
Carnap
(philosophy should be replaced by a logic of science)

PHYSICALISM
(1. atomic [protocol] statements refer to public physical events)
(2. statements that refer to mental events are equivalent to those that refer to physical events)

LOGICAL ATOMISM
Russell
(philosophy is "criticizing and clarifying notions")

(Tractatus)

VIENNA CIRCLE

Ramsay

Wittgenstein
(philosophy is the activity of making "propositions clear")

LOGICAL POSITIVISM
(logical empiricism, scientific empiricism, unity of science, etc.)

Reichenbach
von Mises
Grelling ——→ POLISH SCHOOL
Hempel

Chwistek
|
Ajduciewicz
|
Lucasiewicz
|
Tarski
|
Lesnlevsky
|
Kotarbinski

Gödel
(mathematics is not reducible to logic)
Peirce
PRAGMATISM

PHENOMENALISM

Ayer
(philosophy is logical analysis)
Popper
Stebbing
Braithwaite
Flew
(philosophy is "a family of related but various enquiries and activities")

(G. E. Moore)

(Investigations) ——→ Ryle
J. L. Austin
(every proposition has its own logic)

OXFORD SCHOOL

LINGUISTIC ANALYSIS

Prichard

→ (Carnap) PHYSICALISM
→ (Feigl) LOGICAL EMPIRICISM
→ (Hempel)
→ (Reichenbach)
→ Quine
→ Goodman
→ Nagel
→ Bergmann
→ Bridgman OPERATIONALISM
→ Stevenson

IDEAL LANGUAGE ANALYSIS
(mostly American analysts)

→ Strawson
→ Urmson
→ Hampshire
→ G. and M. Warnock
→ Toulmin
→ Hart
→ Nowell-Smith
→ Berlin
→ Grice
→ Pears
→ Hare
→ Quinton
→ Baier
→ Foote

ORDINARY LANGUAGE ANALYSIS
(Linguistic Analysis)

COMMON-SENSE REALISM

G. E. Moore ——————→
(philosophy is the analysis of common-sense beliefs)

Wisdom
(philosophy "is concerned with acquiring new knowledge of facts, not knowledge of new facts," i.e., a form of conceptual therapy)

CAMBRIDGE SCHOOL

→ Anscombe
→ Paul
→ Rhees
→ Bambrough
→ Phillips
→ Malcolm
→ Lazerowitz
→ Bouwsma
→ Newell

THERAPEUTIC ANALYSIS
(Conceptual Therapy)

Strawson advances the theory that metaphysics should be *descriptive* rather than *revisionary*. According to him, philosophers like **Aristotle** or **Kant** attempt to derive their categories of reality from the forms of language in use and therefore propose descriptive forms of metaphysics. On the other hand, idealists like **Berkeley**, e.g., wish to alter or revise notions about reality. They propose what Strawson calls a revisionary metaphysics.

The main figures in the **Oxford School** are **Gilbert Ryle** and **John Austin**. (For Austin's linguistic theory of meaning, see p. 6.) Both Austin and Ryle put a great deal of emphasis on *ordinary use*. The answer to most philosophical issues—and they hold that there *are* answers—is to be found in the analysis of ordinary use. By this, they do not mean ordinary *usage*, i.e., merely prevalent speech habits. Ryle distinguishes the two by noting that what is needed are the rules by which expressions perform their particular job, i.e., a "job analysis" of expressions such that we can understand what the expression does in its conventionally appropriate task, i.e., ordinary use.

In general, **ordinary language analysis** holds the following:

(1) Natural language must be left as it is, rather than reduced or translated into an "ideal" but artificial language.

(2) Close attention must be given to the forms of common speech especially as they are used "on the job."

(3) Analysis is a *descriptive* rather than a *prescriptive* or corrective activity. The philosopher's task is not to effect reforms, but to analyze use.

(4) Language has many uses that bear a "family resemblance." There is no single meaningful use, such as naming or describing (see pp. 6, 27, 28).

(5) Rules of use appropriate to one category, as, e.g., material things, cannot be applied indiscriminately to other things, such as mental events (the category mistake, i.e., "the presentation of facts belonging to one category in the idioms appropriate to another"—Ryle; see p. 48).

(6) Every statement has its own logic or rules or use (the idiosyncrasy platitude of Wisdom).

(7) Use constitutes the meaning of an expression. *The meaning is the use* (see theories of linguistic meaning, pp. 6, 33, 34).

EXISTENTIALISM AND PHENOMENOLOGY
(Philosophy is the progressively achieved awareness of what it means to be free, responsible, and relevant, i.e., human.)

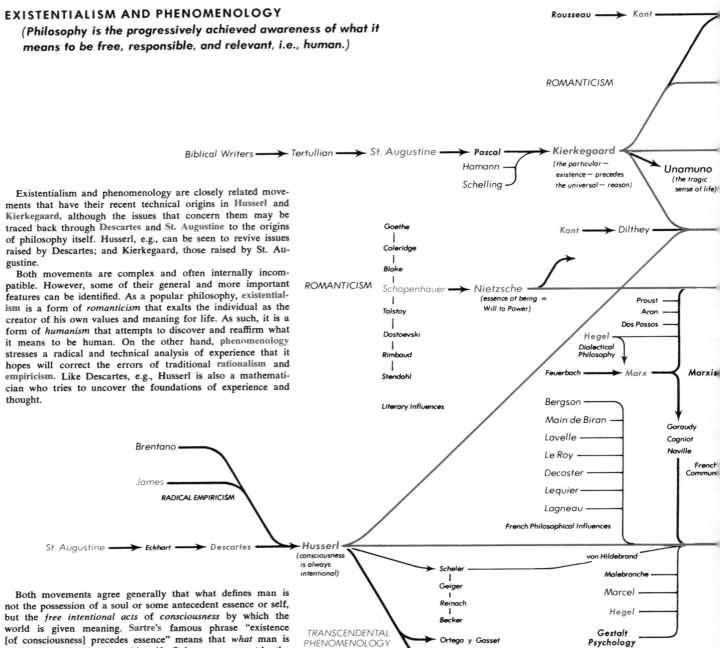

Existentialism and phenomenology are closely related movements that have their recent technical origins in Husserl and Kierkegaard, although the issues that concern them may be traced back through Descartes and St. Augustine to the origins of philosophy itself. Husserl, e.g., can be seen to revive issues raised by Descartes; and Kierkegaard, those raised by St. Augustine.

Both movements are complex and often internally incompatible. However, some of their general and more important features can be identified. As a popular philosophy, existentialism is a form of *romanticism* that exalts the individual as the creator of his own values and meaning for life. As such, it is a form of *humanism* that attempts to discover and reaffirm what it means to be human. On the other hand, phenomenology stresses a radical and technical analysis of experience that it hopes will correct the errors of traditional rationalism and empiricism. Like Descartes, e.g., Husserl is also a mathematician who tries to uncover the foundations of experience and thought.

Both movements agree generally that what defines man is not the possession of a soul or some antecedent essence or self, but the *free intentional acts* of *consciousness* by which the world is given meaning. Sartre's famous phrase "existence [of consciousness] precedes essence" means that *what* man is must be decided by man himself. Only man can settle the question of man and then only momentarily, as he *acts*. Such things as human nature or morality are contingent upon what man chooses to become, how he formulates his future. The idea that mind is an antecedent entity of some sort or an empty or passive "container" for impressions and ideas from an "outside world" is rejected (see p. 46).

Where existentialism is not primarily literary, social, or religious in emphasis, and where it is likely to concern itself with the technical issues of philosophy, it is likely to be a form of existential phenomenology. Heidegger, Sartre, and Merleau-Ponty, e.g., lean primarily on Husserl's phenomenological method. Husserl understood phenomenology to be the study of *experience* or *consciousness*. The subject and object of traditional philosophical problems are "bracketed" out (see p. 43).

For Husserl, consciousness is *intentional* in that it is inherently directed toward an intentionally constituted world, and it arises only as it *acts* as *intentionality*. Both knower and thing known are components of experience. Without the *act* of giving meaning to experience, there would be no subject or object. Existentialism and phenomenology agree in rejecting traditional mind-body dualism or systematic accounts of ultimate reality. On these issues, they also agree with analytical philosophy (see Chart 23). Where they differ with the analysts is on the point of seeing philosophy as an informative discipline. They

do not, e.g., eliminate *metaphysics,* as logical positivism tried to do. Rather, they attempt a radical reformulation of it. Their interest is directed as it was in Kant "to the fundamental structures of conscious experience which constitutes the very conditions of the possibility of any conscious experience whatever" (Edie). Metaphysical entities like the self or independently real objects are "bracketed" out in favor of the analysis of consciousness.

But Husserl's phenomenological method is not to be confused with Descartes's or even Kant's methods. For Husserl and existentialism generally, there is no antecedent self which acts like the character of a play, for example. The "thinker" and his "world" arise in and remain in experience. The categories of experience apply not just to things *as they appear,* as in Kant, but to things *themselves.* In other words, unlike either Kant or Descartes, there is no problem of knowing real things "outside" of minds, since knowers are already part of and inseparable from their "worlds"—the *Dasein,* as Heidegger calls it (see p. 42).

CHART 24

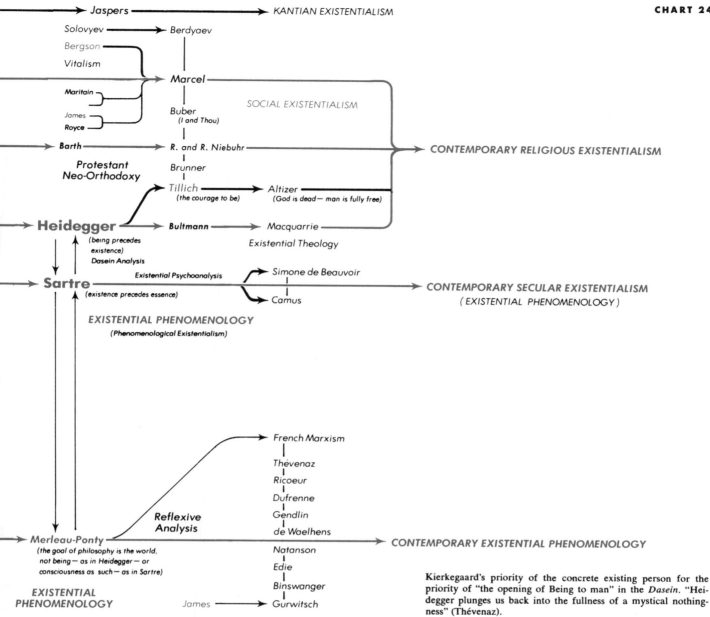

Jaspers ⟶ KANTIAN EXISTENTIALISM

Solovyev ⟶ Berdyaev

Bergson

Vitalism

Marcel

Maritain

James

Royce

Buber
(I and Thou)

SOCIAL EXISTENTIALISM

Barth ⟶ R. and R. Niebuhr ⟶ CONTEMPORARY RELIGIOUS EXISTENTIALISM

Protestant
Neo-Orthodoxy

Brunner

Tillich ⟶ Altizer
(the courage to be)   (God is dead— man is fully free)

Heidegger ⟶ Bultmann ⟶ Macquarrie
(being precedes
existence)
Dasein Analysis

Existential Theology

Existential Psychoanalysis ⟶ Simone de Beauvoir

Sartre ⟶ ⟶ CONTEMPORARY SECULAR EXISTENTIALISM
(existence precedes essence)   Camus   (EXISTENTIAL PHENOMENOLOGY)

EXISTENTIAL PHENOMENOLOGY
(Phenomenological Existentialism)

French Marxism

Thévenaz

Ricoeur

Dufrenne

Reflexive
Analysis   Gendlin

de Waelhens

Merleau-Ponty ⟶ CONTEMPORARY EXISTENTIAL PHENOMENOLOGY
(the goal of philosophy is the world,   Natanson
not being— as in Heidegger— or
consciousness as such— as in Sartre)   Edie

Binswanger

EXISTENTIAL
PHENOMENOLOGY   James ⟶ Gurwitsch

RADICAL EMPIRICISM

An important distinction must be made that marks off the main differences in existentialism by way of Kierkegaard on the one hand (top of chart) and by way of Husserl on the other hand (bottom of chart). The distinction is Heidegger's distinction between existenti*el* (*das Seiende*) and existenti*al* (*das Sein*). The former characterizes the concerns of Kierkegaard, Jaspers, Marcel, and religious existentialism generally for the profound *personal* issues of existence—issues like death, anxiety, and choice. On the contrary, the existential phenomenologies of Heidegger, Sartre, and Merleau-Ponty center on the technical and generally *impersonal* issues of a *metaphysics of experience*—what Heidegger calls *Fundamentalontologie*—which has to do with the existenti*als* or structures of the *Dasein*, i.e., human existence. The psychological and concrete particulars are "bracketed" out.

Since 1950, Heidegger has turned from the study of existenti*als* to the study of *being*, from *Dasein* analysis to being itself as a general principle. Superficially, this interest suggests a return to traditional metaphysics. However, by "being," Heidegger means many things, especially the "to be" of whatever is, i.e., the "to be" as a *verb* of "beings" rather than as a *noun*, not *what* something is as an essence or abstract concept of it, but its *act* of existing. Heidegger seeks the "to be" of being itself and not just the "to be" of man, i.e., the "depth" of man which discloses itself to the "surface" of man. Thus Heidegger reverses

Kierkegaard's priority of the concrete existing person for the priority of "the opening of Being to man" in the *Dasein*. "Heidegger plunges us back into the fullness of a mystical nothingness" (Thévenaz).

By contrast, Sartre goes after the *pure consciousness* that is, for him, *nothingness*. Apart from "being *in* itself"—all there is —"being *for* itself, i.e., conscious human intention of meaning, is nothing. "All conscious existence exists only as consciousness of existing" (Sartre). Since consciousness is "pure spontaneity," it is *freedom*. But the freedom of Sartre is not the freedom of a *self* in the traditional sense. It is the freedom that arises in the relationship of consciousness to its world as it spontaneously *creates* itself in *choice* and *act*, as it forms its future. To *be* is to *act*.

Merleau-Ponty takes exception to Sartre's notion that consciousness is nothingness. Instead, "we are always in *fullness*, in being," he says; and for him, this comprises our inextricable relation to the world in our particular—however ambiguous— *situation*. Thus we do not create meaning from nothing, as in Sartre. Nor does being disclose meaning to us, as in Heidegger. Rather, we clarify "the confused discourse of the world" that characterizes our particular concrete historical situations (see p. 44).

In summary, neither existentialism nor phenomenology denies the *objective reality* of the world, but both do deny the traditional forms of *realism* that speak of a world independent of mind, and they reject all forms of *idealism*. For them, consciousness is always consciousness *of* something, but it is prior to either subject or object. In short, existentialism and phenomenology seek the roots of a subjectivity that is also the root of the objective world.

INDEX OF NAMES

See the Chronology with References for names not included here.
Chart numbers are shown in **boldface** type.

INDEX OF TOPICS

Chart numbers are shown in **boldface** type.

[53]